No Easy Answers
The Learning Disabled Child

"This book is based on my experience with learning disabled children over a twenty-year span. As mother, teacher, school administrator, and professor, I have been involved continually with the problems of the learning disabled . . . with hundreds of intelligent youngsters who have suffered defeat and failure in regular classrooms and needed special help to succeed.

"There are no easy answers. No one way works with every learning disabled child. There are, however, basic principles and approaches that do work. Learning disabled youngsters can learn how to learn. They can succeed!"

—Sally L. Smith

"Sally Smith's *NO EASY ANSWERS* rates a top place on any list of books on this subject. It provides a superb road map to a puzzling and confusing field of knowledge, a field full of questions. Parents, teachers, and child specialists alike will find many of the answers they seek in this concise, helpful, and realistic book."

—Louise Bates Ames
Gesell Institute of Child Development

"She is the Maria Montessori of our day."

—Colman McCarthy
Philadelphia Inquirer

NO EASY ANSWERS

The Learning Disabled Child

Sally L. Smith

Professor, American University;

Founder and Director, The Lab School

Washington, D.C.

BANTAM BOOKS
NEW YORK · TORONTO · LONDON · SYDNEY · AUCKLAND

NO EASY ANSWERS

THE LEARNING DISABLED CHILD

*A Bantam Book / published by arrangement with
the author*

PRINTING HISTORY

Winthrop edition published June 1979

Bantam edition / January 1981
5 printings through June 1987

ISBN 0-553-27095-8

Published simultaneously in the United States and Canada

PRINTED IN THE UNITED STATES OF AMERICA

O   13 12 11 10 9 8

To my son Gary,

who has been my finest teacher
and my hardest taskmaster.

He, who did not read until he was thirteen years old, because of his severe learning disabilities, once said: *"Now* I
understand how people can read to themselves. They have
to share it with their brains!"

Acknowledgments

Elisabeth Benson Booz made this book a reality not only through her constant talented assistance but through her determination that I write it. On every page of the manuscript "Ben's" sharp eye and quick and creative mind have provided useful criticism and editorial correction. She is a dear and close friend, whose love of life is infectious. I treasure the hours spent together and find no way to thank her adequately for all she has done.

To Dr. Edna Small for her valuable help on the psychological material,

To Dr. Grace Gabe for her consulting on the neurological material;

To Mary Mitchell, reading specialist, who has served as a model for many at the Kingsbury Center, and

To Sue Hollis, former Lab School head teacher, for their expert advice on sections applying to reading;

To Helen Colson, who has done so much for the Lab School of the Kingsbury Center, and for the time, energy, and thought devoted to my endeavors;

To Sheila Weiss, Helen Levine, Pete Braun, Karen Vartanian of the Lab School for their continual support;

To Karen Duncan, Lab School head teacher, for the sample IEP's, and

To Judith Zangwill, chief diagnostician of the Kingsbury Center, for assistance on the testing materials appearing in the Appendix;

To Ruth Switzer Pearl for massive technical assistance, substantial help in understanding PL 94-142, and her wicked sense of humor that kept me working on that chapter—

MY GRATEFUL APPRECIATION

I want to thank my two older sons, Randall Alan Smith and Nicholas Lee Smith, who have lived much of this book with me, for their support, deep caring, rich humor, sensitivity, and ingenuity. They have helped their younger brother learn how to learn.

MY ADMIRATION

Contents

Preface

As we enter the 1980s, we are able to control many aspects of our lives by push buttons, levers, switches, computers, test tubes, and nuclear energy, but we still have to deal with many of the human issues over which we have little control. We each wrestle with feelings, relationships, and values daily, and the way in which we deal with them determines the quality of the life we lead. There are rarely easy answers, simple solutions, perfect ways to handle human problems. This is especially true with the learning problems of children. Not machines but the brains and hearts of human beings are needed to help children overcome these problems. Compassion is not enough, although it is always welcome. Knowledge in depth of the child, his particular learning problems, and the tasks we are asking him to do are needed in order to help a learning disabled child to function effectively in school and in society.

This book is an introduction to the world of the learning disabled child. It is about the intelligent youngster who has trouble learning, not about the retarded or the emotionally disturbed child. It is about the child whose nervous system is delayed in maturing. He looks typical for his age but he does not learn as other children his age do because he has a hidden handicap. In some ways, this child is similar to a much younger child, although in other ways he functions at his own age level or above. His wide scattering of abilities and disabilities makes him into a very uneven, inconsistent, unpredictable child who puzzles the adults around him.

DISORDER prevails in a child who is delayed in development. He is scattered in his attention, as well as in his growth. He lacks the tools to organize what he sees, hears, touches, feels, smells, and tastes to make sense of his environment. Normally by school age, a child develops a sense of order, which is the solid base on which future learning is built. The

xi

child with disorder does not have an organized base. He has a learning disorder.

Although disorder is the key characteristic of these children, the term *learning disabled* is appropriate, for they are indeed disabled by their disorder. It is the term educators prefer to describe the intelligent child who experiences much learning difficulty at school. Doctors most frequently use the term *minimal brain dysfunction.*

This book is concerned with the immaturity that causes this disorder and the forces that provide the order necessary to deal with it. It explains how the learning disabled youngster becomes defeated at school, how his movement, language, reading, writing, spelling, and arithmetic are affected by his disorder. It deals primarily with the child who has a severe learning disability, but it is equally applicable to the great number of mildly handicapped children who slide through school getting C's and D's when their potential is for solid A's.

The magnitude of the problem of learning disabilities was forced into national attention in the late 1970s, primarily through the efforts of concerned parents who banded together for action. Public Law 94-142 (effective in 1978) now mandates all states to provide proper educational services for these youngsters. Currently the media are publicizing the problems of these intelligent children who fail to learn properly and who frequently end up as school dropouts. The nation is finally becoming concerned about the wasted potential that ends up on the lines of the unemployed, in the courts, in jails, in guidance clinics and mental institutions. The time has come for us to spot these children early and give them what they need.

This book probes the multiple causes of learning disabilities and postulates that the learning disabled child's prime need is for help in organizing almost every area of his life. He needs explicit teaching of organization skills, along with the three Rs. *Teaching the learning disabled child the approach to a task is as important as teaching the task itself.* This book explores the feelings of the adults closest to the learning disabled child—the many stages and dimensions of their reactions to him. It registers the feelings of the learning disabled child and follows him into his adolescence and preparation for an independent life. Addressed to both professionals in the education field, in health care, day care, recreational and youth organizations, and to parents, the text outlines the problems and offers guidelines and practical approaches.

This book is based on my experience with learning disabled children over a twenty-year span. As mother, teacher, school administrator, and professor, I have been involved continually with the problems of the learning disabled. The body of research that I draw upon is this twenty years of experience with hundreds of intelligent youngsters who have suffered defeat and failure in regular classrooms and needed special help to succeed.

In 1967, I founded The Lab School of the Kingsbury Center in Washington, D.C., for learning disabled youngsters, in co-operation with the Kingsbury Center, a long established and respected center for the diagnosis and remediation of academic problems. Founded in 1938 by Marion Kingsbury, this institution has helped more than twenty thousand children and young adults. When I founded the day school, the Kingsbury Center offered its many resources but gave me the freedom to design my own curriculum, hire and train my own staff and dare to innovate. It was an awesome responsibility and an exciting challenge.

Now, eighteen years later, more than 95 percent of The Lab School's severely learning disabled children have returned to regular classrooms where they are doing well. In 1982, The Lab School—with the same program, staff, and children—became an independent body, The Lab School of Washington. We now have a preschool, a night school for learning disabled adults, a diagnostic and tutoring service, as well as the programs described in this book. A number of students are currently in college and graduate school, and many others, now in the tenth, eleventh, and twelfth grades, are definitely college bound. Nine 16mm educational films and a slide show documenting The Lab School's methods are circulating around the nation. My graduate students from American University, most of whom have had practicums at The Lab School and who have earned their M.Ed. in Special Education: Learning Disabilities, are putting these approaches to use in many other American schools.

This book embodies what I have learned from The Lab School students, their parents, and the teachers and artists who have worked with the children. There are no easy answers. No one way works with every learning disabled child.

There are, however, basic principles and approaches that do work. Learning disabled youngsters can learn how to learn. They can succeed!

Foreword

Sally Smith describes the fourth dimension: What to do! This achievement is made possible only by profound personal and professional experience in the first three dimensions: child, parent, teacher.

As a teacher, Sally Smith has pioneered new approaches and techniques that are both creative and practical. While the classroom is the arena of focus, Mrs. Smith knows that the parent is also a key educator or instructor, who can assist or hinder the work of the classroom teacher. This knowledge is leavened by intimate contact with hundreds of learning disabled youngsters of all ages. With this firm foundation she provides help and guidance for the teachers who must do the work on a daily basis.

This multidimensional adventure, beginning on a personal level, has led to a search for new solutions and new ways, culminating in the founding of The Lab School. Experience as a teacher and administrator led to a recognition of this professional educator who, as associate professor at the American University in charge of learning disabilities, has been able to bring special knowledge to a broad audience. This splendid book will make it possible for many more to benefit from the creative journey of a pioneer.

There are no easy answers for the learning disabled, because persistence and pain go hand in hand in the learning process. This book's triumph is in achieving a synthesis between the emotional and cognitive domains. Careful reading and study will benefit literally thousands of people; and most significantly, it can benefit an individual important to you.

Bertram S. Brown, M.D.
Assistant Surgeon General
U.S. Public Health Service

NO EASY ANSWERS

1

Have You Seen This Child?

He reads *saw* for *was*.
He says a *b* is a *d*, and a *d* is a *p*.
He skips, omits, or adds words when he reads aloud.
She reads well but can hardly spell a word.
  She writes 41 for 14.
  He can do any mental arithmetic problem but can't write it down.
  She doesn't know today the multiplication tables she knew yesterday.
  He can talk about life on Mars but can't add 2 + 2.
    He puts down the same answer to four different math problems.
    He draws the same thing over and over again.
    She asks endless questions but doesn't seem interested in the answers.
    He is an expert strategist in checkers but doesn't understand simple riddles.
      He has an adult vocabulary but avoids using the past tense.
      She starts talking in the middle of an idea.
      He calls breakfast *lunch* and confuses *yesterday* with *tomorrow*.
      He can't tell you what has just been said.
        She can talk about Homer but can't tell you the days of the week.
        He discusses monsoons but does not know the order of the seasons.
        He can remember the television ads but not his own telephone number.
        She can remember what you say to her but not what she sees. She can't picture things in her mind.

1

> She can't see the difference between Africa and South America on the map.
>
> He doesn't see the difference between *pin, pan,* and *pun.*

She is a good child, quiet and polite, but she doesn't learn.

He prefers to play with children much younger than himself.

She says whatever pops into her head.

He rushes headlong into his work, is the first one finished, and does every problem wrong.

She has trouble lining up and can't keep her hands off the child in front of her.

He doesn't stop talking, giggles too much, and laughs the loudest and the longest.

> He doesn't look where he's going, bumps into the door, swings his lunch box into the nearest leg, trips on his own feet, and doesn't look at the person who is talking to him.
>
> > He loses his homework, misplaces his book, forgets where he is to be.
> >
> > She leaves a trail of her belongings behind her wherever she goes.
> >
> > He acts like an absent-minded professor (and has untied shoelaces as well).
> >
> > > She likes routines, is upset by changes, and is reluctant to try anything new.
> > >
> > > He wants everything done the same way.
> > >
> > > He doesn't follow directions.
> > >
> > > She is distracted by the least little thing.
> > >
> > > He doesn't pay attention.

He doesn't look.

> She doesn't listen.
>
> > He doesn't remember.
> >
> > > She doesn't do what she's supposed to do.
> > >
> > > > **HAVE YOU SEEN THIS CHILD?**

Is this a bad child?

> Willful?
>
> > Lazy?
> >
> > > Manipulative?
> > >
> > > > Spoiled?
> > > >
> > > > > Disturbed?

Probably not. This might be a very young child, or it could be a learning disabled child. It isn't that other children don't behave this way. They do! It is **THE QUANTITY, INTENSITY,**

AND LONG DURATION OF IMMATURE BEHAVIOR that make the learning disabled child different. It is the uneven quality of this child which is confounding. He is demanding, bewildering, baffling, and consuming. One day he can do something, and the next he can't. Some of his talents are extraordinary, yet he cannot manage the simplest routines of daily existence. This erratic quality makes the adults around him feel insecure. What will happen next? Is he doing it on purpose? Does he do it to get me mad? These are typical questions asked by the adults who deal with the learning disabled child. They don't understand. His talents and successes give them hope. His distractibility, infantile responses, and disorganization exasperate them. They don't know what is going on. That, in itself, is exhausting. Teachers and parents find themselves feeling drained and inadequate. They want to do the very most and best they can for him, but they don't know what to do. When they are with such a child, adults who are otherwise competent often feel helpless and incompetent.

They Face So Many Difficulties

Imagine yourself to be this child, such a patchwork quilt of "can dos" and "can't dos." Would you believe you are intelligent, as the adults say, when all your buddies can read and you can't? Wouldn't you wonder about yourself if you kept hearing all kinds of sounds but missed what the teacher said? Other kids could remember so much, but you couldn't. Wouldn't that bother you? Might you wonder if something were terribly wrong with you if you were always forgetting things or tripping over your own feet and your friends didn't? Have you ever wakened in an unfamiliar hotel room and tapped that terrible feeling of utter disorientation —"Where am I"? There is nothing familiar to hold on to, and for a brief moment your mind is blank. This is the way many learning disabled children feel in everyday space. And the lack of a sense of time and timing that they feel is comparable to your jet trip to Australia, where twenty hours later, without a watch, you have no sense of what time it is. Try threading a needle with a pair of extra thick rubber gloves on, and you will come close to the feeling of the child whose hands don't work well for him when he tries to hold a pencil and write. Try it while someone is stating firmly that if you only tried harder, you could do it.

If you analyze the process of tying your shoelaces, you will realize how exceedingly complex an act it is. Now imagine trying to tie a bow when you cannot visualize what a loop looks like. It is the feeling of the lost driver who knows his destination but doesn't know where he is starting from, of the frantic mother who is being yelled at but can't locate her car keys anywhere. Frantic and overwhelmed—common feelings of the learning disabled child, who is confused, bewildered, doesn't know where to begin, what to do, how to go about doing a task, doesn't understand what's going on within him, this despairing child overwhelms the adults around him, Frequently he would rather be called "bad" than "dumb," so he will say, "I won't," when he means, "I can't." Often he comes across as negative, hostile, or silly; he may be a loner, avoiding help, laughing at adults, sporting the "I don't care" attitude or saying, "I think this work is boring and stupid" when he can't do it. Sometimes he presents himself as sweet, kind, considerate, overly conscientious. Whatever the outside cover, the inside is hurting. Most adults feel that hurt, and when they don't know how to remove it, they feel helpless. Too often, the frightened child is forgotten along with the precious qualities that the child does have.

They Also Display a Hearty Enthusiasm . . .

There is something extremely appealing about a wide-eyed, open-armed youngster with a beaming smile. "Look, the sun is smiling on us today!" he says as he hugs the world around him. "I'm glad Mr. Rain stayed away," an immature statement for an eleven-year-old but still a pleasure to hear.

There's a sheer joy—temporary though it may be—that many learning disabled children bring to life. Often they seem to embrace life with an enthusiasm and jauntiness that most of us lose with maturity. The spontaneous expression of feelings, the unedited comment, the untrampled-upon gesture are all trademarks of the impulsive child. There's a freshness that he conveys, perhaps because he doesn't see the whole picture, that turns our attention to experiences we have come to take for granted. In the midst of checking the route map, watching the road signs, estimating when the next gas stop must be made, our attention is suddenly diverted to an unexpected delight when the learning disabled child remarks, "How fresh and good the grass smells!"

Often overly sensitive to the feelings and relationships of the people around him, this is the child who slips her hand clumsily into the hand of a troubled adult and squeezes gently. The adult silently wonders, "How did that little girl know what I needed just at that time?" Many adults have commented that learning disabled children seem to have ESP, a certain profound knowledge of emotional states (even if the child can't apply it to himself).

Sometimes a learning disabled child is very shy and retiring, tending to back away from social situations, and especially unfamiliar ones. Often, however, he meets people easily, although he may have trouble maintaining those relationships. In one family of three children, it was always the learning disabled child who knew everyone at the unfamiliar swimming pool, had become a well-known figure in the hotel dining room, and had met every new neighbor within minutes of their arrival. He didn't remember their names but everyone knew his. "Oh, you're Joe's family!" people would say to the rest of them. His friendliness to strangers and his open, guileless remarks enchanted newcomers. In any new situation, this family found it was Joe who made everybody feel at home at once. His impulsiveness may have led him to wandering, but he did get the layout of a new place down pat—that is, if he found his way back to the appointed spot. Joe had a way of heading toward the men's room but along the way discovering all sorts of fascinating byways to share with his family. He was indiscriminate in his choice of companions. He was equally at ease with a beggar and a millionaire, both of whom introduced him to exciting new experiences. Joe would always come back from one of his jaunts (while the family was frantically looking for him) bearing a precious gift somebody had given him—a flower or a candy—or leading some embarrassed but friendly stranger back with him.

Not sufficiently afraid of the dangerous or the unknown, the learning disabled child frequently embarks on adventures that could fill a novel. He's the one who discovers the unbeaten path to the hermit's cottage and has tea with him, uncovers the nest of blue eggs, finds the attic closet filled with treasures (even though he may get locked inside it for a while). Walking along the beach picking up pebbles at random, he finds a half-dollar. He is the one who ducks under the barrier and gets to shake the governor's hand. Important people are treated like any other friends by this child, who is not famous for diplomacy and has no sense of priorities. He doesn't discriminate, to the point that it becomes poor judgment in social situations.

He is likely to be an asset at a party, where he genuinely welcomes people and puts others at ease. Trouble may come later if he meets with a frustration or misinterprets a remark. At school, he often takes on the welcoming role at the beginning of the term or in a new grouping.

. . . and Many Other Special Qualities

Some learning disabled youngsters are not hyperactive, impulsive, or outgoing, but they too have a quality about them that can make others feel good about themselves. Albert, quiet and resourceful, seems to gather children around him. They feel strength in him. They admire his athletic prowess. He seems to have a fund of resources, untried ways of doing things. The learning disabled youngster, because there is so much he can't seem to do like others, must call upon his own ingenuity and use a different perspective. Perhaps learning disabilities have been at the root of some of our most valued inventions. We know that Thomas Edison's learning disabilities brought him failure at school, but they also helped to bring us the light bulb. Auguste Rodin, the magnificent sculptor, had difficulty learning to read and write; he was known as the worst student in his school. Albert Einstein's teachers found him to be a slow learner and socially awkward. And Hans Christian Andersen, who spun all those lovely fairy tales, was an extremely poor student and said to be very immature. Yet his naiveté and his eternal childlike qualities have brought pleasure to countless people.

The learning disabled youngster, along with all the heartache he feels and brings into his home, often touches the family with a freshness, a pure natural quality. When Harry laughed, it was such a full, resounding roar of delight that his family couldn't help but laugh with him. The unscreened pleasure he took in watching the antics of a litter of puppies permeated the whole house. Unfortunately that same loud laugh, and its duration, might send him to the principal's office at school.

Although the learning disabled child is not known for his humor and is often laughed at for his clumsiness of speech, action, or social behavior, many times he coins a phrase that is uproarious. Martin, after suffering along with a classmate who wouldn't stop talking about electricity, said, "That guy is so obsessed with electricity that some day he's going to go to the bathroom and a light bulb will come out!"

Moodiness can bring bright moments too. Just as a young child is very distractible and often can be led out of a bad moment by his own distractibility, so it is with the learning disabled child. The perturbed girl with the storm clouds gathering around her can suddenly change into a sparkling delight if an adult strikes the right chord and provokes her to laugh by imitating her pouting. Within minutes her mood can change, often for the better. Her responsiveness lends itself to adult direction.

Courage is a quality we all admire. With the blind child, the deaf, the paralyzed, the public admires every effort. Such a large part of the learning disabled child's troubles go unseen that he does not receive anything like the praise he so justly deserves. Imagine the effort it takes to operate within the disorder felt by this child. It takes an immense amount of effort every day for the learning disabled child to face the world of school with its meaningless symbols and confused instruction. Not only is he picking himself up literally much of the time, but he is also picking himself up from constant failures and disappointments and keeping going.

It is a wonder that so many learning disabled children have developed strong characters and unique personalities, but they have. True, some of them are quiet, very closed people, called eccentric, but more often than not they are respected for their difference and their specific talents. Many are free spirits, venturing into life with abandon. The brakes are not on enough. The maturity that builds good judgment is not working well enough. But there's a joy, a heartwarming quality that brings out all the good instincts in a person. Many brothers or sisters of learning disabled children (and a sprinkling of parents too) have felt a certain envy and admiration of the free spirit. One older brother said, "I'm so regulated by what I should do and what I have to do, I've lost sight of what I can do or want to do or like to do. And HE DOES IT ALL!"

Teachers often say that they can't get over how good-looking, appealing, and affectionate the learning disabled children in their classrooms are and how unusually creative so many of them are. The learning disabled child has to use other outlets when the switchboard of the brain doesn't make the proper connections; he has to travel new pathways. He has to use all the resources at his disposal to accomplish the simplest of tasks. He has to combat the disorder overwhelming him, making him easily fatigued. He has to work far harder than the rest of us, and still take the abuse of being called lazy.

Have you seen *this* child?

2

Immaturity and the Need for Organization

Organization is the lifeline, the safeguard, the medicine, and the key to learning for the child who is disabled by disorganization, or disorder. This intelligent child cannot filter out and organize the sensations that are coming to his brain from his eyes and his ears and through his body. He is overstimulated, bombarded by every sensation. He cannot sort out that which is relevant from that which is not. He lacks discrimination. The filtering mechanism of his brain is not working properly, and so the mass of sights, sounds, and feelings is coming in unscreened, causing DISORDER. Because the child registers fragments of what is coming in, what comes out is therefore fragmented, disorganized, irrelevant, disordered. He is indiscriminate in his reactions and often in his statements. Although at times he displays a very mature intellect and sensitivity, he is frequently scattered and inappropriate.

A two-year-old is both delightful and exhausting. He runs around a room touching everything in sight. He yells when he is denied a cookie. He rolls on the floor in delight. He spills his milk and breaks his mug. You can tell a home where there is a two-year-old because everything movable or breakable is out of his reach. Unless his environment is arranged to suit his two-year-old ways, he is a menace.

His movements are random—hit or miss. He uses his whole body when one hand would do—everything in excess. His attention, his aims, and his belongings are scattered. He is clumsy, unfocused, and inefficient in anything he does. Nobody expects him to be any other way because he is two. He is funny, his mispronounced words and inappropriate remarks are hilarious, and, although he keeps things hopping and may be exhausting, he is a joy.

But the same behavior in a seven-year-old is not charming. It is a cause of ever-growing anxiety to his parents, and it is not accepted or tolerated by others. The behavior itself is not abnormal, but it is inappropriate to the child's age. It is immature.

For children whose nervous systems develop normally, neural organization happens naturally. They sort out their world. They discriminate between essential and nonessential. They focus. They soon learn to judge distances and lapses of time accurately. They can place themselves and their belongings in their proper places. They can meet deadlines. By the third grade, they know half of everything they will ever know. Most of what follows will be regroupings, substitutions, refinements of categories, the creation of more sophisticated filing systems in their minds.

A child who develops normally learns to control his body and to concentrate with his mind; each new step in his growth lays a foundation for the next. What was random and undirected becomes focused and efficient. If you watch a four-year-old trying to throw a ball, you see him take an exaggerated stance with his feet wide apart, and his whole body, including his contorted face, goes into the act of throwing. He can't speak while he throws. It takes all his thought and energy to accomplish his throw, inefficient though it may be, and he can't possibly do another thing at the same time. A twelve-year-old throws the ball with accuracy and a neat economy of movement, while calling instructions to his teammates. Through trial and error, he has built up a body memory of what works, and he uses only the necessary muscles and energy. His body knows the relationship of its different parts, and his reactions are fast. The superfluous, random movements of the younger child have been replaced by automatic, accurate ones, and he can now do several things at once. Not so for the learning disabled child.

At The Lab School of Washington, the children's difficulty with integrating two or more things at once shows up typically in drama class. When Wayne was playing the part of a bus driver, he could not maintain his pantomime of holding the steering wheel and at the same time asking the passengers where they were going. He would either "drive" in silence or put his hands in his lap to ask the question.

Similarly, at lunch time, Linda could not talk and eat at the same time. Her sandwich remained uneaten because she could not organize herself to speak, take a bite while listening to the response, chew, swallow, and be ready to speak again. Such a child can concentrate on only one thing at a time, and often not for very long.

Indiscriminate Reactions

Nobody expects a three-year-old to sit still for long with a picture book on his lap. In a very few minutes he will be up and exploring—looking, touching everything around him—and any loud noise will draw him to it. This same behavior in a seven-year-old is called *distractibility*, and it is one of the most easily recognized characteristics of a learning disabled child. He reacts indiscriminately to everything going on around him.

Maturity is achieved by separating out the parts from a whole, differentiating them, and integrating them back into an understandable and usable unity, which produces organization. You can't pull things together properly until you can sort out the pieces. You have to know where the parts of your body are and what they can do before you can become coordinated, with all parts working together smoothly. A baby cannot move in a coordinated way, partly because he does not have sufficient awareness of his own body. Just as the infant must babble in a random way before he can speak, so movement begins in a random way before it becomes purposeful and specific. The preschool youngster learns to separate out one part of the body from another, left from right, before he can begin to unify and coordinate his body. Normally by the age of five or six, he knows his right side from his left and can use the two together in actions where both are needed, as in opening a jar. He has freedom of action. The learning disabled child does not follow the normal pattern of maturing. A doctor would say that he suffers from neurological immaturity or minimal brain dysfunction. An educator would say that he has a learning disability. A parent would say, "Something is wrong; he's so inconsistent."

Discrimination

Separating out is at the root of the learning disabled child's problem. Because of the lag in his neural development, he is bombarded by too many sensations at once. Because of his immaturity, he reacts to too much with too much body and mind. He doesn't discriminate. His inability to separate out one idea from another, one sound, one symbol, is related to his difficulty in separating out body parts and one side from the other. This affects his judgment of space and explains why so many of these children spill their milk, drop their papers, and knock over objects by mistake. Physical activities have to be broken down and taught to them in sequence, step by step. Some learning disabled children appear very well coordinated in sports and dance but still have subtle spatial difficulties and cannot coordinate the eye and the hand to work smoothly together.

Random action cannot become coordinated and efficient until the body knows which parts to use. By separating out the functions of the parts, a child becomes aware of the limits of his whole body and himself as a separate entity in space. A baby's first big sorting job is separating himself out as an individual being from all around him. At first he tends to see everything as an extension of himself. Then he sees objects separate from himself. As he grows older, he sees relationships among objects, isolates them, learns to see their differences and also their similarities. From these he makes generalizations and creates abstract ideas. His mind is going through the same process of development and control that his body followed earlier: separation, differentiation, integration.

The ultimate maturing occurs in the transition from adolescence to adulthood, when the young person sees himself both as a unique, differentiated part of a larger society and as a meaningful unit in his own right. The rest of his life will be spent discovering the infinite possibilities in his personhood and integrating them into wholeness.

At the very core of growth is this process of identifying differences and similarities and then pulling them together to give meaning to life. This is the very serious business of the preschooler, his prime developmental task. Through play, he is sorting out reality and fantasy, sights, sounds, and movements. All his exploring, touching, smelling, opening, closing, and tasting are organizing his environment. The preschooler is fully occupied as he discriminates one color from another, one shape from another and identifies sounds, sizes, and sequences. Through play, he is sorting out one item from another; as one puts together a puzzle, he is putting together his world, making sense of it.

Usually the child with an intact nervous system is a well-organized human being by school age. He has sorted, classified, and categorized information into the proper compartments in his mind. He has achieved the maturation necessary to learn efficiently. By age six, most youngsters are ready for formal education (although some cultures believe they are not ready until seven). His equipment can handle it; he has the tools to do the job.

The learning disabled youngster is not ready for formal education on time. He is consumed by disorder and disorganization. He is immature. He doesn't have the internal organization necessary to pay attention. It's not just that he doesn't pay attention; he pays too much attention to too many things. The least little stimulus plays havoc with his concentration. Almost anything can distract this child. It is the creative and scientific challenge to his teacher to capture—and keep—the focus of this distractible child.

Too Many Stimuli

The distractible child is likely to be impulsive. The clamor of stimuli on his nervous system, the overload that causes him to switch his attention rapidly from one stimulus to another, appears as distractibility. His behavioral response to each stimulus that seizes his attention appears as impulsivity. The child can't slow down in order to think ahead and plan the next step. His thoughts come tumbling straight out, and he says the first thing he thinks of without pausing to see if it is really all right to say it. Jerry's mother and father were discussing how to seat their guests at a forthcoming dinner party and shared the impression that Mr. Brown was an old hypocrite. Jerry, whose vocabulary, at age twelve, was large in spite of his learning disabilities, was interested in this new word and asked what it meant. His parents stopped to explain that it meant somebody who says one thing and does another, and Jerry showed that he understood this idea by identifying a child in his class who displayed these same traits. His mother and father were very pleased at Jerry's quickness and turned back to planning the party. That evening when Jerry greeted the guests before he went to bed, he met Mr. Brown with pure delight at his own new knowledge: "Hello, Mr. Brown—so you're the old hypocrite!"

It is not surprising that this child often has a low tolerance for frustration, which causes him either to withdraw or explode. Just as he has trouble inhibiting the intrusive sensations and thought that clamor for his attention, so he has trouble inhibiting his impulses. He will speak before he thinks. Often he will plunge mindlessly headlong into an activity. The job of the teacher is to say repeatedly to him, until he can say it to himself, "Stop. Think. Plan. *Then act*." This is as crucial a part of the teaching as providing the substantive subject matter.

Impulsiveness

He speaks before he thinks, acts before he reasons, and leaps before he looks. Is it any wonder that he is often accident prone? He follows his first impulse and becomes victim of his impulsiveness. He sees a big, fat zipper on a woman's dress and pulls it down before anyone knows what's happening. He does not stop and think about it, weighing the consequences of whether such fun is worth it. The same child, on his way across the room to retrieve his sneakers, stops to play with a toy and forgets all about the sneakers. Not only is he distracted, but he cannot postpone what he feels like doing at that very instant.

Some learning disabled youngsters can't stop what they are doing at the proper time, as though the necessary energy and organization were more than they could muster. The brakes are not working. They can't put their toys away, turn off the television, stop coloring, take off the record. Often they need the help of an adult to take away the crayon or stand in front of the television. The adult does part of the transition for the child by monitoring him, often physically helping him and verbally reminding, "We'll put it away now for we have to leave and go to the playground."

The learning disabled child can't make sense out of what he receives through his senses, even though his sight, hearing, and other sense organs are intact. The messages he receives are jumbled and scattered. The pattern on the tablecloth and the food on his plate come through to him with equal intensity, and he cannot tell which is which. Indiscriminately he gives importance to everything, establishing no priorities or order. He can't ignore the footsteps in the hall, the light tumbling in through the venetian blinds, the hand of his neighbor fixing her hair; the jangling earrings of his teacher remove focus on what the teacher is saying. Everything going on in the classroom distracts him from paying attention to what he is there to do: to learn. He cannot focus on one thing to the exclusion of all others. His nervous system is late in developing, and his immature brain is not yet equipped to filter out the irrelevant and the unnecessary automatically. The chances are that it will mature, however, in time.

A Confusing Environment

Imagine how you might feel if you are in a boat on a rough sea and you see people on the shore waving to you, flags being waved at you, a loudspeaker saying something you can't understand, people in another boat nearby yelling to you—but all you can hear is the roar of the waves. The learning disabled youngster feels that desperation to understand what's going on but is swept up by the surrounding sensations. His immature brain can't automatically relegate these sensations to a subordinate place so that he can focus on the real purpose of the moment.

Have you ever been swept into a festival or a rally where you had no idea what was going on, what the point of it was, what the chanting and movement all around you was about? You couldn't make sense of the whole experience. Have you ever tried to find your way in a strange city following someone's directions that referred to streets you haven't seen—and with the noise of the traffic, screaming sirens, and people shouting all around you, making it harder to understand?

When you want to understand something and you can't filter out what's important, what's meaningful from what isn't, you probably feel overwhelmed, dumb, threatened, perhaps helpless, and then angry. It is frustrating to be unable to separate out the essential parts and pull them together into a meaningful whole. You can't make sense of your environment this way.

For learning disabled children, the ability to organize has somehow been short-circuited, and normal learning cannot follow. If a child cannot be sure what comes first, in the middle, or last, then getting dressed is an ordeal, the days of the week stay jumbled, counting or reciting the alphabet becomes a hopeless chore, and reading is an impossibility. Janet can't get down to work. She's busy putting her lunch away, hanging up her jacket, talking to her neighbor, tying her shoelace, which does not seem to be tight enough and has to be retied, noticing that Alfred didn't put his lunch away in the right spot and that there's a funny groove on the floor next to a crack in the linoleum, and then she's occupied chasing a fly, which she calls a bee. Finally she is led to her seat. Focused by her teacher, she puts on earphones and listens to a book. Soon it is time to stop. The teacher motions to her, taps her, finally removes the earphones from her, and Janet flies into a tantrum. This is a typical story of a learning disabled child. She can't get started, has a terrible time focusing, and then won't stop. The child flits from activity to activity at home, not settling down, getting under everybody's feet, and then— usually near mealtime—becomes engrossed in something and won't, almost *can't*, stop, no matter how many warnings are given. It's as though the activity has taken over the child, and she can't get out from under it unless an adult does it for her. This behavior is called *perseveration*.

A child may draw one circle and continue to draw more all over his paper until the teacher takes the pencil out of his hand. His drawing is an unthinking action, where the mind is seemingly separated from the hand that is circling. Sometimes it is the one activity that a child can do and be successful at. He may fear not being able to manage a new task.

To shift easily from one activity to another demands more flexibility and control than the learning disabled child seems to have. To the parent, it often seems like moving mountains, bringing as much of the mountain to Mohammed as possible. Rather than have Abba create a scene, his mother will bring the clothes to him (instead of insisting that he get the clothes himself) and practically dress him to help him end the activity and be ready to go out for the party on time.

Hyperactivity

A two-year-old can run you off your feet in half an hour. A hyperactive child can do the same thing. However, all learning disabled children are not necessarily hyperactive. If he does happen to be hyperactive, his purposeless, scattered, mindless, disordered activity is exhausting to cope with. All that misguided energy—never concentrating, never resting—makes him an enfant terrible. Yet the child is not bad, nor is he damaged. His development is lopsided and irregular. Nobody calls a normal, energetic two-year-old hyperactive, yet by age seven or eight, the same behavior has been given a name: pathological.

Hyperactivity (*hyper* means "excessive") is frequently considered a disease and therefore a medical problem. In fact, hyperactivity is uncoordinated, random, unthinking, unfocused, restless, excessive movement stemming from an immature brain. It is characterized by constant motion—not necessarily running about all the time but a seemingly endless fidgeting, wriggling, and restlessness. You have probably seen the child whose fingers are drumming on the table, whose feet are swinging, whose pencil is tapping, who continually hums or sniffs, who gets out of his seat ten times in ten minutes. Excessive talking, noise making, and disruptiveness also fit this picture.

The hyperactive child is irritable. Little things that don't bother other children of his age make him blow up in rage or dissolve in tears. He doesn't distinguish big from small issues or blows from affronts. People say he is high-strung or oversensitive. His moods are unpredictable. Within half an hour, he may change from a tight-lipped, stubborn mule to a screaming demon, and then to the sweet, manageable child you love so much, full of regret for the scene he has just created.

Usually the learning disabled child feels terrible remorse after an impulsive act. "I didn't think—I'm sorry," he says sadly. It's as though he is completely gathered up and taken over by overwhelming impulses, helpless to do anything about them or to employ his reason to control himself until he calms down. He is known to have "emotional lability," a swing of moods, big ups and downs. He overreacts or underreacts, but rarely reacts in proportion to the situation at hand.

> Not all hyperactive children have learning disabilities; in fact, many don't.
>
> Not all learning disabled children are hyperactive, impulsive, perseverative, emotionally labile, and visibly distractible.

Some learning disabled children are *hypo*active (the opposite of hyperactive). They have a lower-than-average activity level and are slow to react to everything. Hypoactive youngsters are well behaved, well controlled, and no trouble to manage for parents and teachers. They may daydream quietly in a corner and often seem to be "not there." Hypoactive youngsters who have learning disabilities withdraw because they cannot process what is going on. They may not even be aware of what is going on, with their attention scattered elsewhere, yet they seldom cause the teacher any trouble. They don't disrupt classes but may not be learning anything. Their organization is poor; they reverse letters and numbers. They too have trouble in the regular classroom.

Whereas the hyperactive child cannot tolerate any frustration and will impulsively throw a book, swear, stamp away from the game, or slam the door the moment he can't do something, the daydreamer can either tolerate more frustration without falling apart or else he further detaches himself from the scene. His frustration tolerance is high, while the hyperactive child's is low and borders on catastrophic reactions to even small problems.

The immaturity of learning disabled children is evident not only in their movement, behavior, and disorganization but also frequently in their speech. The learning disabled youngster of school age often speaks in the manner of a much younger child. His pronunciation, his syntax, and his grammar are very immature, reflecting a lack of order. He can't phrase questions. "Why not you said it?" "He gotted it first." "What you think I should do?"

Frequently the immature child will give life and personality to objects. This is called *animism*—the failure to recognize the difference between animate and inanimate objects. A school-age learning disabled child may behave like a small child in the nursery who talks to his teddy bear, says that the car has "gone beddy-bye" when it is in the garage, or greets his breakfast with "Hello, Sugar Pops!" He will admonish his pencil, "Go on—write!" or see his cuisenaire rods as having a fight: "You go in here before the yellow guy gets you. OK, red guy, how are you going to get him?" This behavior is symbolic of an unawareness of himself as a person fully separate from what is around him—a person who occupies a distinct personal space with a precious individuality all his own.

Defining Himself

Ordinarily the learning disabled child is highly egocentric. Like any very young child, he expects to be the center of attention and does not pay attention to others. He wants his parents to himself. Frequently he wants only one friend. Sharing is difficult, and just as he can handle only one thing at a time, so it is that very often he can manage best with just one other person. The learning disabled youngster of seven or eight is frequently similar in his social behavior to the two- or three-year-old. He craves center stage, not out of any base ambitions but because of immaturity. He has trouble defining who he is. He seems to need constant recognition of his existence long after the preschool years are over. Because of his many difficulties (such as being unable to read or write, to tie shoelaces, or to use language correctly to portray his needs and wants), he is dependent longer on the adults around him and must call for help over a longer period of time. The need for attention may equal the need for help, and many learning disabled youngsters have cleverly discovered that helplessness brings swift attention. Also there are many children who would so much rather receive negative attention than no attention that they will purposely get in trouble or act out to evoke an adult response. Some youngsters will provoke trouble with other children to make sure they are not ignored; they can then complain about being teased or picked on, but they have been the center of everyone's attention. This behavior happens frequently with learning disabled youngsters.

The preschool child spouts many unrealistic goals with all the confidence of a believer. "Next year I shall climb the highest mountain in the world," says four-year-old Les. Nine-year-old Hans, who has learning disabilities, also believes he can do it "next year." Many learning disabled youngsters continue to draw Superman as a representation of themselves (long after that stage has passed in most other children) because they are immature and also are looking for ways to feel more powerful and competent.

The chronological age of a youngster simply states how much time he has spent on earth. The developmental age tells us at what stage he is in his growth—physical, social, emotional, mental. The child with learning disabilities is immature in many phases of his development (although not all), and his developmental age is usually several years below his chronological age. He is lagging in parts of his development, but what he is doing is normal for an earlier phase of growth. His behavior is not abnormal, just delayed. We tend to make allowances for the immaturity of a child who looks immature for his age but often expect far too much from a thirteen-year-old who has suddenly become six feet tall. Yet at the same time, we must remember that every learning disabled child's unevenness includes areas of strength, which we must build on, and not ask too little of him.

We have to teach the learning disabled child at his developmental level yet present the material in ways that satisfy his chronological age. His age and the special interests of his age group command respect. Sophisticated use of very primary materials is what is demanded of the teacher to help the learning disabled child acquire a foundation of organizational skills that will allow him to progress academically.

3

No One Cause, No One Answer

It is difficult to say how many learning disabled children there are because the experts disagree. Several believe that 10 percent to 35 percent of America's children have some form of disability and that 3 percent to 7 percent are severe enough to require special schooling. In the spring of 1978, the United States Office of Education, Bureau of the Handicapped, estimated that there are under two million learning disabled youngsters in this country. Most specialists in the field of learning disabilities disagree with that estimate. One says that one American child out of four has some problem in regard to learning. Another estimates that there are at least eight million youngsters in this category. A new book, just published, states there are approximately ten million. Suffice it to say that many of our children have learning disorders and that there are at least a couple in any average classroom.

Learning disabled children range from the most severely handicapped, who cannot function even with a great deal of extra help in a normal classroom, to mild underachievers who get C's and D's when they have the capacity to get A's. They are children whose reading, spelling, and often arithmetic skills are considerably below (sometimes far below) the norms. Often their spoken language, thinking, and behavior are described as very immature for their age.

The United States government describes a specific learning disability as "a disorder in one or more of the basic psychological processes involved in understanding and using language, spoken or written, which may manifest itself in an imperfect ability to listen, think, speak, read, write, spell, and do mathematical calculations."

Although *learning disabilities* is the preferred term among educators, many others are used, sometimes to refer to the same thing, even though, technically, they may not be describing learning disabilities:

Association deficit pathology
Attention disorders
Brain-injured child
Central nervous system disorder
Conceptually handicapped
Congenital alexia
Congenital strephosymbolia
Diffuse brain damage
Dysgraphia
Dyscalculia
Dyslexia
Educationally handicapped
Hidden handicap
Hyperactivity
Hyperkinetic behavior syndrome
Hypoactivity
Hypokinetic behavior syndrome
Language disability
Language disordered child
Maturation lag
Minimal brain damage
Minimal brain dysfunction (MBD)
Minimal brain injury
Minimal cerebral dysfunction
Minimal cerebral palsy
Minimal chronic brain syndrome
Multisensory disorders
Neurological immaturity
Neurologically handicapped
Neurophrenia
Neurophysiological dysynchrony
Organic brain dysfunction
Organicity
Perceptually handicapped
Primary reading retardation
Psycholinguistic disabilities
Psychoneurological disorders
Reading disability
Specific dyslexia
Specific learning disabilities

Strephosymbolia
Strauss syndrome
The child with multisensory difficulties
The interjacent child
The invisibly handicapped child
The other child
Waysider
Word blindness

Learning disabled children for the most part are being educated in mainstream classrooms without extra attention, and they experience much defeat and failure. Some spend the majority of their school time in the mainstream, with extra help from resource teachers and tutors. Others are largely kept in resource rooms and learning centers, going to the mainstream whenever possible. A relative few are in contained classrooms or special schools for the learning disabled. Under Public Law 94-142, the Education for All Handicapped Children Act, which became effective in fall 1978, more specific attention will be concentrated on the needs of each learning disabled child and an individualized program of remediation.

Many Possible Causes

How did they become learning disabled? Are they diseased, damaged, rejected children? Parents often worry that they did something wrong, they know not what, that produced these problems. They fear they gave the child too much love and attention, or too little. Sometimes parents point to each other accusingly about family secrets—the unmentionable relative who may be retarded, emotionally disturbed, or an unlabeled deviate. Teachers often point to the parents as the cause, for spoiling the child or allowing him to be egocentric and lazy. Sometimes neighbors label the child as dull, undisciplined, and manipulative. If it is not his upbringing, parents and teachers may point to his diet and blame too many soft drinks, junk food, or additives. Or they may blame some environmental element like air pollution or a nearby military radar installation.

What causes learning disabilities?
There is no single cause . . .
There seem to be many causes . . .

The following are conditions that have been identified as contributing to a child's having learning disabilities:

Before Birth

Maternal malnutrition
Bleeding in pregnancy
Poor placental attachment to the uterus
Toxemia in pregnancy
Infectious disease of pregnant mother (German measles, a virus disease, influenza, or a chronic disease)
Alcoholism during pregnancy
The taking of certain drugs during pregnancy
RH incompatibility

During Birth

Long or difficult delivery producing anoxia (not enough oxygen in the brain)
Prematurity
Breech delivery
Cord around neck
Poor position in the uterus (such as a left posterior position)
Dry birth (the water broke prematurely)
Intracranial pressure at the time of birth due to forceps delivery or a narrow pelvic arch in the mother
Rapid delivery exposing the infant too quickly to a new air pressure

After Birth

A long time to produce breathing after birth (often occurs with prematurity, difficult delivery, or twins)
High fever at an early age
Sharp blow to head from fall or accident
Meningitis or encephalitis
Lead poisoning
Drug intoxication
Oxygen deprivation due to suffocation, respiratory distress, or breath holding
Severe nutritional deficiencies

Heredity may also be a factor. In many families, reading disabilities can be traced through several generations. Usually the father, an uncle, or other relatives had the problem. (This tallies with the fact that many more males than females have learning disabilities.) Difficulties with spelling, math, or handwriting may also appear at various times in a family's history.

It is not worth agonizing over which of these factors produced the problems of a particular child. It might be something else not even mentioned here, not known yet. Placing blame, feeling overwhelmed with guilt, giving way to fear that some thoughtless action produced a child's learning problems have never been found to help parents help children with the problem. Sometimes it temporarily helps teachers (who feel frustrated by the learning disabled child) to blame parents, but that doesn't help the children either. Teachers, like parents, usually wish to do the best they can for each child and often seek an easy cause that can be remedied fast. The causes of learning disability are beyond teacher control as they are beyond parent control. Teachers waste time and energy looking for causes, valuable time needed for the study of each student in order to discover how he learns best. All races, religions, economic classes; fat, thin, tall, small parents; youthful parents, older parents have produced children with learning disorders. No one group in society produces more learning disabled children than any other.

In proportionately very few cases have doctors found evidence of actual brain damage. In fact, many brain-damaged children do not have learning disabilities. Scientists are working in the area of medical computer science to detect signs of brain damage or dysfunction that previously could not be monitored; these clinicians hope that by locating exact areas and types of dysfunction in the brain, more precise treatments will be possible. The Quantitative Electrophysiological Battery, currently being used at the Brain Research Laboratory of New York Medical College, holds out many interesting possibilities, but it does not yet provide any total answers. Some neurologists point out that stroke victims, adults who have suffered damage to their brains, and those with cerebral palsy show many impairments of language and thought similar to those of children with learning disorders. One theory is that learning disability is an extremely mild and narrowly selective form of cerebral palsy. The Lab School, which admits only intelligent children with learning disabilities, enrolls fifty-six children. Four of them have known brain damage, but thirty-two others act just like these four. Twenty others simply act in a very immature manner. So far, our knowledge of the brain is so limited that we do not know yet what else to look for or how to detect it.

We know only that there is a lag in the development of learning disabled children, their central nervous systems are delayed in maturing. Neurological examinations most often fail to reveal any medical evidence that would support a diagnosis of brain injury. The absence of clear signs of brain injury led the medical world to believe that the constellation of soft neurological signs had to be noted. This is what led up to such medical terms as *minimal cerebral dysfunction, minimal brain injury,* and *minimal brain dysfunction* (MBD). The soft signs include:

> Persistence of some primitive reflexes of the central nervous system, which should no longer be present after certain ages
> Distractibility (lack of concentration)
> Hyperactivity
> Impulsivity
> Perseveration
> Inconsistency
> Left-right confusion
> Irritability
> Talkativeness
> Awkwardness
> Poor speech
> Social immaturity

Scientists, neurologists, and neurophysiologists are seeking answers to the causes of neurological immaturity to pinpoint the factors responsible for this maturational lag that we currently call *learning disabilities.*

Some specialists say that the cause doesn't matter; we must focus on educating the child. True, we must reach the child early and give him readiness. We must find ways to teach him to do the things he cannot do. We can do this, as educators, without knowing the causes. But other specialists say that the cause does matter; when we know the reason, we will be able to treat the child faster and more efficiently. It is possible within the next five to ten years that advances in neurochemistry and neurophysiology will identify the dysfunctioning parts of the brain. When more precise localization of brain anatomy is correlated with various thinking processes, masses of research will have to be done to determine which part of the brain responds best to what type of education. But at this point, there are no sudden cures or easy answers.

The learning disabled child needs more time to grow, more time to do his work, more time to learn. He must work hard. His parents and teachers must work hard with him and provide him with the supports he needs in order to learn properly and to behave appropriately. Those are the only reliable cures at this point.

Larger Recognition of the Problem

The field of learning disabilities, which did not become a recognized field that received government grants until the late 1960s and early 1970s, faces many unanswered questions about causes. Why is there so much learning disability today when there was not fifty years ago? Part of the explanation may lie in the fact that these children were sorted into already established categories of mentally retarded or emotionally disturbed. Many learning disabled children are still being written off as culturally deprived. Disadvantaged conditions and poor schooling are cited as the causes of learning disabilities in inner-city children. Sometimes they are. However insufficient account has been taken of the effect of high fevers, malnutrition, lead poisoning, maternal malnutrition, lack of proper prenatal care, and similar factors, which may contribute to learning disabilities, causing poor performance at school. In fact, there may not be more cases today, but more recognition of the problem. Some specialists claim that until the advent of miracle drugs and the widespread use of antibiotics, many learning disabled youngsters died of respiratory ailments before they ever reached school age.

It is also possible that the one-room schoolhouse of yesteryear allowed for slow maturing. The heterogeneous groupings allowed a child to proceed at his own pace. In the early 1900s, as the frontier disappeared and Americans moved toward the cities, mass education took on a vast, new importance. Public school systems burgeoned, paralleled by the growth of public libraries, and standardization of education at all levels became the new order. No longer could parents direct their children's education. The rise of modern industry required standardized human components in its management, and our upwardly mobile society came to see education as a measurable step to individual success and to a prosperous, enlightened nation. Only in a culture obsessed with the speed of education and measurable results would those who fail to meet these norms at school be considered disabled people. In fact, they are disabled learners and may be fine people.

Our national panic when Russia launched Sputnik in 1957 was merely the latest phenomenon in the trend to standardization, now seen on a worldwide scale. The American public, worried that the Russians were smarter, more educated, and more efficient, exerted pressure on the educators. Out went a lot of the play in nursery schools and kindergartens; letters and numbers replaced motor activities in many preschools. It is possible that the child who needed more time and more sensory-motor activities was deprived of them, and his development lagged further.

As our population becomes more concentrated in cities and suburbs, our schoolrooms have become more crowded. We are surrounded by BIGNESS—the bigness of government, cities, buildings, supermarkets, jumbo eggs, and giant-sized aspirin. Bigness can be overwhelming. Individuality is not prized. Attention to each person's very special needs can become lost. The standardization of quantity rather than quality often determines our values: how much we own, how many high grades we have, how many correct answers we made.

A child cannot always conform within the given time period; if he does not, too often he is classed as a failure. Perhaps because of the uncertainty of our times, the rapid changes in life-styles, the vanishing of accepted traditions, we have become more dependent on the right answer than before and less tolerant of individual differences. Under this pressure, the child with a learning disability may become so burdened with defeat and failure that he doesn't even learn at his own pace and thus widens the gap.

Some subscribe to the theory that our polluted air and rivers, excess noise, and our unclean environment have contributed to the increase in delayed development in our children. Some believe that insecticides and pesticides pollute our children's brains.

Boys are affected with learning disabilities more frequently than girls are. The ratio is seven to one nationally, and some believe that it is ten to one. Some theories hold that the male organism is more vulnerable at birth and is more prone to injury since the infant mortality rate is much higher among boys than girls. Some claim that the male fetus is somewhat larger than the female and thus is more susceptible to injury at birth. One researcher believes that because male heads are larger, boys have more trouble exiting at the time of birth. We don't really know. (As this book developed, it became impossible to keep referring to the learning disabled child as "he or she," so in general "he" has been used since the large preponderance of learning disabled youngsters in this country are boys.)

Why is the learning disabled child much harder to manage and teach in hot, humid weather, before storms, on very hazy days and, some say, when there is a full moon? Educators have noted that weather and seasons affect their performance, but nobody yet knows why.

Is there a connection between hypoglycemia (low blood sugar) and learning disabilities? So far, no substantive connection has been proven.

Doctors have noticed a significant relationship among allergic reactions and hyperactivity and learning disabilities. Some of them have treated the children with antihistamines, corticosteroids, and megavitamins. Some of those children experienced relief from allergies, and at the same time their hyperactivity decreased and their learning improved; some did not.

A few years ago, some doctors felt that learning disabled children had a vitamin deficiency and prescribed large doses of vitamins, with no significant success. There are always a few children who improve dramatically, but, for any method to be considered a cure, it has to cure many. So far, it hasn't.

A few specialists, convinced that the learning disabled children are lacking in protein, recommend a high protein diet (much red meat, eggs, and soybeans). Although some youngsters have demonstrated more energy to learn because of this treatment, no known instant school successes have resulted. And some doctors state that high protein diets are dangerous for they can cause metabolic imbalance.

A current theory is that food additives cause hyperactivity and therefore many cases of learning disability. The affected child is put on a special diet, monitored constantly, and in a number of cases has improved. Still there is no definite proof of this connection and no clear evidence that food additives cause learning disabilities.

Some educators believe that learning disabilities do not exist—that there are simply unmotivated children. Others believe there are merely undisciplined students. Their remedies follow their interpretation of the causes. Every once in a while a child improves under their care, but these hardliners do not have the answer for children with learning disabilities in general.

Today big money can be made by taking advantage of the prevalence and seriousness of learning disabilities. Along with excellent schools and treatment centers, a number of "instant remediation" parlors have opened. From pinching ears, to systematic yelling, to acupuncture, to transcendental meditation, to tactile treatments, to patterning of one sort or another, to helium experiences, parents are being promised substantive help by fly-by-night groups. All kinds of causes are enumerated, and these entrepreneurs usually make parents feel responsible for the problem, as well as for the success of the treatment.

In our culture, where speed is a supreme value, and where we prize the frozen dinners, the freeze-dried coffee, the soup can, we grab for the instant answer regarding learning disabilities. UNFORTUNATELY THERE IS NO ONE CAUSE. THERE IS NO EASY ANSWER.

Focus on the Symptom, Not the Cause

Rather than focusing on the prime cause of learning disabilities, which may be one of the many mentioned above, teachers need to focus on the prime symptom—immaturity or delayed development—and the disorganization and disorder that accompany it. Each child is unique. His problems weave their own pattern. Each teacher must be a detective of sorts to determine how each child learns best, what modalities or channels of learning are a child's strongest ones, what interests can be built on, what specific disabilities are there to remediate. Each teacher needs to learn a multitude of approaches and methods of teaching and to learn the very special skill of being able to match the appropriate method or combination of methods to the individual child's specific needs. (These approaches are gone into in detail in chapters 8 and 9.)

4

The Need to Learn How to Learn

Teaching the learning disabled child the approach to a task is as important as, if not more so than, teaching the task itself. To begin a task, the child has to focus on it, look at it, listen to directions, integrate several processes at once, and establish priorities or at least an order of procedure. All of these constitute areas of difficulty for a learning disabled child, which is why he has so much trouble startig tasks. Teachers often remark that there is no logic to how these children begin something, and they refer to a child's approach as "scattered," "totally disorganized," or "inappropriate." Teachers describe the learning disabled child who begins telling a story in the middle or who starts writing on the bottom of a page or who circles a smudge on a worksheet, obviously missing the point of each exercise. One teacher said, "They don't know what to do with their bodies, no less their eyes, their ears and their mouths. We have to teach them all that before they can get to work."

The very immature child may randomly attack every task in a desultory manner. He may pay no attention to what he is doing, but just do something and do it fast. Jane was so impulsive that she would begin every worksheet before listening to or reading the instructions. She required an adult at her side to monitor what she was doing and to say to her what eventually she had to learn to say to herself: "Stop, Jane. Think. What are you to do? Now begin." Slowing her down, focusing Jane was enough, for she had enough organization skills to draw on after that.

Clive did not. When he finally learned to help set the table and put spoons on the right side of each place, he would ritualistically put out spoons for every meal thereafter, even if the spoons were not necessary. Clive had not yet developed the maturity to distinguish what belonged and what didn't. He lacked the basic skills of discrimination, the organization to select the appropriate way to handle the task. A learning disabled child may find one way to do a particular task and, due to his internal disorder, stick to that way of doing it forevermore, down to the last detail. His procedure may not be right the second or third time he does it, because the situation itself may have changed, but that makes no difference. You could almost give him a new name: the One Way Kid.

> When do we tend to become rigid and inflexible?
> . . . when we don't know what to do.
> . . . when we are most uncertain.
> When do we tend to look for one answer?
> . . . when we are confused.
> . . . when we are most unsure of ourselves and everything seems out of hand.
> When do we want to cling to the familiar?
> . . . when we are overwhelmed.

The learning disabled child is overwhelmed by unscreened stimuli bombarding his brain; he is confused, uncertain, unsure. It is not surprising that he grabs on to one way and doesn't let go, particularly when we think of this child as lagging in development, like a very young child who feels secure only with routine. Swamped by an overload of sensations, in a world that often appears to him as an undifferentiated mass, he opts for one way to do things and rebels if there is a change. This child dreads the unknown and the unfamiliar. There is so little that makes sense to him. Sameness makes sense.

The One Way Kid

The learning disabled youngster is reminiscent of a very young child who cannot deal with alternatives at the immature level of his age. He becomes anxious when he is taken to the park by an unfamiliar route. He is upset on a Sunday morning when his parents have breakfast in their pajamas, breaking the known routine of dress first, breakfast afterward. He won't accept a broken cookie because a cookie is round; if the broken piece is jagged, it can't be a cookie. He doesn't recognize a teacher outside of school. He may appear paralyzed when faced with two equal choices, unable to select either one.

Sometimes the learning disabled child can unintentionally be very destructive. "He breaks all his toys!" says Tommy's sister. He pushes and pulls too hard. He continues to press one lever when he is supposed to press and pull; he can't switch easily from one movement to another. He's often the One Way Kid. He pulls the wheels off his toy cars, he winds too far on the windup robot, he presses too hard on the pencil and breaks it, and he nearly squeezes the life out of the pet turtle. He's called careless, irresponsible, hostile, when, in fact, in his immature fashion, he is continuing an action too long, almost mindlessly. The technical term for this is *perseveration*.

Not allowing any deviation from his one way, the learning disabled child often cannot bear to see another child using a different method to attain the same goal. He will correct the child, insist that his way is the right way, pick on the child, and stand over him to be sure that he does not err. Sometimes the One Way Kid is so busy minding everybody else's business to make sure they do things his way that he neglects his own work completely.

The order he has created around himself is so fragile that he may rush to an adult to announce that Johnny has broken a rule or Suzie has taken the wrong book. Other children see him as a tattletale and shun him. His inability to tolerate differences may make him suspicious of black or white people (whichever he is not), or of people with foreign accents, thereby causing embarrassment to his parents who wonder where he picked up such prejudices.

The Now Child

Anything sudden or unexpected throws the inflexible child off his track. On the other hand, he expects his wants to be met instantly: "I want it right now! Do it now!" The concepts of "later," "in time," "wait" are meaningless to him. The inflexible child who wants what he wants when he wants it, no matter what is going on around him—a storm, a riot, an accident, a crisis—is the same child who doesn't see wholeness. He gets caught up in the details and misses the big picture. Occasionally he sees the big picture but has no understanding of the parts and their relationship to one another.

Any kind of postponement, delay, or change of plans immediately upsets the learning disabled youngster. Bobby said, "People are tricking me. It's not fair," whenever a sudden change of routine, such as a substitute teacher's coming, took place at school. Susan simply cried at these times. Jamie exhibited more excess energy than ever and would ask a series of compulsive, nonstop questions to find out about the change but would not wait to hear the answers. Many a scream in a restaurant, a tantrum on the floor of a department store, a grab at someone else's ball in the playground can be tracked down to the Now Child. In the first years of life, this behavior is understood by the passerby, who comments: "Poor little thing; he's overtired." But the older child is dismissed as a spoiled brat, and his parents are criticized for having done an inadequate job, or the teacher is reprimanded for having poor control of her students.

No matter how conscientious the parents have been (most parents of learning disabled children do a superb, superhuman job), if the child is in a very early stage of emotional growth due to delayed development, he is not ready to delay or postpone. No matter how excellent or outstanding the teacher, a Now Child cannot wait and take turns like others in his age group. He is completely egocentric. The world is composed of his wants, his urges, his impulses. He has separated himself out as an individual, but he has not yet integrated himself into the reality around him. He doesn't think of others and their needs. He's a bit like the child who keeps looking at himself in the mirror to reassure himself that he exists.

The Concrete Child

The very young child has to see what is in front of him in order to make sense of it. We call that child very concrete. A neurologically immature child is also very concrete. In the development of all children concreteness must precede the ability to deal with abstractions, according to the Swiss psychologist Jean Piaget. This child needs to see the material he is taught, hear it, touch it, smell it, feel it, "be" it. He needs to have enough experience with it to know it well. For a word to have meaning, he must associate it with an object, a picture, or an experience. For example, when asked to copy the word *hill*, severely learning disabled Patrick, at the age of twelve, drew a picture of a hill next to the letters, to give meaning to the word before copying it.

The very concrete child is a literal child. Subtleties, nuances, and inferences escape him. Sarcasm goes over his head. "That's just great!" says the neighborhood bully, derisively. "Oh, thank you! I didn't think I did that well," answers Bruce gratefully. "Get him!" laughs the bully, and all the other children join in ridiculing poor Bruce.

Bruce didn't pay attention to the different tone of voice. He didn't separate the tone from the words in order to understand that the tone of voice was not friendly. Abstractions and oblique references pass him by. That's why it is rare for a learning disabled child to have to sparkling sense of humor. Double meanings, exaggeration to an absurd point, distortion, innuendo, taking an unusual perspective—these are some of the ingredients of humor, and they mean that one has to look at situations in more than one way. To have humor, one cannot be literal as so many learning disabled children are. Unfortunately their literalness often provides humor for others. Eight-year-old Rosie asked what the nose looked like when told that somebody "had a nose for business." Nine-year-old Thomas, having just heard the story of John Henry, was serious when he worried out loud, "It must have hurt John Henry's mother when he was born with a hammer in his hand." Ten-year-old Christine wondered where the stack was when she heard that the gym teacher "blew her stack." Eleven-year-old Jason looked anxiously at his feet when an adult remarked, "My, you've grown another foot!"

Eleven-year-old Eugene is also very concrete in his thinking. He was listening to a record that told a story about covered wagons, when he heard the narrator call them "ships of the prairie." Eugene thereupon insisted he was listening to the wrong record because this one was about ships, not covered wagons. He was not able to grasp the metaphor and understand that "ships of the prairie" could mean "covered wagons." Sidney insisted that a mountain lion could not live in a zoo, only on a mountain. Warren was equally vehement about Mount Vernon being the mountain where George Washington lived. These eleven-year-olds were intelligent but very literal because of their delayed development. So was Murray, who could not conceive of a treasure in a story referring to a lobster. "Treasures mean gold," he said, "and so the lobster cannot be a treasure." Fourteen-year-old Janet was furious when she was given a book to read that she thought was about robots. It was a play, and the stage directions telling where the characters were to sit and how they were to act were what she took to be the story. The immature, concrete child is often stuck in the rut of one interpretation. Yet this problem is understandable when we realize how overwhelmed this child is with the indiscriminate mass of information assaulting him.

The Perfectionist

Often the inflexibility that results from extreme immaturity makes a perfectionist of a learning disabled child, who, of all people, does not need that self-imposed burden on top of the others. He can't bear to make a mistake and may react to his error as if it were a catastrophe, dooming the whole of his project. Twelve-year-old Mitchell slowly, carefully wrote a letter to his grandmother. He showed it proudly to his mother who commended him on his very good effort but suggested, in a matter-of-fact way, that he should correct a spelling mistake near the end before he sent it. Mitchell snatched the letter from her hand, crumpled it up, and stamped on it, crying as though his heart would break. "And I could have found him an eraser in two minutes!" bemoaned his mother later, as upset by the incident as Mitchell had been by his spelling error.

Or the child may not blow up. He may simply drop his work and walk away, never to return to it. Blow up or quit—either tendency makes him extremely reluctant to undertake something new, where a surefire one way has not yet been established and mistakes are almost a certainty.

The learning disabled child often equates mistakes with failure. He cannot see that one mistake in a project is not a disaster but can be easily rectified. He may be hypercritical of a teacher who makes a mistake, harping on the fact again and again, making a big issue of it. Her error disturbs his very precarious sense of order, or it may reflect his deep conviction that mistakes serve as living proof of failure, and he doesn't want his teacher to be imperfect. The adults working with learning disabled children need to give themselves permission to make mistakes and thus allow the children to do the same without collapsing.

Fear of making mistakes is unfortunately reinforced almost every time a child watches an ad on television, where intelligent, athletic, stunning, clean, clearly competent people serve as an example of perfection, achieved with no effort beyond buying the right floor wax or the right car. In our world of "instant products," success and perfection occur within minutes, and there's no time for error. "A perfect solution for every householder," "the answer to your prayers," "the way to meet a perfect mate" describe a simple soap or deodorant. The learning disabled child feels very particularly imperfect surrounded by all this perfection. He often projects this feeling of inadequacy by picking on the faults of others. He looks for defects. He tells Aunt Lily that she has a big mole on her chin. He calls everybody's attention to a run in the principal's stocking. He points out the falling plaster, the uneven shelf, the barely chipped cup. He informs each of his classmates as to their ugliest feature. And yet he yearns to be well liked.

It is a rare learning disabled child who can be sportsmanlike in a game. He sees every loss as yet another confirmation of his worthlessness, and he will do anything—even cheat—to win. Occasionally a child will fear winning. A win this time makes losing next time more likely and more terrible. He has been raised from infancy in our competitive society, which emphasizes achievement and winning above all else, where the second best are downgraded as also-rans, has-beens, and losers. There is no way he can simply enjoy an activity for its own sake when everybody around him presses onward toward success and wins because he loses.

The Perseverating Child

Besides wanting to perform a familiar action in his own rigid way, where he can't go wrong, the learning disabled child may start doing it over and over again like a mindless habit. To persevere is good, and learning disabled children are usually very hard workers. They have to work far harder than other children because they must consciously think through even simple actions like sitting down or taking a book off the shelf. But to *perseverate* is to go beyond perseverance and do the same thing again and again, without thinking, without even being aware that the habit exists. This describes that child mentioned earlier who drew circles over and over again.

Often the perseveration is verbal. When a child comes up with a good thought, he has to interrupt you to say it. He's afraid he'll forget it. Then he says it over and over again to be sure you heard. Sometimes he simply says the first thing that comes to mind and repeats it until he is stopped. He may get hung up on a subject—submarines, ambulances, or a trip he took—which he talks about endlessly until everyone is tired of it. Or having accidentally said something amusing, which was appreciated, he may go on saying it in a stereotyped way long after it has stopped being funny.

He may want to wear the same clothing every day, or he may become attached to one color and want blue shirts, blue shoes, blue sheets on his bed, and blue walls in his room. Harry was always in need of bandages for real or imagined cuts; he perseverated on talk of ailments. Monique persisted in drawing Snoopy. Holly gave the same response, modeled on her first response, to all arithmetic problems. Barry wrote the same letter or sometimes the same word down the entire page. Cary sang the same tune over and over again. Frank cleared his throat every few minutes. Mary asked for a drink of water before class one hot day and kept on wanting her drink of water all through the fall and winter as though she could not get into the classroom without it. Paul ate a cheese sandwich every day for a year. Jack kept on hammering so many nails into the boat he was building that when it was time to sail the boat, it sank from three pounds of extra nails.

The Disoriented Child

The One Way Kid cannot deal with priorities, alternatives, or even choices. Choices can produce anxiety, for they demand organization, isolating the prime characteristic or pleasure in each choice. Once the essential factor is extrapolated, then the two choices must be compared. This requires retaining several things in the mind and switching back and forth to study them. The learning disabled child generally experiences difficulty switching gears. It's as though each time he tries, he becomes settled in a permanent position and is thrust out of it and disoriented with the next move. Choices among many alternatives can drive him frantic. Open classrooms, which offer maximum choice and flexibility, can be agonizing for this child. Unstructured time, such as recess or lunchtime at school, can tax his powers of organization beyond the limit. He doesn't know what to do with himself. He may sit and stare, run around aimlessly, talk incessantly, or go from one thing to another. He has to be taught explicitly how to behave and what to do at lunch and recess in order for him to handle these situations properly. He may have to be taught many times over, in different ways, so he can manage the normal exigencies of these periods. The ability to transfer learning from one situation to another is a prime difficulty of the learning disabled child. It is related to his great immaturity, his concreteness, his being the One Way Kid. You can transfer something if the situation is not exactly the same only if you have the maturity and organization to recognize the prime factors, to isolate the essentials, in the situation.

At home, the choices of what to do with free time can be upsetting to the learning disabled youngster. Jeremy's mother complained that every day this eight-year-old came home from school, went to his room to play, and burst into tears within a few minutes. She was mystified: "He had a whole roomful of fascinating toys, and there he'd sit in the middle of the floor bawling!" Finally she discovered that he didn't know which toys to play with. When she structured the situation by asking, "Jeremy, would you rather get out your soldiers or the Tinker-toys?" he was able to relax and start playing.

Substitutions and alternative ways of doing or being baffle the learning disabled child. James made great friends with the janitor, Freddy. When a boy named Freddy joined his class, James became quite angry, insisting that it couldn't be his real name because Freddy was a man's name, not a boy's. James also could not find the cups in the kitchen when someone had placed them upside down on the shelf; with their bottoms up, they did not appear as cups to him. Nor could he recognize the letter *a* if it was written in another type or on a different texture of paper. He could not read the word *cat* because it was printed in red. He insisted that the word *haul* meant to carry something and that the corridor outside his classroom could not be called *the hall*. To say that something is the same as another thing is pure nonsense to such a child. It can't be the same. There can be only one way.

The Naive Child

At this stage of development, a child fixes on one superficial aspect of the thing he perceives and fails to isolate the essential characteristic that binds it to others of its kind. He believes exactly what he sees, and he is easily fooled. In a Lab School class, a group of children made fresh lemonade and tasted it. They poured the lemonade into three glasses, then added orange food coloring to one glass and purple food coloring to another. When they tasted it again, they insisted that only the untouched glass contained lemonade; the others contained orange juice and grape juice. Even though they had added the artificial color themselves, they could not be persuaded otherwise. They clung to a single aspect of appearance—color—and could not yet identify the essential fact that they had made the juice in all three glasses from lemons. Franz banged his package of Fritos against his desk each lunchtime. Why? "I'll have MORE to eat," he said.

Betsy had two balls of clay of equal size. She rolled one of them into a long sausage and then claimed that there was more clay in the sausage than in the remaining ball, even though she herself had rolled it out from the ball. She was beguiled by the new shape and could not remember the two equal balls. The same child understood that $2+2=4$ but found it totally unreasonable that $3+1$ should also equal four.

Garrett gave some dimes to a neighbor's child but clutched on to his nickels. He insisted that a nickel had to be worth more than a dime because it was much bigger. Eleven-year-old Garrett was also the one at school who would bang his bag of potato chips against his desk to break them into small pieces. Why? "Because then I have lots more to eat," he said proudly. Once he got into a fight with his older brother over a similar error. The two boys had agreed to share the job of making brownies. They had the same sized pans and equal quantities of brownie mix. When the brownies had cooled in the pans, the older boy cut his batch into four rows of four big brownies, sixteen in all. Garrett cut his batch into six rows of six little brownies, thirty-six in all. When Garrett compared the two batches, he flew into a rage and accused his brother of cheating by making so few. He fixed on the finished number of brownies and could not understand that the total volume was the same. Such errors frequently lead to misunderstandings, fights, and punishments for learning disabled children because their thinking is at a more primitive level than is expected for their age.

The Developing Mind

Jean Piaget has found that all children's minds develop through four distinct stages in a specified sequence that is the same for all, but the rate at which individual children progress can differ widely. He points out that it normally takes the first six or seven years of life before a child is no longer fooled by the external physical appearance of objects and has finally acquired the logical structure, the mental understanding to recognize the underlying constancy of matter.

Many learning disabled children are very delayed, perhaps by four to eight years, in reaching this stage. They may not have received the benefits of the early *sensory-motor* stage that the two-year-old usually receives. The implication of this possibility for teaching points to a need for more direct sensory-motor experience regardless of the children's chronological age. They need much more teaching with objects and manipulative materials than the average child does before they can start dealing with abstractions, experience being the key to intellectual development. A child who has had physical experience with a concrete object, such as a ball, can then form a mental picture of the ball and act upon it in thought in the same ways that he experienced it in actual fact.

Until children are seven or eight years old, they ordinarily have trouble looking back in time and then forward, in order to make a reasoned judgment. They are more inflexible. Only one way makes sense to them. Doesn't this sound just like the learning disabled child?

Frequently this child develops one way to act in a social situation and applies it across the board to all other situations. He dances into a classroom, waving his arms, going "beep bop—big boy is here—ya dee da!" The first time he amused his classmates, but then he adopted this behavior as his stereotyped entry. "Heil Hitler!" says Albert every time he is given an instruction. "Yes, your majesty," says George perseveratively to each teacher's or his mother's requests. The parents wonder why the child doesn't understand that these remarks or this behavior don't belong in the present situation. The teacher wonders if this is an attention getter, a misfired attempt at humor, or simply rude behavior. The outsider finds it bizarre. Other children label him "weirdo kid."

Just as Sandy has trouble visualizing pictures, letters, and words, he has difficulty visualizing his impact on others. Seeing the consequences of his behavior is not in his repertoire, and he is being truthful when he says, "I never thought about that." Mary, who can't read, also has trouble reading faces; she can't see when somebody is happy, angry, sad, or bewildered. She doesn't look carefully to being with, or she overlooks the clues that are important. Many learning disabled children are extraordinarily perceptive about people's feelings and relationships, but still they rarely can anticipate their impact on others or even recognize it afterward.

Teachers of learning disabled youngsters often live in dread of transitions, for trouble erupts at those times. Those are times of shifting gears, accommodating to change. Putting away what he has been doing starts the storm. The hyperactive child frequently explodes; he shouts, swears, and throws down his work. The hypoactive youngster or the one who doesn't overreact tunes out or daydreams at this time and needs constant reminders to get ready. Many learning disabled children seem not to hear the directions. Lining up to go to the next class brings problems of who has which place in the line, who touches whom, and what's to be taken to the next class. Down the stairs, not watching where he's going, overhearing a remark which he thinks, rightly or wrongly, to be about him, a casual touch on the shoulder misinterpreted to be a hostile gesture—all these may lead to blows. This is followed by entering the next class where his chair may not be in the right place, the materials have been moved, and he is now so furious with the remark and the touch on the shoulder that he can't settle down to work.

Each transition seems to wear out the learning disabled child so that he can't function effectively until well into the next activity. But we know that his neural development is delayed and that he is very slow to integrate more than one thing at a time, if at all. And his difficulties are easier to understand when we realize that planning and preparing oneself for change take organization, the ability to project ahead and to look backward. These are the disabled areas of this child, areas that have to be taken over for him by the teacher until the child can learn to handle them himself. The teacher must be superbly organized herself, be able to see far enough ahead, and be well prepared in advance to help the child plan for the approaching transition. Each child reacts to change in his own pattern and can be helped to discover his own best strategies for coping with it.

Too much going on in the child's mind at once leads to difficulty with discrimination, separating out one thing from another, and then integrating them to make sense. Impulsivity leads to scattered approaches, random action, random thought, or perseveration. A fragile sense of order begets the inflexibility or rigidity of ONE WAY and contributes to a fear of making any mistakes. Egocentricity of the Now Child combined with concreteness, literalness, and relying on appearances as truth are evidences of extreme immaturity. All of these factors contribute to the learning disabled child's inability to deal with alternatives, to choose, to substitute one thing for another, to transfer learning from one situation to another, to switch gears, or even to start a task.

The Teacher's Job

When we are aware of all these factors, what can we do? We cannot change them willy-nilly in order to make the child easier to educate. They will change as the neural development takes place. What we can do is keep these factors firmly in mind while programming for a learning disabled child. If we know a learning disabled youngster cannot begin any task, then we invent ways to help him establish a routine that will work to help him program himself to do it. This is why teaching the learning disabled child how to learn may be more important than the task itself. Part of the teacher's job is to teach him how to sit in a classroom, how to organize his materials, and how to get to work. We would not expect a three- or four-year-old to know how to begin work in a formal classroom setting, yet we do expect a six- or seven-year-old at this developmental level to do so. At first, how to deal with regular school routines becomes more important than learning content, for otherwise the learning disabled youngster cannot survive, much less progress, at school.

5

Managing Space and Time

What's the difference between *1 2 3* and *123*?
What's the difference between *b* and *d*?
What's the difference between *act* and *cat*?
What's the difference between + and ×?
What's the difference between *OIL* and *710*?

What's reading? It involves a series of graphic symbols placed in a certain order in space.

What's math? It involves groupings in space, location of angles in space, order, and placement of numbers in space.

What's geography? It involves land space, water space, relationships in space.

What's history? It involves spaces in time—relationships of one space in time to another

What's art? It involves the creative use of space.

What's learning? It involves exploring new space: discriminating, integrating, organizing spaces in the mind, in time.

The learning disabled child has difficulty with learning in general, usually with reading and spelling and often with math, geography, and history. He experiences confusion in regard to spatial relationships and time concepts.

Space and time are organizing systems. We organize the way we view a room. We organize the way we enter it and choose a seat in relation to what's going on and who is there. We organize our bedrooms for maximum comfort and convenience. We place the furniture where it can be easily reached and arrange our clothes in drawers and closets so that we can find what we want easily. We organize what we will do within a given time period. We organize where we are going in relation to our starting point. We *have* a starting point. The severely learning disabled child does' not.

Children copy the way in which adults use space. They recognize the different atmospheres that exist in classrooms where the chairs are lined up facing the teacher and classrooms where the chairs are placed in a circle. They recognize the feelings and attitudes that underlie the work spaces, play spaces, and eating spaces. They take note (often unconsciously) of a family's way of using space and a community's handling of outdoor spaces. Being able to enter a room and immediately organize it visually so that we place ourself in it comfortably is a skill we take for granted. Knowing instinctively how we'll use space gives us a sense of safety, confidence, and freedom to relate to people or ideas. When we are lost in space, we are groping, stumbling, shaking; with no borders, beginnings and endings, no directions, we feel unsafe, alien.

The learning disabled child is most often lost in space: lost in up-down, left-right, above-below, top-bottom, in-out of, under-over, apart-together. He does not know automatically how to operate in space; he cannot visualize or organize spaces nor can he find his way easily in space. He does not know where the top shelf is since he is not sure that his feet are below his head. He can't make reliable judgments about space since his body is not a reliable instrument of measure.

The learning disabled child is lost in space, so he very often covets one space, one corner, one chair. What if someone takes your chair? Or places himself in a space that you consider yours? What if someone crowds you? What if someone leans on what you feel is your territory? How do you react to this infringement on your space? Multiply that reaction by ten and you can feel what the learning disabled child experiences. His reactions appear to the observer to be way out of proportion to the situation. They are, in fact, that way because his sense of space is so very precarious that the least bit of trespassing threatens his entire being, and too much space is equally threatening.

With a faulty perception of space, this youngster either clings with desperation to an adult or gets lost in a big department store, the supermarket, or at a ball game. A class of learning disabled children from the Lab School was invited to visit the White House with three of their teachers. When they entered the great ballroom with its huge space and vast, shiny floor, the children began running, sliding, rolling in different directions, whooping, and yelling. Such an enormous, unstructured space was more than their senses could manage. "It was as if each of those children had blown a fuse," reported one of the teachers later. "And it was the worst half-hour of my life!"

Without our being aware of it, most of us follow unwritten rules in the way we organize our work space, our recreational space, our conversational space. Space is important in our conversations with others—not just with the words but in our conversational distances. How close do we talk to someone we like (or don't like), to an older person, to a child, or to a sick person? We instinctively know what we want to do. However, frequently the learning disabled person does not. Too often he comes up so close that we back off, or he stands so far away while he talks to us that we can't hear him. Relationships in space cause trouble between people from different parts of the world, even from different cultures within one country. In the Middle East and in Latin America, people usually come very close, often making body contact, to talk to someone. Americans back off, finding these people aggressive, pushy, and fresh. The others feel Americans are cold, distant, hostile. Similar judgments are made regarding the learning disabled child. His indiscriminate sense of space affects how others perceive him. It affects his relationships, as does his poor timing.

Learning about Space

How do we develop a sense of space and spatial relationships? A newborn baby learns about his body little by little, starting with his mouth, which sucks, and by sucking obtains food. Awareness spreads to his face; his eyes follow movements, and he gives a smile of recognition. Then comes awareness of hands and arms, which grope for what the eyes see. Next come the feet, pushing against his mother's lap, defining his length and his place in space, building a body image. A baby who does not yet know the limits of his own body responds to the world with the whole of it, using great energy at random, with no order or pattern. When he smiles, even his feet are part of the action.

His own body is the baby's reference point by which he gauges the whole world—size and shape—far and near. All his judgments about space are related to himself. If his body image is accurate, he is getting good sensory feedback and is integrating it properly. All along, in the normal developmental pattern, he has been gaining a sense of himself by being held, hugged, rubbed, stroked, and patted. He is moving and being moved. If he does not receive this stimulation or if his nervous system does not properly interpret these tactile messages, the baby does not come to feel the dimensions of himself. When he learns to crawl, he tries to squeeze through spaces that are too small. The feelings in his shoulders and sides help him to determine how big he is in relation to the space. He learns by trial and error. As he remembers, he organizes his experiences and builds up a body memory with which he can compare his movements and sensations. His whole body will tell him when he is about to lose his balance, and he will isolate out parts of his body to do different jobs. His mother takes her child's hand and says, "Look at your hand. See Mommy's hand?" She touches it, she shows it to him, waves it, kisses it. Words, too, then become a part of his body image. The information is stored in his brain, pulled together to make a more and more detailed image, organized so as to make sense of his body. Starting with himself, using all his senses, he is beginning to perceive the world.

But if his senses are not conveying accurate information, if the body image is fragmented, if the parts remain scattered and do not relate to a whole, then the body cannot be used as a reliable instrument of measure. The body is not functioning as a prime information-gathering tool; it is not processing, storing, and applying the needed information. If the body is out of kilter, the whole world is out of kilter. If a child does not have complete body awareness, he can't isolate the different parts of his body and make them work together. He must be taught specifically how to do this step by step.

Muscular control and coordination develop from head to foot. A baby can raise his head after two or three weeks but does not walk until he is ten to eighteen months. He throws a ball before he can kick it. As he gains control of his muscles, learns which parts of his body do what, and improves his eye focus, he finds he can do things faster and more efficiently; later on, he can tie his shoelace standing on one foot, talking all the time, and without dropping the tennis racquet under his arm. With good organization, he can do many tasks at once and automatically. He reacts fast. But when a child wastes energy and motion in superfluous movement, then he does everything more slowly, more inefficiently, and more clumsily.

If our body's messages are coming through to the brain clearly, we get quick feedback. If we lean too far forward or backward, we are acutely uncomfortable knowing that we are about to lose our balance, so we straighten up and resume a balanced posture. A child with poor body feedback can fall off his chair easily. Balance and equilibrium develop in stages also. A child of three can usually stand on one foot, at four he can hop, at five skip, but a child with motor learning disability may not have the balance to do some of these things at nine or fourteen. An eight-year-old may swing from one part of the car to another each time it swerves, and a ten-year-old may struggle to ride a bike. They do not have sufficient body control.

Normal development proceeds from bilateral (the use of both sides of the body at once) to unilateral (the use of one side at a time). At first, both hands hold the mug and both feet stand on each stair; but as he grows, a child learns to reach with one hand and to walk downstairs with alternating feet. By age five or six, he shows a definite preference for one hand over the other; he becomes clearly right- or left-handed. As part of average growth, a child develops an understanding of the two sides of his body and learns to use them separately.

The right side of the brain controls the left side of the body, and the left side of the brain controls the right side of the body, with an imaginary midline. Both sides of a baby's body move together toward the imaginary midline but do not cross over. Normally by the time a child is five or six and his separate sides are working together in a coordinated way, with one side preferred over the other, he easily crosses the midline. The immature child, in contrast, has no separate feeling of right and left; he does things on the left side of his body with his left hand, things on the right side with his right hand, and avoids crossing over the midline. Dana is sawing a plank of wood in half. She starts sawing and saws through to the middle of the board, then stops. She now goes to the other side and again proceeds to saw toward the center. Horace tries to conduct music without his arm's ever crossing the midline; the music teacher finally takes his right arm and tries to push it way over to the left, but at the middle of his body she meets rigid resistance. Anne Marie starts writing on the left of her page and then way over to the right; the middle of the sheet is empty. Richard's drawing of a clock is equally strange. All the numbers on the round face—out of sequence, reversed, and rotated—are crowded on the left side, leaving the right side blank.

A true inner awareness of left and right is called *laterality*. If a child does not have laterality, his movements become helter-skelter from both sides. When he writes on a piece of paper, both his hands and arms move. When he kicks with one foot, the other one moves too, and the child falls down. This child frequently mirror writes. Without laterality, he cannot follow directions to find an object or a point in space. Poor body image leads to delayed development of laterality, which leads to poor directionality, so that he is lost in space. He can't put his name in the upper left-hand corner of his page. If he cannot differentiate the left from the right side, how can he memorize a symbol that has a right or left side? He does not even know if he is right-handed or left-handed.

Until recently, and even now, both-handedness (ambidextrousness) has been mentioned as a cause of reading difficulties rather than seen as an indicator of immaturity. It doesn't matter which hand a child uses as long as the maturation has taken place for him to feel two distinct sides of the body, differentiate them, and integrate them. Most of the world is right-handed. Archeologists have dug up ancient tools that show that humans seem to have preferred their right hands as far back as the Bronze Age. Taboos and superstitions have centered on left-handedness. Even the term *left-handed* is called *sinistrality*—a word with the same root as *sinister*—yet there is nothing wrong with a child's being left-handed.

The child who "sights" with his left eye and uses his right hand (or who sights with his right eye and uses his left hand) is said to have *mixed dominance*. For years, doctors and reading experts tended to believe that this was the cause of reading difficulties; then studies showed that half the people who read well have mixed dominance but do not reverse letters and numbers. Thus what had been a convenient answer to the cause of learning disabilities until the 1960s was proven incorrect. Mixed dominance does not matter, but body awareness and the way a body is organized do.

Learning Body Awareness

A child who does not have awareness of his body also lacks mastery over the directions in which his body goes. He would have trouble following directions such as "turn to the right" or "move forward and then come back." He might not know what the teacher means when she says, "Put that aside. Find the paper above the desk and on the shelf to the right." Franklin would say, "Put it *face up*," when he meant "put it *right side up*," and "put it *out* to the center" instead of "put it *into* the center," but even these efforts were a great improvement over his previous inability to give any spatial directions at all.

Frequently the learning disabled child cannot create pictures in his mind. He cannot visualize "up and down" any more than he can visualize *b* or *d* when he tries to write them. He has to do much more looking, touching, and talking to try to remember what he has seen. The difficulty that the learning disabled child faces in visualizing space often causes him to act like a much younger child. He is like the nursery schooler who loses his jacket and runs around to every place he can think of where he has been, looking for it. At a later stage of development, the child can sit still and picture in his mind where he has been until he can logically decide where he probably left it. Until he is able to visualize space, a child cannot plan how to use it.

By school age most children can dress themselves quickly in the morning—if they want to. A few will even lay out their clothes neatly the night before. But not Bobby. Even before he started school and began writing his letters backward and upside down, Bobby had trouble getting his shirt on the right way around. He would habitually put both legs through one leg hole of his shorts and put his shoes on the wrong feet. He couldn't coordinate his muscles. He knew the result he wanted, but he didn't know how to organize to get it.

For a child to plan his movements well, he must know where his body is in space, and he must be able to coordinate several parts of his body at the same time into one action. A learning disabled child with poor laterality may find this extremely difficult. If you have ever tried to mount the obstacles in a difficult obstacle course, you know what kind of planning he needs simply to move around without knocking things over, bumping into the furniture, or falling down. This is called *motor planning*. If you try to write your name backward, you will experience the kind of difficulty in motor planning that a learning disabled youngster may experience in writing his name forward.

Occupational therapists, who traditionally worked with the victims of strokes, brain damage, and cerebral palsy, taught their patients how to dress, how to feed themselves, and how to hold a pencil. But sometimes a patient who was physically able to put on his clothes still could not do so. Occupational therapists found that such a patient had a faulty body image, with so little sense of where his hands or feet were, plus so little organization, that he could not plan his actions or coordinate several things at once.

The occupational therapists developed treatment programs, and they began applying the principles of this treatment to learning disabled children who are disorganized and cannot move in a coordinated way. The occupational therapist works to bring the body image closer to reality by giving the child activities in a step-by-step sequence to encourage the development of movement, balance, and the sense of touch. These activities include rolling, rubbing, pushing, pulling—anything that gives the child a more accurate awareness of his body. She helps the child develop his reflexes and equilibrium, the natural mechanisms necessary to cope with gravity and movement through space. It may be necessary for the therapist to teach the child the most basic concepts of space and direction, for instance, repeating together the word *up* to identify the upward movement of the body as the child is moving. What the occupational therapist frequently does with the body is exactly what parents and teachers have to do with all aspects of learning; she breaks down each task into its smallest units and then puts them into their proper sequence for teaching. This is called *task analysis*. It requires identifying what steps the task involves and which ones the child has already mastered.

Clumsy, Slow, and Inefficient

If a child has nervous-system immaturity, more than likely he has no stable basis for making order of the sensations coming to his brain, because his body, which ought to be providing the basis for all spatial judgments, is not a stable reference point. It does not give reliable feedback and thereby prevents the child from obtaining mastery over space, mastery over directions, and mastery over left and right. A child whose body is not giving proper feedback is receiving faulty information; he has no base to begin from, no steady place to return to, and no frame of reference for understanding time—today, tomorrow, yesterday—no way of visualizing past and future, forward and backward.

POOR SPATIAL AWARENESS,
  MISJUDGING,
    overdoing,
      underdoing,
        poor balance,
          POOR TIMING,
            too fast,
              too slow,
                NOT LOOKING,
                  NOT LISTENING,
NOT BEING ABLE TO COORDINATE SEVERAL THINGS AT ONCE
    breeds

CLUMSINESS

A clumsy child takes longer to learn to remember what he has seen, heard, felt, or done . . . longer to make sense of information from two or more senses . . . longer to get meaning from looking, listening, touching, moving . . . longer to answer a question or repeat what he has been told. His timing and spacing are off. He does not have enough internal organization to put everything together rapidly. This is not surprising when we realize how much excess, random energy the child employs uselessly. His efforts exhaust him, making him slow and inefficient.

Ivan was standing under a cliff when rocks began to fall. His father had to race over and grab him up to save him, scolding him furiously for not obeying. Ivan was not being disobedient or stubborn. He simply could not get himself organized fast enough to meet the emergency. Over and over again, we yell accusingly, "What's the matter with you?" when a learning disabled child does not react quickly. How he wishes he could answer that question! And by asking it, we make him even slower, for under the stress of being pushed and being yelled at, he becomes almost paralyzed.

Distractibility and disorganization can cause clumsiness. Combine this with being lost in space, with poor coordination and poor timing, and what do you have? You have a child who can't look, listen, and move at the same time. Often he can't learn by watching others demonstrate. He can't eat and talk at the same time. When he reads, he can't translate words into sounds and think about their meaning at the same time. He stops all learning in a classroom while he picks a pimple. He cannot integrate several processes at once.

Ruthie always dropped her boots—or her books or her homework or her hat—when she carried them to school. She couldn't organize herself to carry all these things at once. She was clumsy in brushing her hair, brushing her teeth, putting on a kerchief, and she couldn't organize herself to cut meat with a fork and a knife. Hilda literally tripped over her own feet as though they were some alien objects attached to her, having nothing to do with the rest of her. Elizabeth's zeal to be helpful in the kitchen often led to too many, or too few, ingredients in the bowl and rude remarks from her brothers at the table later. Robin wanted more than anything else to be considered grown up and responsible. She begged her mother to let her help dress her three-year-old sister, but somehow the clothes were never put on right, and dressing took so long that her little sister usually ended up bawling.

Friendly and clumsy, an older learning disabled child may long to join the neighborhood children in their games but finds himself rejected, run away from, or the last one to be picked for a team. His awkwardness makes him a liability because he is sure to miss the ball, or drop it, or be too slow getting to first base, or lose track of which direction he is going.

Chuck's family had just returned to America from overseas. They were still living in a hotel, but Chuck, aged nine and a half, was already enrolled in a special school for learning disabled children. One Friday, his mother arrived by taxi to pick him up after school. As Chuck ran happily out the front door, he didn't look where he was going; he tripped on the sidewalk and went sprawling, while the contents of his lunch box rolled into the gutter and under the taxi. Chuck, lunch box, thermos, half-eaten apple, and uneaten sandwich were all picked up and put into the taxi. The following conversation then took place:

"Mom, guess what! I've got a new friend!"

"That's great, Chuck! What's his name?"

"I don't remember, but we're going to meet each other tomorrow."

"Where are you going to meet?"

"At school."

"Tomorrow's Saturday, Chuck—remember? No school."

"Oh . . . Well, that's OK. I asked him to come swimming in the hotel pool. He's gonna come."

"When did you ask him for?"

"Um . . . Oh! . . . Maybe that was yesterday!"

"Well, we'll just have to wait and see if he shows up. Did you tell him the name of our hotel?"

"Sure, the Hilton."

"Chuck! We're staying at the Sheraton!"

At this point the taxi driver turned around and said, confidentially: "Lady, you've got a PROBLEM with that kid!"

The taxi driver may have been right, but the real problem was Chuck's, not his mother's. Who . . . what . . . where . . . which . . . when . . . had all escaped him. With no firm ground under his feet, no fixed points in time to grip onto, he could only stumble and grope, and the result was a well-meaning but inept and clumsy performance. This lack of orientation brings with it a lack of grace. The child is awkward in the disconnected way he moves his arms and legs; he blunders into the furniture and trips over the rugs. He is frequently graceless in his social interchanges with other people—talking too much or too loudly, making an inappropriate spontaneous response, or not reacting when he should. But all learning disabled children cannot be categorized as awkward physically and socially; some appear to be well coordinated, gracious, thoughtful in social situations.

Henry was awkward. He misjudged space and had little sense of time. He was delighted when his mother and father had company because he loved people. He helped his mother set the table, and, in spite of his mistakes, he and his mother enjoyed these times together. Henry would greet the company, and one time he insisted on taking their drink orders. How he wanted to do it well! "Good for his memory as well as his spirit," said his father. But the task turned out not to be too good for his spirit. He forgot the orders and had to ask all four guests to repeat them, several times. Then, when he finally came in, triumphantly carrying the drinks on a tray, he did not judge the space correctly, tripped, and sent the whole lot crashing to the floor.

Typically the learning disabled child can't remember where to go; he frequently gets lost, loses not only himself but also his possessions, and doesn't see things that are in front of him. When he's asked to stand in front of his desk, often he stands behind it. When he's asked to put the paper into the box, he frequently puts it beneath the box. He is disoriented in space. When asked to write something on the bottom of the page, many times the learning disabled youngster turns over the page. It is extremely common that a learning disabled child cannot write his name in the upper left-hand corner of a page; instead he scrambles the letters together in some indiscriminately chosen space or makes the letters so big that they go off the page. When asked to place a dot in the middle of the page, he puts it on the edge—or anywhere else. When asked to touch his left knee with his right arm, he'll frequently mask his confusion with a sneeze or a joke.

Nine-year-old Dean stopped a teacher in the hall and asked, "Where is 'around the corner'?"

"Which corner?" she replied mystified.

"Around the corner!" he insisted.

"There are many corners, Dean. Which one do you mean?"

"I don't know. The sports teacher told me to get the ball from 'around the corner.' "

"Where was the sports teacher standing?"

"I don't remember!"

"When did he tell you this?"

"A long time ago."

Confused by Time

Dean was very intelligent, but he had severe problems with time and space; he had no reference points. Both time and space demand selecting out, remembering, integrating, and sequencing. They demand order, just what a learning disabled child does not have. This is why parents and teachers must immediately provide the structure in space and time for such a child.

Some children need help only in specific areas. Some are good athletes who deal well with their bodies in large spaces yet can't organize space on paper. Others require a clearly defined place and time and space for everything in their lives. Well-marked spaces, or small spaces, spell safety to such a child. He does not know how far his body extends or how much space it takes up. This is why security often depends on the same seat at the dining room table, the same place in the school bus, the same chair in the classroom.

Space is something that the learning disabled child can see; he may see it distorted, out of proportion, and askew, but he can see it. It is tangible. Time eludes him totally for it is more abstract; it is something that happens between two points he can't see. He cannot feel a minute.

An infant's time is body feeling related to his needs—time for milk, time to change his diaper. It is personal or egocentric time. His needs are time. What begins in egocentric, concrete terms moves steadily outward toward an abstract, universal scheme. The child can see a day and a night; he can see a season and know if it is winter or summer. A two-year-old's sense of time centers on the present, but he is beginning to understand *wait* and *soon*. At three, he usually knows *yesterday*, but he is much more able to talk about the future. By then he can tell how old he is; he knows he goes to bed "after supper and after a story"; and he can talk about what he will do tomorrow. At four, he knows what happened throughout a day, what to expect in the morning, what happens before, during, and after lunch, how the afternoon is spent, and he knows the sequence of supper, bath, story, and bedtime. After five, he knows the days of the week; he can tell what day follows Sunday and project how old he will be on his next birthday. He uses the words *yesterday, today,* and *tomorrow* with ease. By seven or eight, he knows the months and the seasons, and he can usually tell the time. The learning disabled child, occasionally as late as age fourteen, still does not know the days of the week. His perception of time is that of a preschooler.

Just as the two-year-old, the Now Child, understands no time but the present, so the learning disabled child becomes sullen or cries, screams, and stamps around when he does not get what he wants now. Long time, short time, more time, less time, do not mean anything to him. Before, after, not yet, soon, later, wait—all this is mumbo-jumbo. Scolding by adults only shows him once more than he is out of phase with everybody else, that he is doing things wrong, and that he is bad. He needs an adult to place him in a time slot, to provide a system for him whereby he can structure his activity to fit into the adult time scheme. Structure of space and time can be lifesaving for the learning disabled child.

Time is order. It is made up of sequences. Because a learning disabled child has no order, he is lost when he tries to tell the days of the week (or the seasons or months), to remember the alphabet, to count or to tell time. Counting is the basis of measuring time. Counting what you don't see is what time is all about, and if you are a concrete child, you need to see it.

A little child who says that Grandma will be coming "one sleep away," is charming, but a ten-year-old who says that is considered peculiar. Primitive people and preschoolers cannot deal with the abstractness of time either. They see it as a time to get up, a time to eat, a time to work or play, a time to sleep. Intervals of time, periods, and durations have no meaning for them unless related to their own life experiences. An abstract time system based on counting does not exist for them. If asked when a story took place, eleven-year-old Norman always answered "in the day" rather than giving a historical perspective or even stating "a long time ago." Ten-year-old Isador wondered if Christmas might come sooner by his coming to school earlier each day. This made no sense, but Isador could not make any sense of time.

On his first day at the Lab School, twelve-year-old Basil was told, "It's two o'clock, time to go, Basil. Your father will be here to pick you up."

"That can't be," protested Basil. "My father works in Virginia, and it takes him an hour to get here."

His teacher explained to him that by starting an hour earlier, at one o'clock, his father could indeed arrive in Washington at two. But Basil, unable to visualize the interval of an hour and connect that to the distance from Virginia, continued to repeat, "Dad *can't* get here at two—it takes him a *whole hour!*" until his father astonished him by walking in.

Basil had no concept of time, even the meaning of *before* and *after;* Basil was also poorly coordinated and lost in space. It was not enough for a teacher simply to work on

Basil's nonexistent time concepts. He needed a whole remedial program of locating his body in space, learning left
from right, working on visual, auditory, motor, and tactile
discrimination, as well as memory.

Intervals of time regulate our lives. People in America and
the industrialized countries of the West are more strictly
regulated by time than the people of Asia are. In America we
live by the clock. Time is precious, hurried, closely watched.
Time is money.

> We invest time,
> save time,
> borrow time,
> budget time,
> charge time,
> spend time,
> steal time,
> waste time,
> lose time,
> check time,
> share time,
> squander time,
> take time.

We hurry our children to grow up and tell older people to
stay young. We hurry to learn. We crave shortcuts, quick
solutions, easy answers.

Speed is a way of life: sports cars, jet planes, instant cake
mix, electronic communications. If you don't get where
you're going today, tomorrow may be too late. Yet with all
the emphasis on speed and saving time, boredom and the
use of leisure time are big national problems today. So it is
with the learning disabled child who cannot tolerate the
pressure of time and yet cannot make constructive use of
leisure time. Sleep is regulated by time. Meals are regulated
by time. We time everything.

Learning to Judge Time and Space

"Hurry up!" How many times a day do we say this? But the
learning disabled child can't organize himself to hurry; he
falls apart instead. With his random, excessive movement
and his immature lack of planning, he expends more time
and effort getting anything done and is therefore slower than
normal. His distractibility and inefficiency keep him from

accomplishing anything on a time schedule. His perceptions are slow and frequently inaccurate.

His failure to grasp concepts of time can cause a wide variety of problems at school. Most obviously, the child may be continually late. He cannot pace himself if he does not have a reliable time sense. He cannot pace himself to finish a job, a paper, or a test on time. The study of history is dealing with time past and sequences in the past. The past is more difficult to deal with than the present or even the future. A five-year-old knows the age he will be on his next birthday but not what it was on his last birthday. Walking backward is harder than walking forward; you can't see where you are going, and you have to visualize what is behind you. Dealing with anything backward is much harder than doing it forward. It takes more organization. The past tense is difficult for many children: "I've got it" and "I'm gonna get it" are much easier than "I had it." Subtraction is harder than addition. Repeating numbers backward requires additional concentration. Double negatives such as "it is not unusual that" are often baffling, for they demand reversing to translate them. It takes years before a learning disabled child can cope with any of these things. He cannot figure out what letter comes before *E* without going back to *A* and reciting forward again. To find out what number comes before 9, he must go back to the beginning and count up from 1.

To apply reason to time, to understand cause and effect, you have to reconstruct time that is past. A child cannot normally do this until the age of eight, usually the third grade. Switching back and forth from past to present to future time demands organization and a great deal of memory. Impeded by impulsivity, distractibility, poor memory, and disorganization, the learning disabled child becomes lost in this process. With no concept of time except what has just happened, he may answer "How was your day at school today?" with "Good" or "Terrible," depending only on what happened during his last activity of the day.

His timing is off in his speech; he doesn't know when to begin and when to stop. He has difficulty perceiving pauses in people's speech and in understanding the implications of those inflections. He has trouble with raising and lowering his own voice. His rhythm may be off. Frequently he can't sing in established tempos. Often he can't rhyme. He's a poor judge of time and lingers after class and then is late to the next one. His timing is off in planning schoolwork. He can't complete projects, can't estimate the time needed for homework, can't judge how much time to allow for each question on a test, can't pace himself to produce a term paper, can't do work on three different subjects in one evening, even when the assignments are very short.

The concept of self is essential in order to locate oneself in space and time. Until a person can see himself as quite separate from his environment, different, unique, yet related intimately to it, he has no real sense of self. Under those conditions, space and time happen to him, and he is helpless. The immature being starts there and slowly achieves a mastery over the present and the past, planning for the future as a defined, independent, fully functioning self.

A very young child believes that somebody big must be older than somebody small because he cannot see time or comprehend age. He does not know whether his mother or his grandmother was born first and cannot imagine them ever having been children. He senses only that he himself is growing; he expects to catch up and overtake his older brother, his parents, and his grandparents.

By seven or eight years old, children with normal development are accurate judges of both time and space, and it is this ability above all others that gives them the solid foundation on which to base formal school learning. Some school systems, such as Switzerland's, devote the first two years of school to intensive readiness activities—the arts and handicrafts—postponing formal learning of reading, writing, and arithmetic until the children are at least seven years old. Since a school-aged learning disabled child is delayed in his development, he remains at the stage of a preschooler who is not clear about the location and use of his own body, who is not yet ready to undertake the tasks of formal schooling. He gropes in time and space. He is lost without two of the major support systems of daily life. Lost in the space and out of pace with life around him, the learning disabled youngster falls many times along the path of progress and, yet, most often gets there . . . in time.

The implications for teaching the learning disabled child how to manage time and space mean giving him much more experience with motor development—more dance, more sports, and more perceptual-motor activities in the classroom activities to make him aware of his body and teach him to use it in a more organized fashion. His body then becomes a more reliable instrument of measure through which to gain accurate feedback about the space he moves in. Organization of the body helps the child ready himself to begin mastering the organizing systems of our society: space and time. The foundations necessary for this mastery are the same foundations necessary for mastering the three Rs at school.

6

Learning the Three Rs

Henry was so smart that he could guess a word from all sorts of clues—pictures, the name of the book, his teacher's expression. It was only when he was faced with plain words on a page that he developed a mysterious bladder complaint that obliged him to flee, tripping and stumbling, to the bathroom as soon as the reading lesson began.

Katie said: "I don't want to read. You can't make me!"

Andy was a good boy. He was quiet and well mannered in class. Much of the time he was off in a daydream. He was a whiz at sports, and the other children admired him. But he could not speak well. It was so embarrassing for him to talk that his teacher let him read silently rather than aloud in front of the class, and she missed the fact that he couldn't read at all.

Teddy lost everything. He lost his pencil. He lost his homework. He lost himself going from one classroom to another. He lost interest in the middle of a project. And he lost his memory for the words that he could read perfectly well yesterday.

Here are some of the comments their teachers sent home about these four children:

> "Henry does not take the time to be careful or neat. His large vocabulary indicates a high degree of intelligence. He will not sit still long enough to master his reading thoroughly although he could easily do the work if he tried harder. He needs to be more motivated."

"Perhaps the source of Katie's uncooperative attitude toward language arts may be found in her home environment."

"Andy has adjusted well to the group. He is academically a 'slow bloomer' but his shyness in class is more than compensated for by his outstanding abilities in the gym and on the playground, where he assumes responsibility and leadership. It is a pleasure to have him in class."

"Teddy is all over the place. He seems to make things deliberately harder for himself. Teddy is a careless student. His handwriting is messy and illegible. Unless he is threatened with punishment, he will not do his work. We have found no other way to gain Teddy's cooperation."

Henry's teacher knew he was intelligent; his large vocabulary and lively interests convinced her of it. She recognized that he was clumsy and restless, but she was sure that if he could just be made to concentrate, he would read as well as any other child in her class. He needed only to try harder. She did not see the need for any special testing or tutoring.

Katie infuriated her teacher by her attitude. The teacher was at her wit's end and felt the parents must have fostered this degree of stubbornness in Katie. The teacher did not recognize that a learning disabled child will most often say, "I won't" or "I don't want to" rather than admit the truth: "I can't."

Andy's teacher thought there was nothing to worry about. The fact that Andy could assume responsibility and even leadership in his area of competence led her to believe that he was basically doing all right and that time alone would do the trick for his reading. It did not occur to her to have him specially tested or that he might need tutoring or other forms of special help.

Teddy's teacher could not believe that Teddy wasn't

being so disorganized or having some of his accidents on purpose. More discipline was her answer. She found that he would sometimes go through the motions of working when he was under threat of punishment, and she fell back on this method more and more.

As a preschooler, Henry knocked over the blocks and spilled the juice while he talked in an adult manner about unidentified flying objects. And Katie had a tantrum every time she was asked to perform for her nursery school class. Andy sat quietly in kindergarten but was inattentive to the stories that were read aloud. Words were as unmanageable to him as zippers, buttons, and coloring books were to Teddy. None of these four children was identified as learning disabled because many preschoolers have these same problems and soon grow out of them. It was only when they started to fail in school that people panicked.

A child with an outstanding talent, like Andy, can manage to slide by for a while, with goodwill around him. A child who can sit still, who can follow directions, talk appropriately, and who has a good memory, can also get by. But sooner or later,

> failure to learn to read
>> usually spells
>>> failure at school,
>>>> which usually spells
>>>>> a feeling of failure in life.

What are some of the common school characteristics of a learning disabled child?

1. Erratic, inconsistent, unpredictable. Appears to be lazy. Good days, off days. Forgets what was learned yesterday. But without reteaching, he may remember it two days hence.
2. Poor attention span. No sustained focus.
3. Works very slowly. Never finishes work in allotted time or works carelessly, finishing in half the expected time. Feels need to hurry, without thinking.
4. Poorly organized. Desk a mess. Always losing his coat or lunch.
5. Late to class. Lingers after class.
6. Loses homework, or hands it in late and sloppily done. Doesn't understand or forgets assignments.

7. No study skills. Doesn't know how to organize work, how to plan in regard to deadlines, how to organize time.

8. Low frustration tolerance. Gives up easily or explodes.

9. Freezes when required to perform on demand. When he volunteers information, he can tell what he knows; in responding to questions, he appears dull and ignorant.

10. Can't plan free time. Daydreams, acts silly, or repeats same activity over and over when given free choices.

The school difficulties of the learning disabled child revolve around organization, sorting out, differentiating, remembering, and integrating. Learning means doing more than one thing at a time. It means making many connections and plugging them all in at once. It's connecting sounds and symbols. Sounds and symbols linked together in the proper order have to be perceived correctly in the first place.

Perception is the ability to read the environment. It is making sense of the environment through the stream of messages coming into the brain from the eyes, ears, nose, mouth, hands, skin, and the whole body. It is the brain's picture of the world and the organized relationship of one sensation to another. *Perception is the foundation on which all learning is based.*

School Readiness

A baby under a year old with a cookie holds the cookie in front of him, beams, and looks at the whole satisfying treat. It looks round, feels round, is round. He experiences totally the cookie with his whole body. He proceeds to suck it, smell it, smear it around, drop it, and perhaps sit on it. He has seen the whole cookie, and now only part of it is left, a morsel. Does he still know it's a cookie? If he is handed a square cookie, he may not know it is a cookie until he tastes it, smells it, and remembers, recognizing its prime characteristic—its good taste.

When he grows older and yells "Cookie!" he has a picture in his mind of how it tastes, feels, and looks. He creates a mental picture, a visual image, of the object. This is his visual memory, stored in his mind and ready to be recalled for future use. He learns by experience with other objects to recognize what makes them identical, similar, or different. This discrimination later is transferred into seeing the difference between *want, went,* and *won't* (visual discrimination). And the same discrimination must be applied to the sounds he hears—hearing the difference between *berry* and *very,* between *think* and *drink* (auditory discrimination).

His memory is trained during his preschool years as he remembers what he's seen, what he's done, and the names for everything; he memorizes labels of all kinds. This, though he doesn't know it, is visual and auditory memory training, the underpinning of reading readiness. He will need to remember not only individual letters with their names and sounds but total configurations of letters:

In the early years of a person's life, listening is the first way of connecting meanings to words. A baby can stop when he is told "no" as early as ten months. He can respond to "Give me that" by fifteen months. Soon after that, he can point to his own nose, eyes, and hair. But his brain is not ready for him to start speaking until he is close to two years old.

After the age of three, language is the most important tool a child has. If he does not have adequate use of language, then he continues to communicate through pointing, gesturing, and other body language. If language develops normally, he uses it to discover more and more about the world he lives in, to develop concepts and ideas about the world. He uses it to express his feelings and opinions, to transcend the now world of things he can see and touch in order to talk about things which are out of sight in another place or another time. Eventually he uses language to reason and to discuss ideas.

But in order to use this amazing tool of language properly, a child must have an intact nervous system. He must be able to receive language: listen and hear, understand what he hears, and store it away in his memory, ready to be recalled and used later (the same system of sorting out, differentiating, integrating, and remembering that applies to every other mode of perception). He must also be able to express language by finding the right word in his memory and speaking it correctly—but this skill depends partly on having heard the word correctly in the first place. Speech reflects hearing. A toddler says *aminal* for *animal* or *pisghetti* for *spaghetti* because he hears it that way. Amusing in a three-year-old, it's a sign of poor auditory perception and sequencing difficulties in a seven-year-old.

Good listening is demanded of a child when he enters school. He has spent six years listening to dos and don'ts, to television, records, and songs, to toys with bells, beepers, and squeaks, to stories and counting games, to people talking all around him (happy talk, loud talk, angry talk, gentle talk), and in the normal way of development he is now ready to sit still, listen carefully, and follow directions.

In kindergarten he is taught many skills that are designed to make him ready. He learns to listen and look. He learns to count, although he probably won't be able to remember his own telephone number until he is seven, and he may not yet comprehend that four is bigger than two even though he sees that two here, and two there, make four when they are all put together in one pile. If his teacher taps her drum three times, he learns to answer with three taps on his own drum. He learns to speak clearly. If he is still saying *aminal*, he now learns *animal* as if it were a new word, and he puts it in a new place in his memory. Most important of all, he learns to follow directions. This ability requires the child:

1. To be able to stay still and pay attention.
2. To hear all of the directions so as to get the main point and know what he is supposed to do. This also means understanding the sequence, getting the details in the right order.
3. To remember what he's heard—the main point of it and the parts of it in their right order.
4. To translate it all into terms of himself, organize himself accordingly, and turn those instructions into action as he carries them out.

The child whose nervous system is developing at an uneven rate may meet his first troubles in the area of sounds. He finds himself bombarded with noises, and he pays equal attention to them all, slow to sort out the meaningful ones from the background. He may not talk until after he is two and a half or three, and then he may use only a limited number of words with no connecting links. When he gets to nursery school and kindergarten, he may not be able to repeat a sequence of three claps after the teacher. He may not understand what his teacher says to him because he was distracted when a fly flew by his face, or he may have heard the first part fine but started thinking about that instead of listening to the rest, or he may have heard it all but forgotten it right away, or he may have confused some sounds or not known the words, or he may not be able to get himself organized to do what he's been told. He may be called willful, stubborn, or uncooperative because he doesn't follow directions.

Language Difficulties

He may also be unable to organize his speech so that it has a clear beginning, middle, and end. A learning disabled child's mind often leaps through many ideas before the words can come out. The struggle is similar to that of a child who can't get his body organized and moving in time to react properly. He may speak slowly, groping for words, making him the butt of many jokes and imitations. His immature speech may make him sound ignorant. Ten-year-old Sidney, from an educated family, claimed, "He got dead," when he was trying to say, "He was killed." He would say, "I buyed it," "My footses are wet," and "My notebook is gooder than his."

Often a learning disabled child cannot make his wants clear because his phrasing of words is clumsy. Anne tugged at her teacher, saying, "Come quick! He wants you because it hurts him!" while her teacher tried frantically to find out who was hurt, where he was, and what had happened. People often do not understand what the learning disabled child is saying, for he begins in the middle of a story, at the end of an idea, or at some point that is unclear. He can't seem to recount the events that happened in order for them to make sense to a listener.

The immature child, beset by distractions and muddled in his language, has a limited ability to control his environment through words. He cannot make reasoned requests or explain his problems, so he uses actions, the way two-year-olds do. Perhaps those older youngsters who feel alien in the world of words resort to action in the same way. Maybe for the nonverbal learning disabled child, his hyperactive or impulsive behavior are substitutes for his limited language, by which he tries to gain a measure of control over what happens to him. Or conversely, perhaps his immaturity forces him to remain in the concrete now world of the two-year-old, and his immature behavior inevitably follows. It's like the question, "Which came first, the chicken or the egg?" Does immaturity prevent him from acquiring the language that would allow him to transcend the here and now? Whatever the cause, the nonverbal child encounters escalating difficulties at school as he grows older and often increasing social problems as well.

Speech makes mankind human: words spoken and listened to, meanings exchanged, questions asked, orders shouted, complaints voiced, tales told. Hunched in their caves three million years ago, our ancestors could make do with pointing, gesturing, and grunting until they needed to call attention to something out of sight, something that happened yesterday, something about tomorrow. Then a symbol—a spoken word—was needed. The caveman didn't choose pebbles or scratches on the ground to be the symbols that represented objects to him. He chose sounds because his hearing was his most highly developed sense. It was his survival sense, his scanning system. He relied on his ears for the first warning of danger, picking up sounds from all directions, around corners, in the dark, through walls. His ear placed against the ground could detect sounds from far away. His ears were always alert, even when he was asleep. He would wake up at any hint of danger, just as today a parent wakes up at the first cry of the baby or the tiptoed steps of a teenager coming in late.

The cavemen and women developed speech when they wanted to leave messages or make plans. Presumably they began with naming concrete objects and moved to abstractions. Languages evolved with different grammars and vocabularies, and language became the channel for culture. Words transmitted knowledge, intelligence, education. For more than two million years, listening has been the chief way of learning; and language has been the primary means of communication.

Language arts are taught to children from the moment they start first grade, yet there is now ample evidence that in any school population there will be some children who are not ready for the standard language arts curriculum. These are some of the typical language problems that impede the academic progress of learning disabled children:

1. Cannot state something in an organized, cogent way. Tends to muddle; starts in middle of an idea. Cannot organize words properly into a question.
2. Has immature word use and ungrammatical phrasing.
3. Has trouble following directions, particularly long sequences of them.
4. Doesn't enjoy being read to, but does like looking at pictures in book.
5. Becomes distracted in class when instruction is presented orally. Learns from watching, not listening.
6. Is very literal. Misses inferences, subtleties, nuances, innuendos.
7. Has poor sense of humor; doesn't understand jokes, puns, sarcasm.
8. Has trouble with abstract words. Defines words by their concrete attributes or function.
9. Can't deal with multiple meanings of words; very rigid.
10. Can't tell a story in sequence or summarize; can only recount isolated and highly detailed facts about an experience.
11. Forgets names of things that he knows and has to describe them (word-finding problem). Later, when not under pressure, will recall the word he wanted to say.

The confusion in what the learning disabled child hears is reflected in his speech and use of words. He often is Mr. Malaprop. He may reverse words without knowing it or use words with similar sounds to the ones he means. Twelve-year-old Morton said that his dog ate *god food*. Eleven-year-old Clyde was explaining that every time he went to the drug store, he sneaked over to read *Boy Play*. Thirteen-year-old Brian said he played with a pair of twins who were not identical; they were "eternal." Molly's Sunday school class finished the first part of the Bible, and she was excited that they had just started reading the "New Intestine."

When he begins school, a child is expected to be able to listen well, to speak clearly, to pay attention, and to take the second great step in the process of civilization: writing. For more than two million years, speech was the overriding skill of man and made all other developments possible. Only in the last five thousand years did a further need arise: the need to say things to people too far away to hear. A symbol was needed for the sound of words, and writing was invented. And so reading and writing became the primary goals of a child's education.

In a society where productivity is prized and a child no longer plays an economic role as he did up through the early 1900s, there is only one area where a child is required to produce, and that is at school. "How's school?" is the question all adults ask.

Reading and Writing

Going to school is equated with learning how to read and write, and reading and writing, in the minds of many people is equated with intelligence. If a child can't learn how to read and write, he must be dumb. This is very far from the truth; learning disabilities can occur in children who test out in ranges from normal intelligence to unusual brilliance. Yet parents feel that there is a stigma on their child if he does not learn to read quickly. No matter how much they love him, parents take the child's failure as their own, so they try by every means possible to make him do better. They tell him, as his teacher has told him before, that he is not trying, or that he is not trying enough, that he's too used to getting his own way, that it's time for him to stop being a baby and grow up and to take responsibility by learning to read. They talk to him at length. They bribe and punish, spend hours going over his schoolwork with him. And they can't understand why all that extra effort doesn't bring him more success with the written word.

What is involved in learning to read? Organization of thought, all the perceptual skills, spatial relations, and timing. (See chart.)

TO READ...

SPACIAL RELATIONSHIPS AND SPACING
- left to right progression knowing left from right
- eye-hand-foot coordination
- directions in space directionality
- judgment in space (motor planning-sequencing)

ORGANIZATIO
- ability to sort information classify, categorize, label
- appropriateness (what belongs, what's missing)
- ability to recognize parts that make up a whole

EYE TRACKING

EYE, HAND AND FOOT COORDINATION

VISUAL PERCEPTION
- observation skills
- discrimination
- memory
- sequential memory
- understanding to give meaning

form constancy

figure ground

size

shape

color

TACTILE PERCEPTION
- discrimination
- memory understanding

SELF CONTROL TO SUSTAIN ATTENTION

INTEGRATING SOUND AND SIGHT TO HAVE MEANING

CHILD NEEDS:

**THOUGHT •
ORDER**

bility to break down
he whole into parts

recognize sequences

mall	first	beginning
g	next	middle
igger	last	end

SYMBOLISM—
VERBAL SKILLS

- vocabulary
- comprehension—understanding of
  concepts expressed in words
- verbal reasoning
- recognizing the oneness of objects,
  symbols, words—separate identities
- understanding that a mark, a
  sound, a pattern, represent
  an object or idea

**AUDITORY
PERCEPTION**

listening skills

discrimination

memory

sequential memory

understanding

RHYTHM
TIMING
SENSE OF TIME

INTEGRATING SEVERAL
PROCESSES AT ONCE

What is a written word (*wrod, sojb, drow*)?

A word is a message.	It carries an idea, an object, a person, a place, an action, which links up with an experience you can remember.
A word is a symbol.	Those black marks on a white page mean something; they stand for something specific.
A word is a pattern.	Like a code, each symbol in the pattern can be translated into a sound, and the series of sounds in their proper order make sense.
A word is a sequence.	The shapes that make up the word have an organization of their own—a beginning, a middle, and an end; they cannot be switched about and keep their same meaning.
A word is a total shape.	It is a total configuration. It may have more than one internal pattern, but the sequence is fixed, and when the symbols are translated into sound, the meaning is fixed and does not change.

A word consists of a series of graphic symbols in space that have meaning when a series of sounds are linked to them in the proper order.

The process of decoding the symbols can be taught in many ways—by sight, by sound, and by touch. Most important is to match the method to the child. Identify his strengths. If he seems to learn more from what he sees than from what he hears, begin with a visual method of teaching reading. Perhaps his ears are his best channel. In this case, begin with an auditory method. Maybe seeing or hearing have to be combined with touching letters of different materials and textures, or with writing and tracing the shapes of letters to reinforce the learning. One builds on a child's strengths while remediating his weaknesses.

For the new reader, there are two basic methods: visual and auditory.

Visual method.	Instant recognition of the total configuration of a word: "look and see" or "look and say." Visual analysis of spelling patterns, leading to pronunciation of the whole word.

Auditory methods.	Hearing the sounds in a word. Sounding out unknown words. Learning the beginning, middle, and end sounds of words.

Some children cannot use the visual method because they don't have the visual perception—visual focus, visual discrimination, and visual memory—for immediate recognition of words. They have not yet learned to look carefully, find the visual similarities and differences, and remember them. They are most incapable of this when they have laterality problems—rotations, reversals, and problems with their eyes tracking left to right. Reading involves moving the eyes smoothly across a line of print, then back again, a bit lower down the page. This is a hard task for a child with space difficulty, and it is why some youngsters need to guide their eyes with a marker—a finger or a moving pencil—to avoid losing their place.

Some children can't use the phonic method because they don't have the auditory perception, the focus, discrimination, and the memory to attach new sounds to new words. Because they have not learned to listen carefully, they don't hear the differences between two sounds, or, if they do, they forget them right away.

But no matter which strategy works best for a child, reading is still a visual-auditory association. Therefore even though a child is taught through his area of strength, progress may still be slow until the weaker area does its tasks automatically and ensures the association. Some children are fairly well developed in their ability to see and hear differences, but they cannot link the two. In many ways, the ability to make the proper connections is the most crucial of all. It is the only way that experience can become usable. The process of combining and digesting the messages from two or more senses into one coherent meaning is like the process of cooking. You can mix butter, flour, eggs, milk, and spices together in a bowl, but they do not become a cake until you bake the batter. Understanding comes through making connections between things that did not appear connected before.

Once a child has begun to read, structural analysis is introduced. He analyzes syllables, breaking a word into its elements and then pulling them together; he learns prefixes and suffixes. He also uses his reasoning powers to guess the meaning of a new word from the rest of the sentence; he learns to figure from contextual clues what's missing, what belongs, what's appropriate.

These are some of the most typical reading problems encountered by learning disabled children:

1. Confuses *b* and *d*, reads *bog* for *dog*, and often confuses *b, d, p, q*.
2. Confuses the order of letters in words (reads *was* for *saw*).
3. Doesn't look carefully at the details in a word and guesses from the first letter (reads *farm* for *front*).
4. Loses his place on a page when reading, sometimes in the middle of a line or at the end of the line.
5. Can't remember common words taught from one day to the next; knows them one day, not the next. Most frequently forgets abstract words (*us, were, says*).
6. Has no systematic way to figure out a word he doesn't know. Guesses or says, "I don't know."
7. Reads without expression and ignores punctuation. The mechanics of reading are so hard for him that he has no awareness of the ideas expressed by the written symbols.
8. Reads very slowly, and reading tires him greatly.
9. Omits, substitutes, or adds words to a sentence.
10. Reads word by word, struggling with almost each one of them.

Listening decodes sound into meaning. Reading decodes symbols of sound into meaning. But writing puts it into code in the first place. This is called *encoding*. To write something down means going into the mind, plucking out a series of visual symbols with sounds attached to them, putting them in the right order (going from left to right) to produce the word you want, then putting several words in the proper order (also going from left to right) to convey the message you want. It takes more organization, more differentiation, more remembering, more sequencing, and more integration than reading or many other skills. It is one of the most sophisticated activities devised by the human brain, and it clearly demands maturity. Whereas a child may be able to read on an adult level as early as third or fourth grade, only a very rare child can write well, with precision, clarity, and expression, before the seventh grade.

The learning disabled child with all his disorder, his visual and auditory problems, his connecting problems, is indeed defeated when he must produce the written language. It has been the experience of many teachers in special classes and special schools that even though a child may reach or surpass his grade level in reading, arithmetic, and language, spelling will still tend to stay below grade level. Spelling seems to be the last residual area that needs remedial help.

Some of the learning disabled child's typical spelling problems follow:

1. Writes *b* for *d* and vice versa.
2. Transposes the order of letters (spells *was* as *saw* or *the* as *hte*).
3. Doesn't hear the sequence of sounds in a word and writes isolated parts of it (writes *amil* for *animal*).
4. Has no memory for common words that are not regularly spelled. May try to spell them phonetically (writes *sez* for *says*).
5. Does not hear fine differences in words (writes *pin* for *pen*).
6. Has trouble with consonants (writes *wif* or *with*).
7. Often disguises poor spelling ability with consciously messy handwriting.
8. Uses no capitals and no punctuation in sentence writing.
9. Leaves words out of sentences; can't express himself in complete written sentences.
10. Avoids writing whenever possible because it is so difficult and so demanding.

Handwriting

To compound his other problems of writing, this child frequently has poor handwriting too. His immaturity causes him to confuse his left and right sides, and he has trouble crossing the midline, trouble tracing letters, trouble staying inside the lines. He leaves no space between letters and words and can't visualize which way the letters go and what the letter looks like, much less a series of letters. He doesn't capitalize the beginning of a sentence and rarely uses punctuation. Punctuations are visual symbols that have to be remembered, that mark endings, or that represent pauses (that a child with poor timing doesn't have). He presses too hard, or not hard enough, on his pencil. His thumb does not help to maneuver the pencil; he has to use his whole arm to write. (This is known as visual-motor difficulty, small-motor difficulty, or eye-hand coordination difficulty.) The child who has severe difficulty with handwriting is often the child about whom the teacher says, "It's as though his brain shuts down when his hand has a pencil in it." All his energy goes into the writing, and there is none left over for thinking.

Here are some typical handwriting problems of the learning disabled child:

1. Holds pencil awkwardly, too tightly, inefficiently. Tires easily by writing.
2. Can't write without lined paper. Spacing is poor. Leaves no space between words. Leaves no margins.
3. Writes letters backward, upside down. Has incomplete formation.
4. Mixes lower-case letters with capitals. Memory for the forms of letters is poor, so he uses whichever form he can remember.
5. Writes letters above and below the line. No size consistency.
6. Writes in very large hand; can't control pencil enough to write small.
7. Holds pencil too tightly and writes very small. Can't relax hand and pencil. Also hides poor spelling.
8. Writes incredibly slowly. Takes five minutes to write a sentence; each letter must be perfectly formed.
9. Can't remember how to form letters so uses his own way. Forms letters inefficiently.
10. Erases often and writes the same letter several times.

It is not infrequent that one finds a learning disabled child whose handwriting is extremely legible, well formed, and neat. He does not have visual-motor or fine-motor difficulties, but he still may not be able to spell or read. His good handwriting ability can be used to help him learn to read.

The child who puzzles many teachers is the one who can't remember which way the letters go (he reverses them and rotates them), yet he may be able to draw very well indeed. His problems are much more related to his visual-spatial perception than to eye-hand coordination.

Mathematics

The writing down of math problems causes many learning disabled children the same trouble as the writing down of letters and words. The number *14* becomes *41; 6* and *9* get mixed up, and so do *2* and *5, 3* and *E*. Then *7* comes out looking like *r*, and *4* looks like a swastika. Somehow the child cannot picture in his mind what the number looks like and thus can't write it.

A child may be very talented at mental math but defeated every time he has to write down his answer or work out his processes on paper. In long division and long multiplication problems, he puts his figures in the wrong columns. Signs like + and × are hard to differentiate and even harder to reproduce, and a page with too many problems on it is too confusing. The child's wrong answers result from visual perception problems plus eye and hand not working together rather than a failure to understand the math.

Sometimes a learning disabled child does superbly in math (though not in reading and spelling) if the math problems are read to him. Perhaps his superior reasoning and memory make this possible. Or perhaps it is because numerical symbols, once learned, mean a fixed set of things. Number 4 means a certain quantity, and there are no inferences, subtleties, or multiple meanings as there are with words.

If a child cannot differentiate sizes, quantities, or measurements and cannot categorize them or put them into sequence by size, we cannot expect him to understand abstract number concepts. Organization to the extent of understanding sequences (first, next, and last) is essential to the awareness and recall of a succession of numbers.

To begin with, a child must understand that one object = 1, that one person = 1, that one symbol = 1. If a child cannot separate himself from the environment to become a single self, we cannot expect him to gain an understanding of this one-to-one correspondence or one-to-one association. Yet we cannot proceed in math without it.

Counting is at the root of all computation. Adding is a shortcut to counting forward; subtracting is a fast way to count backward. Since addition and subtraction are counting forward and backward from a given point, then multiplication is counting forward in groups and division is counting backward in groups. Counting is sequencing. Counting is order. But the learning disabled child cannot remember sequences. He has disorder.

The concepts of *more than* and *less than* are dependent upon our perceptions of larger, longer, big quantities, as distinct from smaller, shorter, little quantities. To know that three is more than two, you have to understand one in relation to the other. Math consists of seeing relationships, and that's what many learning disabled youngsters can't cope with; they can't group one set together as distinct from another set. Math requires focus on the main principles, the binding force, and a disregard of unessential information.

For the One Way Kid, math may be very upsetting. Four plus six is the same as five plus five is the same as nine plus one, but in his pure sense, there can be no equivalencies and alternatives until he has matured somewhat. The inflexibility of the learning disabled child makes it difficult for him to shift gears, and yet much of math is switching from addition to subtraction and multiplication. What if Maria is asked this word problem: "Ms. Brown had five apples in the cellar. She had twice that number in her kitchen. She bought a dozen more at the store and gave six to the neighbor to make an apple pie. Her little boy ate three of the apples in the cellar. How many apples did Ms. Brown have left altogether?" Even if Maria had no language problems, even if she had no problems clearing away extraneous information, still she might have considerable difficulty translating "a dozen," figuring out which computation process to use, and then switching from multiplication to addition to subtraction. If she had memory difficulties, as most learning disabled youngsters do, you can comprehend the magnitude of the problem.

Holding in the mind several things at once, remembering and integrating them are part of math. Sheer rote memory, such as memorizing the multiplication tables, is part of math, and many learning disabled children have no rote memory;

and some do have rote memory but can't understand the principles. The very concrete child can reason only on the basis of what he sees and in regard to objects he can move around. He cannot deal with abstractions and numbers are very abstract.

These are some typical math problems of the learning disabled child.

1. Counts on his fingers.
2. Cannot commit multiplication facts to memory.
3. Reverses two place numbers (13 becomes 31, for example). Also reverses numbers (5 to ꙅ) or rotates 6 to 9.
4. Doesn't understand place value.
5. May solve addition and even multiplication problems by counting on fingers, but cannot subtract, the reverse operation.
6. Subtracts smaller number in a column from larger number. In the problem $25 - 7$, he subtracts the 5 from the 7 simply because the 5 is smaller, not seeing the 5 as representing 15; thus he arrives at the answer $25 - 7 = 22$.
7. Often understands concepts but can't work the problem in written symbolic form with paper and pencil.
8. Occasionally can do rote arithmetic on paper, but it has no meaning for him and he can't solve math problems in daily life, such as making change.
9. Can't remember sequence of steps required to multiply or divide. Has trouble switching from one process to another, such as dividing and subtracting in long division.
10. Solves problems left to right instead of right to left.

Thinking Patterns

If he has trouble grouping like objects or like numbers, if he tends to get caught up in details and miss the main point, or if he has trouble understanding relationships, then he may reason that $4 + 3 + 2$ cannot be the same as $5 + 5 - 1$ because one problem has subtraction in it. Jessica has difficulty seeing the relationships between number facts. She knows that $7 + 5 = 12$, but she can't solve $12 - 7$. This may be the same youngster who at a later age does not understand that cats, alligators, and hippopotamuses are all alike in that they are animals, four legged, and vertebrates: she can focus only on alligators being in water or hippopotamuses being fat. When Gus was given a list of animals—dog, cat, tiger, bear, horse—and asked what they were, he answered "pets" instead of "animals," focusing on only one or two clues. The child deals with one part of a situation without relating it to the whole. "You're missing the point," or "You failed to pay attention" are criticisms he hears over and over again.

The sorting out of the essential from the unessential characteristics causes him a great deal of difficulty. In order to compare two items, he must define the main characteristics and find similarities and differences. He must rely on his ability to classify and categorize, which in turn demand that he sort the information properly. If he is to compare a red pencil and a green pencil, he must understand first of all that they are both pencils, that they both have the same function, and both are approximately the same size and shape. The difference is their color. He has to avoid being sidetracked by the fact that one may have a broken point and the other may have words printed on it. Organization of information makes possible the drawing of conclusions and the building up of generalizations. But the learning disabled child can't do either if he hasn't organized the information correctly in the first place. His assumptions make little sense and can cause him ridicule or failure at school. Many learning disabled youngsters cannot even come up with a simple assumption because they do not yet have the equipment to tie all the information together, let alone attempt a summary or a generalization. This child is often labeled as "preoccupied" or "refuses to try."

A child may have trouble with analogies because he can't remember a word or because he can't focus on the prime characteristic under study. Ten-year-old Letha said, "*Swim* is to *fish* as *hop* is to . . . *jump.*" She offered her first association to the word *hop* rather than focusing on the basic structure of the analogy. "*Grass* is to *green* as *snow* is to . . ." produces an answer of *ice* or *sleds* from twelve-year-old Mary, who says whatever is uppermost in her mind or what relates to her life. Mary is egocentric. Her world does not yet include many things other than herself. She is very concrete, and she reasons about what she sees in front of her, not abstractions. If she can't remember facts and she can't organize either, Mary cannot participate effectively in a discussion on how the French Revolution differed from the American Revolution. And we cannot expect Mary to be able to predict or foresee the consequences of being a revolutionary.

"The cause was oppression. The effect was revolution." Understanding this kind of statement demands organization. It relates one thing to another—a condition to a consequence, motivation to incidents. It takes a certain maturity to state, "This happened because . . ." The learning disabled child is not a frequent user of connecting links like *because* and *therefore*. In general, he has trouble with linking one thing to another and, specifically, relating cause to effect or vice versa. He doesn't see the effect of his own behavior on others or anticipate its impact. Often he does not understand why he is being castigated or punished, for he does not understand the connection between what he did and what happened. His problems in making connections bring him further defeat at school.

The ability to make decisions, to select choices, and to make judgments rests on being able to weigh several alternatives at the same time, compare them, and choose the one most appropriate to the situation. One alternative has to be seen as more valuable than the others. But the learning disabled child, bombarded by too many impressions at once, cannot tell what values to apply; he is overwhelmed and thrown into a greater state of disorder.

> Delayed and uneven maturation
> > causes
> > > delayed and uneven perception, which
> > > > causes
> > > > > delayed and uneven conceptual growth.

Often the learning disabled youngster has average or above-average reasoning abilities, but he cannot put them to use when his perceptions of situations are off. He fails at school not only on the evidence of his worksheets but by failing to demonstrate good reasoning and intelligence.

These are some of the typical thinking problems of the learning disabled child.

1. Has difficulty sticking to the main point. Brings up irrelevant, extraneous points.
2. Doesn't grasp cause-effect relationships. Rarely uses the word *because*. Doesn't anticipate and evaluate.
3. Is rigid. A word can have only one meaning. Or knows $5 + 7 = 12$ but can't answer $12 = 5 + ?$. Or knows $8 \times 7 = 56$ but can't solve $56 \div 8 = ?$.
4. Has trouble seeing similarities and differences and understanding relationships.
5. Doesn't see patterns. Must memorize all words because he can't see spelling patterns. All multiplication facts have to be memorized one by one (that's why he gives up) instead of seeing patterns that simplify the task. Doesn't group ideas together to form patterns of thought.
6. Has a poor memory. Can't remember names of people or places and has trouble also with faces. Reasoning often gets sidetracked because of poor memory.
7. Doesn't organize the facts and concepts he does have and thus can't mobilize them to solve problems, to predict or foresee consequences.
8. Can't categorize or classify. Each experience is an isolated event. Doesn't summarize. Can't generalize from the concrete to the abstract.
9. Doesn't transfer learning from one lesson to another. Has to relearn each concept anew.
10. Understands concepts too narrowly or too broadly. All four-legged animals are dogs. Only black and white cats (like his own cat) are cats. Or he may call all cats Puff, the name of his own cat.

Programming for Success

The learning disabled child is often very immature in his thinking, as he is in his movement and language. His disorganization betrays his fine intelligence. Frequently this child has not reached the stage yet where others of his age are ready to take off academically. This child does not automatically develop a filing system in the brain that allows the information to be quickly slotted in logical compartments of the mind and retrieved at will. He lacks the internal organization to classify and categorize information or put it into proper sequence, to understand time, or to perceive and use the space around him accurately. Therefore he cannot acquire the skills for academic learning by school age as most other children do and consequently cannot meet the expectations and requirements of his grade. Without the organizational foundations, he cannot approach the norms of knowledge and achievement against which children are measured annually, and he lags further and further behind.

Defeat means losing. The learning disabled child is much too frequently a loser at school because the people around him don't understand what's preventing him from learning. Often he's trying as hard as he can while the world tells him, "You're not trying hard enough." He's doing the best he can, yet we tell him he's not.

Academic success is dependent upon the acquisition of the foundations, the readiness, and the maturation necessary for mastery. Obviously motivation is an important component and motivation is nurtured through successful experience. Success breeds success. In every tangible way, we need to program learning disabled children for success and pleasure in learning. Nothing is more effective than the experiences that produce that unique and exhilarating excitement within a child of "I CAN DO IT!" To provide students with the tools for mastery, a sense of competence, and confidence is what teaching is all about.

7

Teachers: Their Concerns and Feelings

There are definite principles of teaching and techniques for structuring the learning materials, the space, and the time of a learning disabled child who can't sit still or remain in focus long enough to concentrate. Some specific methods have been tried over many years with hundreds of severely learning disabled children at The Lab School. (They will be discussed in the next chapter.) Before a teacher can apply the techniques effectively, she must be able to reach the child. She needs to provide an environment where learning can take place, and she needs to understand the feelings of anger, frustration, and defeat that both she and the learning disabled child will inevitably face. This is true whether she is a specialist with a whole group of severely learning disabled children or a regular classroom teacher with one or two such children who disrupt her class.

It is difficult to set limits on a child when the training and inclinations of a teacher make her want to expand, rather than narrow, his world. A high degree of organization and persistence is required to put boundaries on a child's behavior as well as on his work. This includes the way in which children enter and leave the classroom, their seating, and their ways of approaching their work. The teacher must decide whether the group is sufficiently threatened by one child that he must be sent out, even though she wants to bolster and support the child. She must know how to set the tone in class so that the children feel good about themselves and about each other. She must learn how to avoid confrontations where nobody comes out the winner and how to find ways that allow the child and herself to save face. In the end, she must try to teach the child to monitor himself, so that, in time, it is no longer the teacher who must tell him, once again, that he has acted inappropriately or has been careless, but rather he who can think, "Is that what I meant to do? Is that what I meant to say?"

The needs of learning disabled children are so great that the demands on their teachers are very great, and they need solid support from their supervisor, principal, and the school administration in general. Learning disabled youngsters, without meaning to, consume their teachers, exhaust them, and bring out all their fears of inadequacy and incompetency.

The teacher of a learning disabled child must be willing to give and give and give, in turn receiving criticism and facing defeat and failure. She has to absorb the child's frustration, anger, guilt, and defensiveness, all of which seem to be directed against her. A learning disabled child can give a teacher the constant feeling that she is doing the wrong thing, which only adds to her frustration in trying to find the right thing. It is painful after hours to effort to give success to a particular child and then to hear that same child say, "You always work with the others; you never work with me." A learning disabled child can make an adult feel that nothing she ever says or does is good enough, and in the end she finds herself with no more to give. He is like an insatiable sponge, draining off all her effort and energy. In fact, that is the effect he often has on adults in general. They find themselves worn out by his constant demands. The teacher is exhausted by the amount of anticipating she must do, the planning, the extra preparation, and the perpetual tension that never lets the atmosphere in class become relaxed. In a classroom of thirty-two children, one or two who can't sit still, who keep interrupting, who demand help incessantly, who constantly drop, lose, mess up papers, can easily extend this exhausting quality into all its activities and drive the teacher almost to distraction.

Not all learning disabled children are hyperactive, disruptive, and vocally demanding, however. Yet in some ways the quiet daydreamer is equally draining because he is very hard for a teacher to reach and very easy to forget. When a hyperactive, scattered child can be made to focus, he usually responds quite fully. The quiet one may be simply "not there," unavailable for response. He may be a reliable, well-behaved child who has no friends but never bothers anybody; he can fill a teacher with guilt because she has never had time to give him her extra attention. Or she may become overprotective of him, finishing his sentences for him, shielding him from the gibes of other children, inadvertently bringing him the label of "teacher's pet" and further rejection. The daydreamer may avoid focusing or trying to put in a word for fear of being wrong, making a mistake, and risking failure again. It can be exhausting for a teacher to attempt continually to get any reaction from this child.

Although at first a teacher may feel very positive about what she can do for all the students, the normal response of a classroom teacher faced with one or more severely learning disabled children in the class is:

> Either this kid goes or I go. The principal has to do something!
> This child can't learn.
> He won't listen to me.
> I can't teach him.
> I can't control him.
> I can't reach him.
> He takes all my time from the other children.
> He destroys my class.
> He distracts the others.
> He keeps me from doing my best.
> He doesn't belong in my class.

Catching the Child's Feelings

It is common for a teacher to feel completely helpless to deal effectively with the learning disabled child. It is common for her to feel woefully inadequate as his teacher. It is normal for her to feel resentful at being placed in that position and then be ashamed of her resentment and anger. Her attitudes are understandable, for none of us likes to feel incompetent. Beyond the deep wounding of her feelings of competency, the teacher is also prone to catching the intense feelings of the learning disabled child. They are very contagious.

When the teacher says, "This child will never learn!" she has caught the child's own feelings of defeat.

When she says, "No matter what I try, it doesn't work," she has caught his frustration and mixed it with her own.

When she says angrily, "There's no point in trying to teach

him!" she is probably reflecting his angry feeling that there's no point in trying to learn.

When she says, "If only I could do better by him, make more materials, give him more time!" she is probably mirroring his guilt at not learning.

At one moment she feels she can help him; at others she knows she can't. These feelings correspond to his own ups and downs.

When she says, "He's impossible. There's no way this child will ever learn," she reveals her feelings of total inadequacy, the same feelings as the child.

Parents and teachers of learning disabled children know all too well the experience of coming into a room feeling cheerful and competent and, after five minutes of work with the child, feeling angry, guilty, helpless, and exhausted. They have caught precisely the feelings of the child. But they cannot help him effectively if they are caught up in his cycle.

Usually a teacher's feelings about a student
  tell
    how the student is feeling.
Therefore a teacher's feelings about a student
  are important diagnostic tools.

This is why it is important for teachers of learning disabled children to be in touch with their feelings, to recognize them, and to acknowledge them.

When the teacher can say, "I'm not feeling angry. But the moment I'm with Agatha I feel anger, so Agatha must feel angry," then she is in a position to help Agatha. If she does not recognize that it is Agatha's anger she is feeling, the chances are good that she will become really angry herself and make Agatha angrier, until the two become locked in a battle for supremacy.

A psychologist spends most of each Wednesday at The Lab School. Rather than work with the youngsters who have severe learning disabilities, she meets with their teachers, individually and in groups, and talks with them about their feelings. She helps them to identify their feelings, trust them, and relate them to their students. She prefers to employ this process rather than working with children directly because the teachers are on the front line daily and can do the most for the students if they know how. In this school, the director sits in on these sessions so that she can reinforce this work throughout the rest of the week. The more the teacher understands of herself, the more she can understand her students. The more support a teacher receives, the more she can support her students.

Learning disabled children produce anxiety in teachers. And when teachers are anxious, they become more tense, more demanding, more punitive, more scattered, more clumsy, less patient, less humorous, less sensitive, less organized, less confident. Anxiety can wear out the best of teachers and reduce effectiveness.

Parents often do not understand how infuriating these children can be for a teacher. Conversely teachers usually do not realize how utterly exhausting and consuming the children are at home. Parents tend to blame teachers for not providing their child with the proper educational experience and for letting him bring home his feelings of failure. Teachers frequently blame parents for the child's inattentiveness, his rudeness, and his messiness, feeling that these qualities would surely improve if he were properly cared for and disciplined at home. Teachers and parents alike are exceedingly vulnerable when they try to deal with a learning disabled child because much of their pride and their feelings of self-worth depend on the child's performance.

The Teacher's Self-Esteem

A teacher's ego is closely tied to the responsiveness of her students. It is unfortunate, but too often true, that some teachers measure their success by their popularity, by the degree to which their students show their appreciation of them. Others measure it by the degree of control they achieve over the students. Occasional teachers feel uncomfortable with other adults and at ease with children; such a teacher may tend to depend excessively on children for ego support. However, if her ego depends on a learning disabled child, a teacher is in trouble. She will be up one minute, way down the next—and she will feel defeated.

If there ever was a field that needed teachers with intact egos, whose gratifications are gained elsewhere, it is the field of learning disabilities. The learning disabled child has so many desperate needs of his own that he cannot be burdened with an adult's needs as well. He cannot tolerate the pressure, and he can only make a needy adult needier. There is already more than enough frustration, fear, anger, guilt, and anxiety that the child is passing on to his teacher. She is asking him to learn, knowing full well that his equipment for learning is faulty. This is a difficult situation at best, but it is impossible if the teacher's feelings of worthiness as a person depend on that child's succeeding immediately or the child's showing appreciation or affection for the teacher.

Miss Bayard, in charge of a special education class, wanted to be loved by her students. She would let them do whatever they wanted and did not help them to control themselves for fear of losing her image as a lovable person. As a result, children were hurt more than once in her classroom during the one semester that she taught in the resource room.

Mr. Toby tried to impose discipline by behaving like a military commander with his learning disabled class of ten. He nagged the students for every small infraction of his rules and was always looking for any possibility that they might be contemplating trouble. He spent very little time teaching. Like his students, he was indiscriminate; he did not set priorities; he did not identify the most important issues that deserved reactions or consequences.

Mrs. Martin would whine in front of other teachers, "But Jerry won't listen to me!" Her feelings of helplessness made the other teachers uncomfortable and alerted Jerry to the fact that his teacher couldn't cope with him. To make matters worse, Mrs. Martin would seek Jerry out at the end of the school day, saying, "Let's talk about our relationship." She put an unfair responsibility on the child, who was carrying more than his share of problems anyway. Mrs. Martin's needs were too great for her to be working with learning disabled youngsters.

Young Andy Cole, straight out of college, had an idealized view of learning disabled children. He claimed, "They see life in its purest form. They've got the right idea, man. They can teach the rest of us." He romanticized the lack of control to represent a positive expression of spontaneity and vibrancy. He saw the child's inability to follow instruction as an admirable way of flouting authority, and he encouraged it. Andy was too much an adolescent himself to assume an adult role. He felt that the children could enrich him and help him to "find himself." He lasted in a learning disabilities classroom for one month.

A superior science teacher in a public school system was given the title of master teacher. He taught and supervised other teachers in the system and demonstrated new methods and curricula. At age thirty-five, he was clearly one of the best in his field. Yet when he went into a special school for learning disabled children, he could not cope. In addition to his supervisory work, he taught six severely learning disabled, hyperactive youngsters three times a week. He talked with the principal about how difficult the work was, and they developed some new approaches together. The third week came, and he did not show up for his appointment with the principal. He did not show up at his next scheduled class, and he did not telephone. He could not be reached. Unable to face the fact that he, a master teacher, had been defeated by a handful of children who didn't learn, he ran away from the job. The principal, to whom this reaction was no novelty, tenaciously pursued him, called him back, and helped him to see that he had caught all his feelings of frustration and despair from the children themselves. She helped him to separate out his own feelings from theirs and aided him in programming for his success as a teacher in this special situation.

Deep concern and love for children (particularly for those who provoke rejection) is necessary, but it is not enough by itself. Many caring teachers have failed with learning disabled children because they have not been able to provide the borders for the children's scattered attention so they can focus, provide the control that will help them behave appropriately, and provide the tight organization and structure that will allow them to approach a task successfully. For solid learning to take place, a teacher needs to limit the amount of material she gives to a learning disabled child, being sure that the child thoroughly learns each part before moving on to more and using as many creative ways as possible to repeat and reinforce each step. It is common for a new teacher to introduce too much, to cover too much material because she wants the child to move ahead quickly. The faster the student learns, the better the new teacher feels about her teaching abilities. She is pleased with the child and pleased with herself as he seems to move along at her pace, but too frequently she is serving her own shaky ego rather than his needs. A child knows when he has not learned a lesson, and his failure makes him feel bad, but he may hide the fact to please his teacher and maintain her enthusiastic approval of him.

Howard slid along like this for a whole term with a new teacher. When the same material was reintroduced the next term, he resisted it vigorously. He refused to go over it and reveal his inability to grasp it, insisting instead that he had done all this before and it was boring. The new teacher had ended her term feeling that she has succeeded where others had not, but she had done a real disservice to Howard.

Since many learning disabled youngsters are very concrete, sometimes teachers need to explain difficult situations to them in concrete terms. Leroy was ridden by so much anxiety that he could not learn He seemed to carry the whole weight of his many problems—his inability to master reading, writing, and arithmetic. His teacher longed to ease the burden of responsibility he felt. She wrote two columns on a page:

Your Strengths	*Your Problems*
You work very hard.	Reading
You are determined.	Writing
You care.	Spelling
You are a good artist.	Arithmetic

Then she tore the paper down the middle. She handed Leroy the list of his strengths. "You keep these," she said, "and it's my job to take care of the others." Leroy could see and understand the division of responsibility, and it went a long way toward relieving his anxiety. As he was more able to deal with his problems, his teacher was able to engage him more in the process of learning, and pass more of the list to him, but her first job was to relieve his anxiety.

Because of their disorder, learning disabled children need the certainty and safety of a confident adult in charge. But this is quite a different matter from the dogmas of the self-proclaimed experts. These are more like the great black and white truths that we discovered in college and that our exasperating parents insisted on seeing in shades of gray. Growing maturity allows a teacher to define what she doesn't know, to rely confidently on what she does know, and to make occasional mistakes.

Setting a Model

It is crucial for adults to give themselves permission, frankly and out loud, to make mistakes, so they can give learning disabled children permission to make mistakes too. Miss Rockford, who gave one of her students the wrong workbook, said, "Whoops, I made a mistake here. I'm sorry about that. But there's something I can do about it right away." Mr. Hart, who sawed off the wrong end of a board needed for the puppet theater, said, "Well, look at what I did! I wasn't thinking properly. But now I am thinking well and I see there's a way to fix this." Neither mistake was the end of the world. When a teacher is dealing with the One Way Kid, she must remember that he cannot visualize alternatives and that each mistake, to him, means total defeat. A teacher needs to demonstrate through her behavior and her reactions, as well as her words, that mistakes can be useful and that they can lead to new solutions.

Similarly a teacher must be willing not to know all the answers. By being able to say, "I really don't know but I can look it up and find out," she sets a model for the child who fears that every admission of ignorance is a confirmation of his worthlessness. Often the learning disabled child will not admit that he doesn't know something and will not dare to say or do anything unless he is sure he is right.

Frequently the learning disabled child is so defensive that it is easy for his teacher to become defensive too. Defensiveness in students shows through comments like these: "I don't care," "It's boring," "I don't want to do this anyway," "I've done it before," "It's too easy." The child is always making excuses for why he can't do something, and often we hear his teachers making excuses for why the teaching materials aren't easier, more interesting, or more relevant. The defensiveness of the learning disabled child appears at the hint of criticism. If a teacher says, "It's windy in here," a learning disabled child may say, "Well, *I* didn't leave a window open." The teacher may respond with, "I didn't either," catching the child's overreaction to a simple statement about a cold day when nobody, in fact, left a window open. Some teachers become so caught up in self-defense of this sort that they are continually apologizing, a device that does not help the very unsure child to learn. Others show defensiveness through an exaggerated response to a simple question, comment, or criticism. The ultimate defeat occurs when a very caring teacher says, "I don't care."

A lot of the child's intelligence and his good reasoning are devoted to manipulation: how to get out of work, how to get somebody else to do it, how to hide his fear that he can't do it, and how to irritate the teacher or cause a disturbance that will change the focus from his accomplishing a specific task. Every teacher likes to keep control of her classroom and to engage the cooperation and respect of the children. The people who go into the teaching profession usually are interested in minds; they like sharing; they enjoy ideas. The word *education* from its Latin derivation means "to draw forth" (not "to fill up a container" as, alas, it has sometimes been interpreted). In drawing forth a child's ability to use his mind, a teacher counts heavily on the child's response, his demonstration of understanding for her professional satisfaction. In the learning disabled child, too often she meets a blank wall.

Traditional educators—many of them excellent, caring, fine teachers—have a body of information that they want to impart to their students. They like their subject, and they like to see it become part of each student's intellectual formation. This teacher meets nothing but frustration with a learning disabled child. Progressive educators—many of them excellent, caring, fine teachers—hope to spark the student's imagination so that he can take off on his own and chart his own course. This teacher, too, meets only frustration with the disordered child who can't organize himself or his work.

What keeps the average teacher working with such difficult children above and beyond her regular, overloaded classroom schedule? For one thing, the learning disabled child needs her help badly; in some cases the teacher believes that her efforts can make a difference and improve the quality of his life. Sometimes she can succeed, and that makes all the other efforts worthwhile. There is a great reward in the pleasure the child may feel when he finally succeeds in making a step forward. His guileless enthusiasm and his sweetness emerge visibly, and for a little while his teacher can forget the exasperating, slogging hard work that led up to this moment.

A teacher can sometimes become militant on behalf of a learning disabled child. Mrs. Higgins took on her whole school administration in battle, demanding a speech therapist, extra tutoring, and special books for a child whom her supervisors would prefer to have forgotten about. In this case, the extra help was sufficient. The child was able to catch up; Mrs. Higgins had indeed rescued him in time. That knowledge bolstered her and gave her the courage to take on many more learning disabled youngsters.

Becoming an Advocate

Learning disabled children need a committed advocate to explain the special situations arising from their handicap. For instance, the behavior of a child who talks aloud to himself, reminding himself not to forget his homework or repeating key words to keep his mind focused, may irritate those around him. When it is interpreted for other teachers by the advocate, the behavior can be seen as helpful to the child and tolerable rather than bizarre.

The advocate, like Mrs. Higgins, needs to muster the necessary services available to the child, coordinate them, and act as a clearinghouse for parents, school, and outside professional services. The learning disabled child's advocate needs more than normal courage in the face of inadequate resources and often insensitive institutions. She must be willing to step boldly forward and, if necessary, take leadership.

Miss Pendle, a regular classroom teacher with many years of experience, had rarely seen a child as disorganized as Jake. She found him annoying, infuriating, and worrisome yet challenging. She was puzzled by him because often his remarks were brilliant, yet he couldn't add 4 + 2 or read beyond the preprimer level in second grade. She tried every approach she knew, read some new books, turned to colleagues for help (unusual for her), and finally consulted a specialist in learning disabilities.

Mrs. Higgins had become an advocate for a mildly learning disabled child who needed extra services from specialists. Miss Pendle, who was faced with a much more severely learning disabled child, needed help in how to manage and structure this child to learn within her classroom. She met regularly with the specialist in learning disabilities who knew how to manage, reach, and teach these children effectively. Miss Pendle became Jake's best ally by providing the very structure and limits that he needed.

Setting Up a Structure

"Jake has the attention span of a flea!" said one of his former teachers. Miss Pendle found she had to stand right in front of him, use a louder or softer voice, a bigger or smaller gesture, a touch on the shoulder to catch his attention even for a minute. Besides Jake's inability to focus on any task for more than a few seconds, he was in a moment, if given half a chance, at the pencil sharpener or putting gum into his mouth. He would then have to be told to sit down or be reminded, once more, that chewing gum in class was against the rules. By the time Jake arrived in class for the first period on a typical morning, he was already frantic. He had thrown one tantrum while he was getting dressed and couldn't find one shoe. By the time the shoe was found, it was time for the school bus, and he had missed his breakfast. An older child taunted him on the bus and brought him close to another tantrum. In his anxiety to get off the bus, he tripped and fell on the sidewalk. As he entered the classroom, he was chattering a mile a minute and not looking where he was going.

First, Miss Pendle would catch Jake's eye and stop him talking; then she would point him in the direction he must go to find his seat. She had placed Jake's seat closest to her desk, and she had marked out an area around his chair with masking tape on the floor. The outline of his own space helped to curb his restless wandering, and he was close enough to her to put her hand on him for reassurance or restraint. When the children moved their desks around, Miss Pendle made sure that Jake's place faced a wall, where distractions would be minimized. As his ally, she helped hold him together until he could learn to hold himself together, and she helped to supply the emotional brakes. Yet Miss Pendle knew better than anybody else that what worked yesterday might not work today.

All children need the security of predictable rules and limits. They need to know precisely what to do and when to do it in which order. Structure provides a framework that can be changed to allow the child to succeed. Teachers often confuse structure with rigidity. The latter inhibits growth, for it doesn't allow for any flexibility. Every child needs supportive structuring of his time, and for a learning disabled child it is essential. He needs a time and a space for everything. Routines are the backbone of his structure: how he enters the room, where he sits, what he puts on his desk.

These must all be structured for him. He must be taught routines, step by step, until he's mastered them and can do them almost automatically. The things he uses must be kept in the same place. The place for puzzles is on the shelf by the window—big puzzles on the right, small puzzles on the left. When the child takes a puzzle to use, he must always put it back just where he found it. Miss Pendle's masking tape on the floor around Jake's own space served the same purpose. Jake knew exactly where he belonged and where he would always find himself. Three squares of masking tape on Jake's desk visually organized his work space. The upper left-hand square held the papers he was going to work on; the lower center square was for his current work; the upper right-hand square was where he put his finished papers. Later Miss Pendle removed his squares, one by one, as he internalized the organization.

Classroom materials, such as puzzles, worksheets, counting blocks, and a book, were introduced to Jake one at a time whenever possible because he could not integrate several things at once. Miss Pendle made a card with a picture on it to represent each material. When Jake was given a card with a picture of a puzzle on it, it was his cue to fetch the puzzle, put it in front of him, work it, and put it away. Then he would turn over his card and wait for another. When the other children in the class were given their assignments for a period, Jake would receive three or four cards from Miss Pendle, which she put into a special holder on his desk. It had a pocket for each card, clearly marked to show the order— first, second, last—in which the assignments should be done. This was his schedule, his checklist, his review of accomplishments.

Whenever a child in her class did something he had never done before, Miss Pendle made a point that not only she, but the children as well, show recognition of progress. She set the tone and gave the word so that each child's accomplishment, whatever it might be, was acclaimed. Besides progress in the three Rs, she pointed out that Russell now came into the room smiling instead of scowling, that Betty had remembered to water the plants every day, that Jake had sat still and listened to her instructions all the way through. "What do we say to Russell, Betty, and Jake?" she would ask. The answer from the class was a resounding "Well done!"

Due to his distractibility, Jake was always knocking things

off his desk. Pencils and crayons would always find their way onto the floor. Depending on the total class situation, Miss Pendle would point to them, thereby giving Jake a nonverbal clue, or she might ask him directly to pick them up. Or she might gain his cooperation by using a light touch and pretending to talk to the pencils, "Hey, you pencil under Jake's chair—can't you get back on his desk? Don't you think he'll help you?"

Dispelling the Tension

Humor is an important teaching tool. If a child can begin to see the funny side of a bad situation, he can often find his way out of it. A teacher who can laugh at herself in an easy, accepting way is an important model for the children who see themselves only as a source of worry to others and despair to themselves. The use of humor and the absurd, with a light touch, can be effective tools for discipline, teaching, and testing. A school where laughter abounds among staff members and permeates classes is usually a place where children are given many opportunities to enjoy learning and living. The problems of learning disabled children are serious and need to be treated with utmost concern, yet nothing dispels an atmosphere of tension faster than laughter.

Some of the dilemmas that a teacher faces are not funny, however, and seem to have no easy answers. The child who craves attention, for example, makes noise, says inappropriate remarks, and throws erasers, forcing the teacher to interrupt the lesson and reprimand him. If she does so, she gives him the attention he is demanding, thereby rewarding his negative behavior. If she doesn't, he disrupts the class to a point where it is impossible for her to teach the others. She frequently ends up sending him to the principal's office. What to do about a defenseless child who is being teased? If she steps in to rescue him, he will not learn for himself how to handle one of life's recurring situations. If she doesn't, she risks allowing his weak ego to be eroded even further, making him still more defenseless next time. Both solutions can seem wrong. How to handle the child who can't bear to be touched? There are many such dilemmas with no one solution.

All teachers know that a transition causes difficulties. When the children are changing classrooms, moving to the

library, or going to the cafeteria, the most trouble occurs—
pinching or hitting, teasing, or cruel remarks. A buddy system often works best at these times for a learning disabled
child. A well-controlled child can be asked to be his buddy,
to help him find the way, help him to remember his books or
his lunch box, be his friend during the transition. The learning disabled child can hold up his end of the bargain by
saving a seat for his buddy or by rendering some other
little service. Even when the children make their transitions
in an orderly manner, the change and the relative lack of
structure and focus can cause considerable anxiety to the
disordered child.

Physical education or gym can be extremely upsetting to
the learning disabled child because these times may have
less structure. Routines are likely to be looser and the level
of noise much higher than in the classroom. If he is consistently upset and behaving badly after such a period, it is
sometimes preferable to excuse a learning disabled child
from physical education and use the time for special tutoring. The daily trip on the school bus can be more stimulating
than some learning disabled children can handle. If teachers
are on the lookout for trouble in this area, they can sometimes help parents to arrange car pools and avoid an unnecessary upset in the day. Walking to school in a group can
also be overstimulating. Walking alone can lead to many
adventures for the distractible, impulsive youngster who
might follow a stray cat or walk along a new trail. Parents and
teachers need to analyze the strengths and the hazards involved in how a child comes to school and then build in
ways to make the trip a calmer, more focused, pleasurable
experience. Arrival and dismissal times, unless they are very
orderly, can also be periods of great stress. Learning disabled children may be helped to cope if they are assigned a
particular place to wait until the hubbub dies down.

Unexpected changes of any kind can devastate a learning
disabled child. Over one Christmas vacation, Mrs. Henry
decided to paint and redecorate her classroom as a New
Year's surprise for her class. Although some of the children
were delighted, the ones with learning disabilities met her
efforts with tears or tantrums. Halloween, Christmas, Valen-
tine's Day, and other holidays need a long lead-in period, so
that when the change in routine occurs, the learning disabled children are well prepared and expecting it. They tend

to perseverate on holidays, becoming obsessed with one aspect or symbol of it. The day on which such a child is going to a birthday party after school can end up being a wasted one for him because he can think and talk of nothing but the party. This is one reason why special schools or classes, with totally integrated school days and the minimum of over-stimulation, are necessary for seriously learning disabled children.

Giving Instructions

Most learning disabled children experience great difficulty in listening to, remembering, and following a series of oral instructions. Most teachers are unaware of how wordy they are and how fast they tend to speak. It's important that teachers listen to themselves. One school requires each teacher to be taped so she will hear herself. If a child has language problems, he cannot deal with many words. If he is learning disabled, usually he cannot remember a sequence of directions that exceeds two or three steps.

Count the steps that are involved in the following set of instructions given to a fourth-grade class last year: "Please sit down, take out pencil and paper, write your name on the upper left-hand corner of the page, put the date on the upper right-hand corner, draw a picture of a man in the center of the page, fold the paper in half vertically, place it on the left side of my desk, and return to your seat." A learning disabled youngster could not carry this exercise out effectively.

In giving oral directions, it helps to have the children look at the teacher, to catch the eyes, to reinforce the sound. For some, it is necessary to give the reinforcement of being touched or held in a position facing the teacher. It's important to be clear, precise, and succinct with directions. It is vital to speak slowly enough and yet loudly enough to be heard. Often it helps to limit directions to one or two steps until a teacher is sure of a child's capability in understanding directions. Sometimes it helps to break down directions, giving one small part at a time. This practice follows a basic tenet of remedial education that one goes down as low as is necessary to discover what a child can do and then it's possible to move up from there.

It may be helpful to have the children repeat the instructions before carrying them out. "First we'll put away lunches, then we'll line up at the door, next walk quietly down the stairs and out to the playground. Now what will we do first? Second of all, we'll line up. You tell us what's next. Last of all, we'll walk to the playground." And the next set of explanations takes place at the playground. When the child follows oral directions properly, he deserves much praise and encouragement.

Sometimes teachers have to say the same things over and over again, in different ways, to help focus the children, to interpret to them what they are doing, to deal directly with their fears and their learning disabilities. Here are some stock phrases that might be helpful to teachers of learning disabled children.

Focusing

Look at me. Eyes on me. Now think through what things you need to bring with you.

Stop. Think. What are we going to do first?

Are you ready now? Ready to sit down? Ready to concentrate? Good!

Calm down. Pull yourself together.

Slow down now. Organize your thoughts. We have time.

Is that relevant?

Keep your eyes on what you're doing.

We'll do it step by step, systematically.

It's hard for you to stop what you are doing, so I'm going to give you a warning and then ask you to stop.

Let's review what we did. First we went outside. Then what did we do? I remember what we did next . . .

Dealing with Frustration

It's OK to be angry. Everybody gets angry at times. It's how we handle it that counts.

I know it's hard for you, but you can master it. I'll help you. You try first. I'm here.

When you're frustrated, it helps to tell us about it, and then we can help you deal with it.

You may have learning problems, but that's no excuse for poor manners!

When you say something is too easy, it really isn't. It's hard. I know it is, and I can help you do it. (Also a response for "It's boring" and "It's babyish.")

You and I know now that when you say you are too tired to do this that you are afraid that you can't do it well. Let's try it together.

Encouraging Appropriate Behavior

Yes, I am bossy and I'm going to continue to be bossy until you can boss yourself a little better.

That's not appropriate behavior. (It does not fit the situation.) This is the appropriate behavior. Let's try it.

I'm helping you to help control yourself. It's hard for you to control yourself. Sometimes it's best for you to be away from the group for a while until you can pull yourself together.

When we see you tease others that way, we know that someone has hurt you very badly with teasing. Let's talk about that hurt. When people tease you it's because something really bothers them. They have a hurt.

Dealing with Disabilities

Some babies walk at nine months, some at a year and a half, and others don't walk until they are two years old. They walk when they are ready. The ones that walked earlier don't walk better than the others. Some children read earlier than others. You will read! You need more time but you will read!

It's good thinking that counts in this world. You have a good mind, and I like the way you use it. That's what's important!

The most important thing about mistakes is that we can learn from them. Don't worry about making mistakes for you can learn so much from them. Many great inventions have come as a result of mistakes.

You don't have to be perfect. Nobody is perfect. How dull the world would be if people were perfect.

How great that you can laugh at yourself.

First, let's look at what you are good at, what you can do. Then we are better able to tackle what you can't do.

It's hard to lose a game, but I'm sure you'll win one soon. This is a game of chance anybody can win or lose. It has nothing to do with how smart you are!

Nobody likes to lose a game (of skill). That's hard for you! Let's work on it together for a while. You'll see that you'll improve. (Or: "Let's change positions. You take the one that is ahead and I'll take the one that's behind.")

Sometimes it's hard to win, too, because you worry about whether you can win the next one as well.

You don't have to cheat to win. You're winning as a person, and you'll get better at the game!

Try to accept my knowledge that you're making progress. You will see it for yourself soon.

Remember how hard this was for you in September. Look at your work now!

Teacher Support Systems

Just as the teacher must build on a child's strengths, interests, and unique talents, so must principals and supervisors. The tone of a school is set by its top administrators, by how willing they are to look at themselves and listen to their reactions, by how they deal with problems and uncertainty. The teacher of the learning disabled child is dealing with an uncertainty—an erratic, inconsistent, misleading, puzzling youngster. She may need help in sorting out what she knows from what she does not know. One of the significant signs of a mature person is the ability to recognize the areas where her knowledge is insufficient, be able to state it, and ask for help. This skill is crucial for teachers of learning disabled children because at times there is a need for help, since the job is so difficult and demanding.

A teacher is thrown on her own resources when schools do not recognize the special problems of a child with faulty perception who cannot learn normally despite normal intelligence. Where schools adopt *mainstreaming* (regular schooling) as a philosophy, the responsibility of meeting the special needs of a learning disabled child falls upon the regular classroom teacher. She has rarely had special training, and often she does not know how to proceed. She cannot be expected to perform this job proficiently without proper support and guidance.

Schools need to build in more supervisory services that are less judgmental and more supportive. Teachers need supervisors who will listen to the details of their worries about a child. Often the process of talking clarifies problems for them. Sometimes a fresh view helps. Teachers frequently need the help of a supervisor or master staff in designing new materials for the child, creating a model lesson, making a learning game, or constructing learning aids together with the teacher, instead of just hearing advice on how to do it. At times they need inspiration. The nourishing of teachers needs to become a top priority of school administrators because then the children are assured of being well nourished educationally.

School support systems that encourage the sharing of ideas and feelings are essential for teachers. Staff need to be trained and treated in the same way they are expected to train and treat children—by drawing on their experience, building on their strengths and interests, by helping them to overcome areas of weakness, by establishing trust. Tapping their hidden resources, giving them experiences that tickle their intellect, excite their imaginations, stimulate hearty laughter, and give satisfaction need to be a conscious part of staff training.

If administrators don't want the staff to stand in front of their classes and lecture all the time, then they must not do this with their faculty. If the goal is to provide more experiential learning, then administrators need to set up situations for the faculty to explore new situations using as many senses as possible. When teachers are asked to develop programs that totally involve their students, they will be helped if they see models provided on an adult level where they have been totally involved themselves. Too often school faulty meetings deal with immediate logistical concerns and announcements, not with the true issues of education, with great ideas, with a myriad of ways to solve a certain problem. They don't bring out the best of the human resources that fill the meeting room. They don't bring out a commitment to inquiry, a seeking of new knowledge.

Staff need to be helped to prize each other's uniqueness, recognize each other's special talents and rely on one another for help in those areas. Brainstorming in small groups within an established time frame to work out new systems for the operation of the school or teams that present alternate ways of solving a particular intellectual or behavior problem, are ways in which a faculty can learn to work together.

The more ways a faculty is helped to grow . . .
   the more a faculty can do for its students . . .
      the more students grow.

Teaching Teachers

Teachers serve as models to most students. The ways teachers carry themselves, react, speak, and handle their own feelings are emulated by many of their students. All students, learning disabled students even more so, pick up the emotional atmosphere of a school, feelings about the institution, the relationships between and among teachers, attitudes toward authority. Too little of our teacher training attends to these human factors. In fact, not enough attention is devoted to the quality of those applying to be a teacher or for teacher training. Too much attention has been paid to grades and prerequisite courses. In ancient times, the purpose of education was for children to be near the finest adults possible to absorb their wisdom, their values, and the way they dealt with feelings and relationships. Should it not be so today?

We want all of our children, and particularly those who are disabled in learning, to be near adults who are constantly learning and growing and are excited by the very process of living. Universities need to select human beings to become teachers who care deeply about children, who desire to probe ideas in depth, who want to built up a storehouse of knowledge, systematically, layer upon layer. Teacher training programs must prize the ingenuity, creativity, problem-solving attitudes of adults, so they can draw on those reserves when there are no set paths, no predestined routes. Liking children is not enough. To develop fully the intellects and imaginations of their students, the adults need to be mature, growing people.

As the job market for teachers shrinks, as the birthrate falls, and as the mainstreaming of handicapped children becomes common practice in schools, universities should become much more selective in their admissions to schools of education, seeking out more candidates who are multidimensional people. Teachers need solid training in theory, a vast exposure to methods and techniques, and then highly supervised practicums under master teachers to put the theories to practice and to develop their own unique styles and teaching approaches. They need experience in creating their own teaching materials, worksheets, and games to be able to meet the specific learning needs of each child. At the same time they need exposure to all the commercial materials available so they can select appropriately.

Helping Teachers

School is more than an institution for the acquisition of information and knowledge. It needs to be thought of as a place for students to experience mastery in all areas of learning and human relationships. For learning disabled students, school needs to be a source of comfort as well as a challenge. It can be thus if teachers are resourceful and imaginative, well trained in the needs of children and in a vast array of teaching methods, and thoroughly supported by the school system.

Evaluations by supervisors need to detail everything positive they observe and to provide constructive help in the areas of need demonstrated by teachers. Very specific suggestions, brainstorming with the teacher, fueling her up to get on with the job are ways to a better teacher. In some schools, supervisors merely rate the condition of the room, how the bulletin boards look, how well the children are behaved, and if the lesson plans seem neat and in order. One classroom teacher with five learning disabled children in her class of thirty-two first-graders said, "All my supervisor told me was that she rated me highly on how nice my room looked and how green the plants were but she thought my behavioral control was only fair. She never had the time to listen to my plight with these five kids who aren't learning anything. Mrs. Jones reminds me of my mother—too busy to take the time to really help." Fortunately most supervisors aren't like Mrs. Jones. Nevertheless the roles of supervisors need to be examined in depth. Perhaps the nomenclature is too judgmental. Maybe school systems need advisers, backup support provided by master teachers who welcome the challenges of helping teachers deal with their most difficult students and produce learners. Those who advise or supervise teachers need to present examples and to pose questions. They need to help make lesson plans for these youngsters and, with the teacher, seek out the most effective methods. The advisers need to be part of the process to support the teacher.

It may be helpful for a teacher with learning disabled children in her class to make a checklist of questions to ask herself. The following examples might be typical:

What did I do that worked today?
What did I do that should be avoided?

Am I looking at the strengths each child brings with him?
What are his interests?

What are the areas of my strengths, my weaknesses?
Am I too tough on myself?

Do I have enough change of pace in my program?
Do I always have enough alternatives to fall back on when the program is dragging?

How flexible am I?

How important is it to me to be right all the time?

Instead of merely disapproving of negative energies, am I finding ways to divert these negative energies into more constructive channels?

Am I devoting so much attention to negative behavior that I am reinforcing it?

Can I remember to praise positive behavior, the things we tend to take for granted?

Am I talking too much?

Am I unintentionally encouraging their "answer-grabbing syndrome," their feeling that they must have an answer for all situations?

What kinds of questions am I asking the children?

Am I a good listener?

Am I encouraging the children to ask questions?

Since the basis of all relationships lies in the feeling of trust, what can I do to establish it? Can I rush it?

What are the cues that the children are not being reached? Can children be listening even when they seem to be focused on something else?

Do I bring humor, laughter, and smiles into my classroom? How can I make more use of the absurd mistake, the absurd example, both as a learning tool and a source of humor?

What do I do with the child who stands on the perimeter?

What do I do with the hyperactive child or the child who may leave the room?

What do I do with the very aggressive child?

At what point do I send a child to the "crisis teacher"?

Is it helpful for the children to be told at the beginning the goal or goals for that period and to know if they reached them?

How important is it at the end of each period to repeat, rephrase, refresh, and restate the concepts, vocabulary, and information that have been taught?

How do I know when a child is really tired or using fatigue as an excuse to escape work? Why does he need to use an excuse?

What special plans must I make for a rainy day?

How can I stimulate the children to recognize not only their own progress but each other's and to praise their peers?

What can I do in my classroom to foster respect, to promote a positive look at what each child can do?

Am I setting a model of inquiry?

How do I approach the unknown?

How can I help the children to see that mistakes are useful, not to be laughed at, but to be learned from?

Do I fear failure?

Basic questions

What will I teach? (What do the children need to know?)

Why should I teach it?

How will I teach it?

How will I know I taught it?

8

Teaching Approaches

Every child can learn. It is up to us, the adults, to seek out and discover the routes by which he learns. Detective work is required. Vital clues can be found through precise observation of the child, keen listening to the child, and careful study of his work. Patterns of learning can be discerned through close scrutiny of all formal and informal test results, teachers' records, and the history and information given by parents. Experimentation is needed to decipher what works and what doesn't. Astute analysis of all the evidence demands strong reasoning, alertness, attention to detail, and precise record keeping in order to uncover a child's unique learning style. All this detective work does not imply that it is a crime to have learning disabilities, of course. The crime is allowing a child to go through years of schooling without learning the basic skills.

To program a child for success, the necessary starting point is to ask very basic questions:

In general, what are the child's strengths?

What are his interests, his hobbies, his pleasures?

What does he have going for him?

Does he seem to learn best through his eyes, his ears, his hands, his body, through associating one thing with another, or through a specific combination of these?

What can this child do?

We have to know in detail what a child can't do, but some teachers concentrate only on what a child can't do. It is too easy to say that since we taught him and he didn't learn, the child is dumb, lazy, willful, manipulative, or badly brought up. Sometimes the child does have limitations on his intelligence, or he is disturbed, or he has learned to manipulate adults to avoid working. Usually, though, the child desperately wants to learn and doesn't know how to do it. *It is our job to find out how he learns and then teach him how he learns.*

School needs to be a place for a child to experience mastery. Our teaching approaches must *program for each child's success and pleasure in learning.* No matter how far down we have to go to find an activity that a child can do, and can do independently, we must find it to offer him success. Each success leads to further success. That exultant feeling of "I can do it!" needs to become part of each child's daily school experience.

Knowing the child and defining his *learning profile* is necessary but not enough. It is only the beginning. *Knowing what he needs to know* is next.

The child needs specific educational tasks to learn. Clear, precise objectives are a must. No matter how the child learns best, or which teaching methods are used, a tightly structured treatment program must lead to a well defined goal. The teacher must analyze first whether the child has the skills to reach the goal or which skills the child has and which ones must be built in first.

A child may need to be taught a whole spectrum of readiness skills before any attempt can be made on the goal itself. He may not have the foundations on which to begin, and so the building up of these foundations becomes the short-term goal. A ten-year-old learning disabled child, for whom the objective is learning to read, may not yet have developed the most primitive, preschool abilities. For instance, he may not be able to distinguish loud from soft sounds, to recognize similar sounds, to know left from right, above from below, to discriminate shapes and forms, to see the background of a picture as separate from the foreground, to be able to classify and categorize on a simple level. He may first need very specific instruction in one or several of such areas, and a learning prescription that pinpoints these precise needs must be produced for him.

Task Analysis

Any task presented to a learning disabled child must be explored in depth by his teacher. For this, *task analysis is* required. The teacher may find performing the task herself to be a good starting point. After noting what she did and how she did it, she breaks down the task into its components and isolates the steps that were involved, ranking them from the simplest to the more complex and putting them in logical sequence.

Marie wanted to skip, but she lacked the coordination. "Teach me to skip, Mrs. Willis!" she pleaded. Mrs. Willis analyzed what skipping entailed. Before Marie could skip, she must know how to hop. Before she could hop, she must know how to stand on one foot. Before standing on one foot, she must stand on two feet. Marie could hop, so Mrs. Willis began by having Marie stand on one foot, the point where she could succeed with ease. She explained that Marie would have to practice standing on one foot and hopping, first on one foot and then on the other, before she could skip. They started out the same way each time, and then Mrs. Willis varied the routine, creating games to help her hop on alternate feet, and finally to combine forward motion with alternate hopping. Much repetition ensured that Marie could skip automatically. Marie was involved in the learning process with Mrs. Willis; she understood what was going on to help her reach her goal. Each time she was able to hop on one foot and then the other, she would fill in a colored square on her graph paper. She built up colored squares into a bar graph and kept a visual record of her progress. Each step required a more sophisticated set of readiness abilities than the step before. Each step needed to be broken down into its own components and examined in the light of Marie's readiness.

To ensure the child's success and keep his enthusiasm, the place to begin teaching is just below his point of mastery. From there, each step can be structured into a lesson plan and taught systematically, one step at a time, reintroduced and repeated again and again until the goal is reached and the child responds automatically.

The chart entitled "To Read . . . A Child Needs," shown in chapter 6, shows a beginning task analysis of an extremely complex task. Only the largest components appear on it. Each one of those could make the subject of a chart of its own. Each part needs to be magnified until the teacher thoroughly understands what is involved and what, precisely, the child needs to be taught.

In preparing a task analysis, a teacher might ask the following questions:

> What am I asking the child to do?
>
> What are the main components of the task?
>
> What are the smaller components within the larger parts?
>
> What parts come first and which later?
>
> Can I rank them from simple to complex?
>
> What does the child have to know in order to perform each stage?
>
> At what point in the sequence of the hierarchy does the child have mastery?
>
> What steps will I teach him, one by one, from there?
>
> Can I set clear, precise goals for each step?

The task analysis combined with the profile of the child serves to prepare the way. The teacher then must have access to and be familiar with a multiplicity of teaching materials and their various levels of difficulty. No one method or set of materials is foolproof. Many of the very best teachers subscribe to no one method but draw on the many that they know, matching a variety of materials to the child's age level and interests, as well as to his developmental level. Methods and approaches must fit the child rather than the child having to adapt to a particular method or approach.

Still another ingredient is necessary. This is the part that challenges all the resources of a human being and makes teaching exciting. It is *problem-solving ingenuity*. Creativity is needed for a teacher to present material so that it entices the child and lures his participation. Inventing materials to present the same lessons in hundreds of different, imaginative ways until it is learned and has become part of the child's very being is surely the spice of teaching. There are many excellent commercial materials available today for teachers to choose from but teacher-made materials are also necessary. "You made this game just for *me!*" said nine-year-old Jane Ellen, who loved games and relished the fact that something had been designed especially for her. Not only can teacher-made materials focus on a specific child's interests and needs but they motivate the child's focus right away.

Preparation for the Task

Before he starts his task, the learning disabled child needs to be *structured to focus*. He needs to be told the purpose of the task and what is expected of him, told what to look for, what to attend to and what to ignore. He needs to be shown explicitly how and where to begin a task. Things that we take for granted with children who have no learning problems must be spelled out, step by step, to the learning disabled youngster. If he is approaching the task of circling all objects that begin with the letter *t* on a page, the preparation may include teaching him how to sit most conveniently for the job, where to look first, how to begin in a systematic fashion, what to say to himself as he does it, and what to do when he comes to the end.

Overloaded with stimulation when faced with complexity, the learning disabled child needs to be given only one thing at a time to do. He does not need widening horizons and enrichment. He needs limiting. *By limiting the amount of materials, the number of words used, the quantity of procedures, the choices, and the amount of work,* we are not limiting the child but, in fact, allowing him to learn. Establishing *regular routines, familiar procedures,* and *prescribed ways of behaving* are ways of giving parameters or borders to the child who is disorganized and distractible.

By *establishing a time, a space, and a place for everything in the classroom,* the teacher is providing the structure that gives the child the safety to learn. Then he does not have to expend all his energies on where to put his body, so often lost in space, where to put his belongings or his work, or how to organize his time; this careful structuring helps him to concentrate on his work. Structuring the day for the learning disabled child in terms of events, instead of hours, helps the concrete child. Preparing him for the end of class and *giving advance notice of changes in routine* helps make the transition for a child who has so much trouble switching gears and who has such a precarious sense of order.

The child who has difficulty processing language hears most of the instructions he receives in the course of a day like the gabbling of a record that is played too fast. *Clear, precise directions* that use a minimum of language and are delivered one direction at a time—and never more than two or three—ensure his success in following them. The learning disabled child needs eye contact, a teacher's gestures, modulation of her voice, and, at times, a certain animation on her part, to help him focus.

The child with disorder, whose energy is as scattered and random as his attention, tires quickly. Many learning disabled adults who have achieved professional success tell us that their hardest job remains to block out the extra stimulation. They have to work very hard to contain the overload of their senses; they talk of the enormous energy this takes and the consummate fatigue that results. In teaching the learning disabled child, professionals must take account of this fatigue that results from so much inefficient functioning. It is therefore helpful to *change the pace of instruction* frequently, to prepare several different activities for a given time period, to give *short-term assignments*, and to *alternate energetic activity with a more restful exercise*. The child's fatigue cycle forces a teacher to *prepare alternate plans and backup material* to draw on when necessary. She needs to acquaint herself with the fatigue cycles in order to reserve the most intense teaching for the time when the child tends to learn best. Many learning disabled children are most alert the first hour of the morning; others need an hour or two to become organized to learn. Most learning disabled youngsters *need extra time* because of their slow processing. Many cannot finish a paper or a quiz in class within the time limits but, if given extra time, can do exceedingly well. Recognizing this fact, the College Entrance Examination Board and Educational Testing Service now can make provisions for certified learning disabled students to be given extra time for finishing their SATs and other standardized tests. It is acknowledged that the abilities and performance of these youngsters cannot be properly evaluated when held to a time limit.

A Multisensory Approach

Learning disabled children need to use every available channel for gaining knowledge and retaining it. By using their whole bodies, by learning and reinforcing what they have learned through experiences of touching, tasting, smelling, seeing, hearing, and doing, they seem better able to organize and integrate information in the brain. The *multisensory approach to teaching* is effective with most, but not all, learning disabled youngsters. For some children, the use of too many senses produces confusion. The total-immersion approach is too much for them, and the use of the senses has to be limited. However, all learning disabled children *need repetition* of lessons until they are fully learned and have become automatic.

To be able to transfer the learning of a task in one situation to a totally different situation causes great difficulty for most learning disabled students. It becomes part of the teacher's responsibility to *attempt to teach transfer,* the recognition of the same task in many different forms. This means encouraging the pupil to discover relationships and structuring the lesson so that the child is led to the place where transfer becomes the logical next step.

Whenever possible, a teacher must *link what is unknown to a learning disabled child to his own experience and knowledge.* He is helped to learn by referring back to himself and to his familiar world as often as possible. A child who was making a simple musical instrument in the Lab School woodwork shop was taught the word *vibration* and its concept. Her teacher encouraged the child to hold her hand against her own throat as she made a series of sounds in order to feel the vibrations. She then felt vibrations on the teacher's throat and on the musical instrument. The word *vibration* proceeded to have meaning for the child when the function of a musical instrument was explained. A history teacher wanted to get across the idea of *preservation* when her class began to study Egyptian mummies. She demonstrated the concept by using a concrete object that the children knew well. She asked them each to take an apple, slice it in half, and encase one half in plastic wrap. In a couple of days they saw one half of an apple rotted and one "preserved."

Concrete Examples of Abstract Problems

Many learning disabled children have difficulty remembering, and some have a word retrieval problem. If they can't find the right word when they need it, the teacher can avoid unnecessary frustrations by supplying the word immediately. *Memory can be jogged by experience with concrete objects.* An artist, who was also a very creative teacher, found that her class of learning disabled children could not remember basic historical facts. For example, they could never remember what Columbus was looking for when he discovered America. One day, she came to class with a heaping bowl of plain, boiled spaghetti, which she promptly offered to the children. Nobody wanted any.

"Why don't you want it?" she asked.

"There's no sauce!"

"What is sauce made of?"

"Tomatoes and stuff."

"What stuff?"

"Spices and stuff like that."

"Aha! Spices! Now you know what Columbus was looking for!" And the children never forgot it.

Because learning disabled children are so concrete, they need to be introduced to *abstract ideas through their bodies and objects and pictures*. Evolution is a topic that is not only complicated for six- to eight-year-olds but contains the added difficulty for learning disabled children of many sequences that have to be remembered in their right order. At The Lab School it is taught by games played on an ordinary flight of stairs, with each step representing a stage of life—fish, amphibian, reptile—each with its own objects and pictures to identify it. The physical action of going up the steps, following the stages from fish to man, and touching and seeing the objects at each level helps to make the ideas and sequences stick.

Very sophisticated material can be presented to these children only when the teacher thoroughly understands it herself and breaks it down into simple parts to teach it step by step. Conversely *very elementary skills*, which are ordinarily introduced to much younger children, need to be and *can be presented in a sophisticated way* so as to lure learning disabled children who are older into doing what they must. When a group of eleven-year-olds at The Lab School needed the nursery school experience of touching and discriminating among textures, we set up the Tactile Museum. The children helped create the museum out of a wide variety of materials for touching—Styrofoam, sponge, velvet, fur, and metal, among others. They guided visitors around it, having them identify different surfaces, and they helped to develop scavenger and treasure hunts and all kinds of other games that seemed adult to them. In short, they provided for themselves the very preschool experiences they needed.

The children were very proud of their Tactile Museum since no other school had one, and they felt that they were performing an adult activity.

Keys to High-Quality Teaching

The secret to high-quality teaching often lies in the imaginative presentation of what appears to be a grown-up activity. Learning disabled youngsters need every possible opportunity to feel pride in what they are doing, to be able to share some of it with the rest of their family. Six-foot-tall, fourteen-year-old Van was mortified when his eight-year-old brother saw that he was plowing through a second-grade reader for homework. Twelve-year-old Kristina crumpled up the homework of simple addition and subtraction problems that she took from the resource room into the school bus so that none of her peers would see it. A wide variety of teaching materials are available that are pitched at very elementary levels but appear sophisticated and are tuned into the times, reflecting interests close to the child's chronological age. A teacher can also make her own, for format (as well as suitability of content) is an important consideration if we wish to secure a child's full cooperation. Children must feel good about what they do. Yet they need to know that there are some very elementary exercises they need to do, but that work is better left to the privacy of a classroom desk.

Often teachers face a dilemma when a child must be taken out of class to meet with a tutor or a resource teacher or to receive other supplemental services. The child needs the extra help, but he is resentful of being separated from the group. Ways must be found to help him save face, such as scheduling his remedial sessions during periods when some of the rest of the students are out of the classroom. It may mean doing battle with specialists who are on tight schedules, but it can be worth it for a sensitive youngster; his lower level of resentment may allow the remediation to become more effective.

Mr. Backral found that Jeff seemed to learn best when he was lying down on his back to read or listen to a story. At home, Jeff always listened to the radio or watched television lying down. Learning while sitting up presented a real problem for Jeff; the occupational therapist who worked with him speculated that Jeff's vestibular system did not allow him to deal easily with gravity, and she felt it was justified to have him lie down in order to be more productive. However, Mr. Backral had a problem when Jeff refused to be the only one in the class lying down. His solution was to place a number of big, comfortable, brightly colored pillows and a rug in the back of his classroom and announce that anybody could make himself comfortable there during silent reading time. Jeff was never alone there.

When a child makes slow progress, it is necessary for him to *have visible proof of his progress*. He has heard too many easy platitudes—"Come on, you're doing fine," "You're doing great; keep trying." He needs to be convinced. If his teacher keeps a folder for each month of his work, in February he can look back on his September work and see the progress. He can be encouraged to keep bar graphs, charts, or stars pasted on a page. With each tiny accomplishment, he can fill in each step up to the grand prize on top, paste in each slice of pizza that will lead to that treat, complete each part of the electric system until the light bulb goes on. His teacher can help him draw a train, with a new car to be added for each achievement, a caterpillar that grows longer with each book he has read, or a simple checklist to check off if he can read well enough. How many words did I learn today? How many times did I raise my hand instead of blurting out a question?

Fernando's teacher decided she wasn't doing her duty unless she recorded every failure too, and she made him put them in his graph alongside his less frequent successes. As Fernando started to see his graph go down, he became disruptive, he made frequent trips to the bathroom, complained of headaches and tummy aches, and stopped trying. Marie's teacher neglected to put down most of the failures, and that chart, as well as Marie, continued upward. Sometimes a child simply cannot do a task, in which case it is better not to continue it and certainly not to keep a visible record.

Do we *value a child's intangible achievements* enough? Do we praise effort, hard work, and perseverance, even when the result may be less than we hoped for? The willingness to be taught (availability for teaching), constructive enthusiasm, and sensitivity to others are qualities that deserve recognition and encouragement. When a child becomes aware of their existence in himself and has them pointed out for him with appreciation, in a specific situation, he is more likely to try and draw on them again. Even when he does not fully succeed, he needs praise for attempting to make a change, for making progress in learning from mistakes, for getting started more quickly, being better organized and following through a bit more. Recognition of each little step spurs the child on.

An important approach that helps a child keep track of his own progress is *self-monitoring*—evaluating what he is doing as he goes along. A child may have to learn stock phrases to repeat to himself. "This is what I just said. Is that what I meant to say?" "Before I go outside, have I got on my jacket, my mittens, and my cap?" Mr. Constable trained his students never to say they had finished a piece of work until they had said to themselves, "Look carefully at what I have done. Now look again. Did I do what I was asked to do? Am I satisfied?"

A Problem-solving Approach

The teacher acts as a *model* for a child in how to approach situations, how she treats others, what she says. But the learning disabled child often needs more than a model. In certain situations, he must frequently be taught carefully and systematically *how to react appropriately and what to say*. For example, Jenny had to be explicitly taught that when people said "Hello" to her each morning, it was important to look at them and respond. Besides handling such everyday situations as riding on the school bus, eating in the cafeteria, and using the playground equipment, a learning disabled child also needs to *be taught how to deal with unexpected situations*. If he is lost, he must know whom to ask for directions. If he doesn't know what is expected of him, he must know how to get clarification; he must know whom to go to. Coping with this sort of uncertainty before panic strikes requires familiarity with some strategies. It becomes part of a teacher's role to teach alternative options. Taking typical life situations of the children's age group, she can create exercises with one solution, then provide alternatives and try to have the children produce even more. Problem solving—not just in arithmetic or social science but in the children's own lives and concerns—is an approach that needs to be used more in our schools.

Television: A Teaching Tool

When there is *any activity learning disabled children thoroughly enjoy doing, then teachers need to use it to teach the children the skills they need.* Television appeals to all children. They become enthralled by its magic, fun, silliness, excitement, and humor. To the learning disabled child, television can also be a haven, a safe place to escape from a difficult world that makes exhausting demands on him and makes him feel picked on and confused.

While the learning disabled child relaxes in front of the television, it is bombarding several of his learning channels at once. He can see it, hear it, and associate his own experience with it. He knows and learns to predict the sequence of the program formats, the plots, jingles, and ideas. The repetition endears television to this child who loves familiarity, who loves to know what will happen next. He can absorb what is presented with no fear that he will have to perform in response to it. It is safe and sure.

Teachers need to show parents that they can help a learning disabled child best through television by helping him to organize in his mind what he has seen. The parents will occasionally have to watch his programs too so they can get patterns of thought started, an exercise that can be extremely valuable to him.

What was the show about?
What happened—first, next, last?
When did it happen? Where? How?
What was the result?
What was the main point, the theme?
What do you predict will happen next?
What do you predict the ending will be?

By asking these questions in different ways again and again, over a period of time, the parents can help the child to build up the patterns, understand the logic of sequences, and link cause with effect. If the child can't put his thoughts into words that make sense, the adults need to do it for him until he can do it for himself. This may take quite a period of time, even a year.

Police and detective shows are very simplistic, logically organized, and easy to understand. They show a clear relationship between cause and effect. A child who has difficulty with abstractions can see everything in concrete terms. He can be asked why the action occurred and what resulted from it. If parents are worried about the violence in police shows, television can be a good way to explore these values together.

Family and situation comedies also have strong learning possibilities. The relationships between people touch the child's own experience and are a fruitful base for discussion. The plots tend to follow the humorous ramifications of a single event. The child can be helped to recognize and isolate the repeated patterns. The people in the stories are usually predictable stock characters, each of whom has one outstanding attribute: the kind, helpful person with a heart of gold; the insensitive bore; the efficient, impatient boss; the flighty scatterbrain. These oversimplified characters can be used to help a learning disabled child understand cause and effect in social situations, especially his own. Perhaps for this reason comedies about hip teenagers hold such a fascination for learning disabled adolescents.

The role of adults concerning cartoons often has to be one of interpretation or a conscious decision to leave this area alone. Although the drawing is usually clear and the animation is simple, the narrative is often far too sophisticated; the dialogues are full of adult nuances and adult humor, which are incomprehensible to a learning disabled child. Yet he seems to enjoy cartoons. Many of the good educational specials, which delight most other children and adults, can be resented by children with learning disabilities. It is as though the television, which has been his friend and fortress, is suddenly seen as a traitor, allying itself with teachers and schools, trying to teach him something! Educational programs, like "Sesame Street," are likely to have some parts paced too fast and include too much, although he does enjoy and profit from other parts. Newscasts can interest a learning disabled child if he develops some expertise in an area such as politics, the environment, or the stock market and follows it closely. From one special interest, he can be helped to find similarly engrossing qualities in a second area and then a third.

Medical shows offer parents a chance to talk with their child about illnesses in general. They can discuss the causes, the symptoms, and the cures. This may be a good time to reassure him about his own troubles, which he may identify as an illness or a terrible injury. Quiz shows may help him to add to his fund of knowledge (but are more likely to add to his interest in money or the prizes). Sports programs can be a source of real interest and growing expertise. Once they have been taught the rules very explicitly, the youngsters can frequently understand football games better on television than on the field, where they have trouble locating the ball and following the action.

Some parents look on television as a pure waste of time for children. They may demand, "Why aren't you reading a good book instead of looking at this junk? Why aren't you out in the fresh air instead of cooped up in front of the television? Why aren't you doing your homework?" Professionals can help parents realize that *television is not a waste of time for a learning disabled child if he is helped to use it properly*. It can serve to expand his vocabulary and train him in the skills of focusing, observing, and listening carefully. It can help him sustain and lengthen his attention span. It can reinforce the skills of readiness that he needs for academic learning—classifying and categorizing, seeing parts in relation to a whole, and improving language skills. Parents can make extensive use of television as a teaching instrument and enlist the willing cooperation of the child as well. Parents can build on their child's interest in order to work on his weak areas, *programming what he needs into what he likes to do.* Sylvester needs to organize, he needs practice expressing a sequence of ideas clearly, and he needs a larger vocabulary. Sylvester's favorite program is "Star Trek," so frequently at dinner, his mother, father, and older brother ask him to describe the latest episode in a straightforward, concise way. Sometimes they try to predict how the show ended, and he has to correct them.

Teachers can use television constructively for homework by creating simple forms that the child has to fill out, requiring him to name the program correctly, write down the day of the week and the time it appeared, categorize it as a mystery, a comedy, a quiz show, or science fiction, name the main characters, and describe the main theme in one or two sentences. Furthermore teachers can play category games by having the children group their favorite programs into medical shows, detective shows, quiz shows, and so on. Comparative thinking games can be built around television programs.

The same activities can be done with movies. Learning disabled children enjoy being movie critics, and those who can write may spend hours writing movie reviews and illustrating them. Class discussions on movies can be organized to teach a myriad of skills.

Radio programs also offer many opportunities for teaching. The child has to listen and has no pictures to help him remember what he has heard. A soap opera, a special broadcast about a famous person, a sports program, or a newscast can be used as assignments.

Challenge the Intellect

It is vital to *challenge the intellect and imagination* of the learning disabled child, to tempt his curiosity and spur his reasoning. When I founded The Lab School, I was determined to *find ways to keep youngsters enjoying fine literature* even if they could not read. I wanted to keep them hooked to books. It was important for them to have access to the information that others of their age group were learning from reading. They needed to hear good story construction, fine use of language, and an expanded vocabulary. I wanted the minds of Lab School children to be stimulated, and The Lab School Media Center emanated from this wish. In 1967, the Library of Congress allowed "medically proven word-blind children" to use Talking Books for the Blind. Tapes were made by the director of The Lab School Media Center of books that had not been recorded previously.

Precise teaching objectives and a set of procedures were developed by the director of the Media Center. Twice a week, children come to the Media Center to develop their listening and expressive language skills. In an interview with the teacher, they have to relate the main point of a story, identify what came first, next, and last, and describe an episode in detail. Understanding motivation and cause-and-effect relationships are emphasized. When the students finish hearing a book, they have to locate on a map *where* the story took place and on a pictorial time line *when* it took place. The books are chosen by the Media Center director, keeping in mind the children's age, their interests, their ability to listen, and their comprehension. Children with poor listening skills can listen to only forty seconds of a tape. Some can do so for a few minutes and others for half an hour or forty minutes without discussion. The Media Center is not only teaching them in a systematic way the skills they need for academic success but also exposing them to high-quality literature, universal ideas, and the great concepts of history.

An intelligent child does not stop learning because he can't read, write, and spell. The intelligence of the child must be respected. Too often our schools stop offering education to students who cannot read. They work on remedial techniques and give the students manual work while neglecting the educational journey into great ideas. Learning disabled youngsters need quality education. The world of inquiry is wide open to nonreaders if teachers are given the training, help, and support to grapple with the difficult task of teaching exciting content without the students' reading any of it themselves.

While the slow process of remediation in reading, spelling, handwriting, and math is taking place, the intellect of the child has to be challenged as far and as fast as it can go. Reading is the passport needed for effective entry into our society. Yet too often we equate it with intelligence and stop educating.

9

Teaching Through the Arts and the Academic Clubs

The arts have been a universal language among human beings since the world began. Gesture, movement, dance, rhythm, paintings, music, and masks carry symbolic meanings that often have no verbal equivalents; they are understood without words.

It took the human race a long time to develop an oral language and far longer to evolve a way to write it down and read it. Children in their early years reenact the history of mankind. They understand gesture, rhythm, tone, and movement before they understand words. They sing and croon before they speak. They draw and paint before they form letters. They dance and leap and act out stories before they read. We need to make more use of this developmental sequence in our schools. Our elementary school children need to be immersed in the arts, which are considered essential to quality education. They foster intellectual, physical, social, and emotional growth.

Almost every child can be reached and taught innumerable skills through the arts. Yet rarely do schools take advantage of the rich and full education that can be derived from them. Schools tend to sideline the arts by relegating them to after-school activities or allowing drawing and music to be taught only once or twice a week. But some schools allow artistic activities to be scheduled in conjunction with a social studies or science project, or they employ the arts as preliminary training for eventual careers. In special education, the arts are sometimes treated as adjuncts to medical treatment, as therapy. The Lab School of Washington has pioneered in using the arts as vehicles to teach academic skills.

When I founded the Lab School, I wanted the arts to be central to the education in the school's unique program. I not only believe in the intrinsic value of the arts to better the human condition, but also that children love to participate in most of the arts. They become totally involved. Further the arts provide activity learning, and immature children need a great deal of this type of learning to gain that total involvement and to ensure their understanding of the material. The arts lend themselves to the imaginative use of concrete materials and experiences to teach abstract ideas. Neural immaturity makes it very hard for the learning disabled child to grasp abstractions. He has to be introduced to them through his body, through objects and pictures, and then through symbols. The arts offer opportunities to strengthen visual, auditory, tactile, and motor areas. Through the arts, a child can order his world, make sense of what he knows, relate past experience to the present, and turn muscular activity into thought and ideas into action.

An Arts Curriculum

I developed a curriculum where half the day is spent in the classroom and half the day in the arts. Woodwork, all the arts and crafts, music, dance, drama, puppetry, and filmmaking offer pleasure and tangible results to children. Highly structured, clearly determined objectives have to be pursued through each art form. I programmed organizational skills, essential for approaching academic tasks, into the arts curriculum just as they had to be programmed into the classroom curriculum. If a child has not acquired the basic skills, he cannot learn to read even if he is taught reading several times a day. Reading readiness must be taught in the classroom, but it can also be taught successfully through the arts, and the two together form a more solid base.

Artists, art teachers, and art therapists can work on the same basic skills as a classroom teacher but in different and captivating ways. The same training in discrimination that is required for reading in the classroom is provided by discriminating one shape, sound, color, or direction from another in the arts. The skills for academic readiness are inherent in the arts: organizing and remembering sequences; assembling diverse elements into a meaningful whole; gauging relationships of size, shape, color, or volume; using and recognizing a symbol in varying contexts; and many more. With a prescription of precise objectives, the artist concentrates on the learning process while the child, doing what he enjoys, concentrates on the product he is creating.

There is a discipline underlying every artistic endeavor. People think of the arts as being very free; they are, but they become so only after one has mastered a set of basic skills. These skills must be taught in an organized, purposeful way. Learning disabled children need to be introduced to the arts in a step-by-step progression, as with anything else taught to them. They need to sort, to differentiate, and to integrate several things at once. The special genius of artists must be tapped to offer these experiences in systematic ways.

The most resourceful of artists are needed to teach the learning disabled youngster who cannot cope with the freedom that is usually ascribed to the arts. His attention is so unfocused and scattered that freedom is chaos for him. The overload of unrestrained stimuli on his senses calls for just the opposite of free choice and unrestricted opportunity; *his world must be limited to allow him to learn and create.* The artist and the art must do the work of the faulty "filtering mechanism" of the brain to allow focus, discrimination, and organization to take place.

Tom: A Lab School Student

When Tom first came to the Lab School, he was a handsome seven-year-old with above-average intelligence, and, in some areas such as verbal reasoning, he was in the superior range of his age group. He used adult vocabulary correctly, although he often reversed the sequence of syllables. "I gather this decision is *umanimous*," or "The *emenies* are encroaching upon us!" he would say, with great authority. He could talk about the galaxies with the knowledge of a ten-year-old but couldn't recite the days of the week or the seasons or count to ten accurately.

Tom could make no sense of written symbols. He could not perceive the difference between a straight and a curved line; dollar signs and percentage marks were mere decorations to him. His eyesight had nothing to do with the problem. He could not link sound and symbol to recognize letters or read a word. He could not write or spell. He was not able to follow directions, and he interpreted everything in its most literal sense—when he paid attention. But in fact he could rarely pay attention in class for every little noise or movement distracted him. Tom was totally unpredictable; sometimes he was very alert, and at other times he was very slow. He was inflexible and unwilling to try new things— even to the point of bringing the same kind of sandwich to school every day for a year. Tom threw himself indiscriminately into every activity with inefficient and exhausting energy. He would run around the classroom and climb on his desk while simply getting a book from the shelf, quite unaware of what he was doing. He was clumsy as well— knocking things off his desk, forgetting his homework, tripping over his untied shoelaces—for everything about him was totally disorganized and scattered. If you had seen Tom, you would have said he looked like a normal, bright child. He in no way appeared handicapped. His was no hidden handicap of learning disabilities. You would have been surprised only by his age, for he behaved most of the time like a child much younger than his age, and he looked younger too.

It took Tom five years to begin to read at the Lab School. It took two more years before he was reading ahead of his grade level and before his math skills were catching up. Today, aged eighteen, Tom is a senior in a regular high school and is bound for college. His SAT scores in English place him in the ninety-ninth percentile nationwide and in the ninety-third percentile in math. He is still having trouble with spelling, but he organizes his work so as to give himself extra time for heavy use of a dictionary. He continues to have difficulty organizing his studying for six courses. He is an Eagle Scout, a member of the school soccer team, and a confident, well-liked, all-around young man.

What was he doing at the Lab School during those five long years before he began to read?

Tom's Curriculum

While the slow, laborious process of reading readiness was being systematically taught to him, Tom's lively intellect was fully engaged; his imagination was being challenged and stimulated. He was learning history, geography, and civics—covering material from the Old Stone Age through the Renaissance to American history in a special Lab School program. He was encountering the literature of his own age and going way beyond it through Talking Books for the Blind and tapes in the Lab School Media Center. While he learned the difference between *b* and *d*, he was listening to *A Tale of Two Cities* by Charles Dickens. He was building a desk and a chair, a xylophone, a go-cart, and a six-foot boat in the woodwork shop—planning, measuring, and proceeding step by step to completion. (In order to bring home each tangible proof of his success, he had to teach another child how to do the same thing.)

He was playing rhythm instruments in music class, distinguishing high sounds from low ones, fast from slow, loud from soft. Tom was playing games that linked sounds to symbols. At the loud bang of a drum, he would pick up a red poker chip, at a soft tap a yellow one. When his music teacher held up a card with two red circles and a yellow one, Tom could "read" it to mean "loud-loud-soft" and play those sounds on the drum himself. Tom's music program was challenging and fun for him. Every bit of it was planned to teach him reading readiness skills.

Always on the move, Tom was constantly crashing into doors or tripping up the stairs—partly because he was impulsive and didn't look where he was going, partly because he did not judge the space around him properly. Like a child of two or three on unfamiliar turf, seven-year-old Tom had no sense of what was in front of him, behind him, or above or below him, nor could he tell left from right.

To help Tom understand his own location in space, his dance teacher at the Lab School (a professional dancer with his own company) always made sure that Tom—like his classmates—began each exercise at an appointed place against the wall so he was clear about his own point of departure. Similarly Tom's classroom teacher marked the space around his desk with wide masking tape on the floor so he could see where "in front of the desk" or "beside the desk" really was.

Tom's well-formed body was a stranger to him. He had no sense of its parts or how they connected. Without being able to identify arms, legs, head, or back, he could not make them work as a unit. In dance class, he had to isolate his hands and feet separately to become a puppet like Pinocchio. He learned to use his arms and legs as though they were pulled by imaginary strings. In front of a silhouette screen, he had great fun stylizing his movements and guessing what the movements of his classmates represented. As he grew older and the dance exercises became more sophisticated, he moved as part of the gang in *West Side Story*, isolating body parts and unifying them within a dramatic and exciting framework. From the beginning, imaginative obstacle courses demanded that Tom look carefully in front of him, judge distances, and plan the movements of his body.

The ancient Greeks knew that educating the body as well as the mind led to an educated citizenry, yet we have eliminated much of the work with the body from our elementary schools. Few schools have dance or drama in their curriculum. We know that the ordering of the body leads to organization in the mind. It is imperative for the progress of learning disabled children that great attention be paid to teaching organization of their movements, which will help organize their minds.

As Tom began to plan better and move more efficiently, his use of paper space in the classroom also improved. The orderly placement of his math problems on a page was a welcome change from the previous scramble, with all the problems usually crowded down one side of the page. He was able to follow directions such as, "Write your name in the upper left-hand corner of the page."

In graphic arts class, Tom printed repetitive designs, always proceeding from left to right and establishing order. Collage helped him to organize visual experiences and to separate foreground from background.

Tom learned the tools of drama with puppets, masks, hats, and other props. A radio station, a spaceship, and a restaurant were among the many settings. Tom could use words like *majestic* and *feeble* correctly, but he couldn't act the parts of a strong king and a weak king and show any difference between them. His drama teacher, an actress, helped him to isolate the main characteristics so he could exaggerate and communicate them by his walk, his gestures, his facial expression, and, in time, his voice. Learning disabled children have great difficulty organizing and integrating several actions at once—skills that, when worked on in drama class, can carry over to the classroom. Tom didn't look at words—and he didn't look at people. He couldn't decipher expressions of anger, sadness, or fear. He had to be taught this skill. It's difficult to size up a situation if you're a poor judge of size, shape, or direction. Through drama, Tom was focused on looking at people's faces, walks, and gestures and matching them to an emotion. The immature, egocentric child doesn't look at the reactions of others. Drama is an effective tool for teaching this skill.

In filmmaking, Tom's class made Super-8 films from their own scripts about slapstick characters who were jinxed or were mummies (wrapped in rolls of toilet paper) and who never knew what was going on, and about battles with a runaway alphabet trying to take over the children.

When Tom and two classmates decided to make a movie melodrama about a hero and a villain, the filmmaking teacher helped them to focus on the main point: the hero wins, and the villain is defeated. When the children started shooting the film in the park with three more classmates playing the hero, the heroine, and the villain, the professional filmmaker frequently reminded Tom to focus and frame, to keep his camera on the main action. The purpose of such constant attention to visual focus in filmmaking was to build more attention to visual detail in the reading program, to see the difference between *stick, stock,* and *stuck.*

The filmmaker had the children edit their own movie, organizing the sequences to make the action interesting, exciting, and understandable. Their work required that they think out the thread of the story and decide what should be shown first, next, and last. The addition of music and sound effects and the animation of titles called for intense concentration and organization. (All of Tom's film titles were delightfully animated.)

In all the arts activities—in Logic Lab where games of logic and strategy were played, in the Media Center, in the academic clubs, and special classroom projects—Tom's reasoning, language, and general knowledge were developing at a fast clip.

Creating and Reinforcing Order

In every area and at every level, Tom was immersed in the learning of ORGANIZATION—the organization of his belongings, his time, his work space, his body, and, above all, his mind. A system had to be created in his brain where all information could be slotted quickly and retrieved at will. What most children achieve automatically by school age and need never think twice about, Tom had to be taught step by step, over and over again.

Throughout the day at the Lab School, every activity had the purpose of creating and reinforcing order. Even while lining up to go from one room to another, the children represented the different days of the week or the months in order and formed the correct sequence in the line. Tom was constantly immersed in patterns and sequences, sorting and classifying information in dozens of different ways through all the arts. He continually was asked: "What comes first? What comes next? What comes last?" "Stop. Think. What are you going to do? Where do you begin?" "Make a picture in your mind to help you remember." "Look—then speak." "Listen—then react." "Now plan." "Tom, this is what you just said. Is that what you meant to say?" or "Tom, this is what you just did. Is that what you meant to do?" Tom's teachers were providing him with the information that people can normally give to themselves—the monitoring that we do automatically. His teachers were continually asking Tom the questions they hoped he would learn to ask himself.

When Tom started to build his chair in the workshop, his teacher, a sculptor from the Corcoran School of Art, had him look at chairs and then pictures of chairs and then gave him a choice between making a straight chair or a rocking chair. The sculptor helped him to draw the straight chair that he chose. Since Tom could not visualize well, all the dimensions were measured against his own body. The teacher started him on each phase of the work and stopped him, helped him through the change from measuring to sawing, fitting pieces together, to hammering, to sanding, then painting. Together they rehearsed what must be done first, next, and last, so that Tom thoroughly understood the parts that contributed to the whole and the order of procedure. The artist imposed the order and the limits that Tom needed until he could do it for himself. Like all the other arts programs in the school, this one was carefully structured for the child's success and pleasure. Any time a learning disabled child can have the experience of competence, he is developing the confidence to try new things and take new risks.

Any good teaching is diagnostic. The nature of a child's

mistakes, difficulties, and confusions point out to a skilled teacher the areas of development that are lagging. We gain diagnostic information by analyzing a child's approach to a task. With spelling, we need to notice the child's body in relation to the paper, his posture, how he holds a pencil, how quickly he writes, how he forms the letters, whether he scratches out or erases continually, sounds out every letter, closes his eyes and tries to see the letters and writes in the air first. We need to look at his face as well as at each hand, where he starts on the page, how much of the page he covers, at what point he becomes frustrated, and how he handles his distress.

The Artist's Contribution

Often an artist can make important diagnostic observations that alert a classroom teacher or reading specialist to a particular difficulty or can confirm a previous diagnosis. A woodwork teacher-sculptor observed that a child who could not hit a nail on the head with a hammer could not line up his body in a position that made it possible for the eye and hand to work together; the same child could not focus on a printed page. When the sculptor shared his observations, the reading teacher recognized that the position of the child's body in relation to the task of reading (no less writing) interfered with what he saw, and she was able to help him find a position for his body that helped him focus.

The art teacher who discovered an eleven-year-old's confusion between the colors blue and purple, and his trouble in differentiating pink from tan, added another dimension to the classroom teacher's picture of the child who was stumped by all nuances and inferences in language and thinking. It is often said that learning disabled children can't understand subtleties. The drama teacher who observed that a ten-year-old child could not pretend to stir a pot and speak like a witch at the same time underlined the teacher's analysis that this child could not integrate several functions at once; he could manage one thing at a time, but other components must be added slowly. This actress identified which children could not focus on the main pont and were continually lost in details.

A dance teacher found that four of his eleven-year-olds could not move backward. Their classroom teacher discovered that they were the same four who were unable to do subtraction. Together the dancer and the teacher recognized that these same four could not use the past tense in their language.

The music teacher listed all the children in her class who could not discriminate differences in pitch; the list tallied with those having auditory difficulty recognizing vowels. The musician found that some students were excellent in discriminating sounds but that they could not link sounds with visual symbols. In filmmaking, the children who had a hard time focusing the camera on a particular object and framing it in the viewfinder or who had trouble distinguishing foreground from background were all demonstrating visual perceptual difficulties. The filmmaker also identified the children who could not organize the content of their Super-8 film, when they edited it, as to which part came first, what should follow, and what came last. This observation agreed with the classroom teacher's diagnosis of sequencing difficulties for these particular children.

A child who cannot work easily in one art form but succeeds admirably in another is telling something significant about what he can do and indicating where his strengths and abilities lie. *An analysis of the art form in which he excels gives clues to the components needed for the child to learn most effectively.*

Although the arts at the Lab School have been used to ensure quality education and to teach academic readiness, they have sometimes unearthed artistic talents that become vocations or important leisure-time activities. One former Lab School student, now in his second year of college, is majoring in music, playing in the college orchestra, and making flutes on the side. Another is a drummer in a band. One is a high school student known for his artwork and cartooning. Another high school student is heading for the stage. Several others have continued their filmmaking for pleasure and profit.

Practicing artists, art therapists, and art teachers are all needed in the field of learning disabilities, and they are often willing to make their time and talent available. But they must have that unusual spark that is excited by the challenge of trying to reach and teach the children who puzzle most adults. When that spark is present, their unorthodox approaches, originality, and ability to create with whatever is on hand make them uniquely suited to teach children who defy usual school practices.

Artists working part time in a school bring freshness and relief to regular teachers. Learning disabled children consume their teachers, as anybody who has dealt with them knows. One teacher cannot possibly give her best to these youngsters five hours a day, find time to develop individualized materials for each child, and use her resourcefulness to the fullest.

Educators and artists share many common goals. Joining together means a pooling of talent and techniques. When it passed the Education for All Handicapped Children Act in 1975, Congress intended that the arts should be an important part of the education of handicapped children. The Senate Committee on Labor and Public Welfare stated,

> The use of the arts as a teaching tool for the handicapped has long been recognized as a viable, effective way, not only of teaching special skills, but also of reaching youngsters who had otherwise been unteachable. The Committee envisions that programs under this bill could well include an arts component and, indeed, urges that local educational agencies include the arts in programs for the handicapped under this Act. Such a program could cover both appreciation of the arts by the handicapped youngsters and the utilization of the arts as a teaching tool per se. [Senate Report 94-169]

The developing of organization skills helps strengthen memory, which in turn helps language development. All the arts offer opportunities for the child to talk about what he is doing or expects to do; verbalization comes naturally in the arts. Drama works specifically on language. However, woodwork, the graphic arts, music, filmmaking, and dance can be taught in ways that make the children describe what they have done, tell the order in which they did it, and then summarize the experience. All the arts work on helping a child to visualize. Frequently a learning disabled child cannot create a picture in his mind—a picture of a toy, a product he wants to make, an experience he had. No wonder that it is hard for him to visualize letters and word configurations. To visualize helps a child to remember vocabulary, which helps his language development.

A child with part-whole confusion may become quickly fatigued while working on syllables of words in the classroom; but he may pick up energy and motivation in the music room as he taps out the syllables of a musical phrase with a different teacher. The child with poor auditory discrimination may find such intrinsic pleasure in linking color to sound that he is spurred on toward linking sounds to letters and the ultimate goal of reading.

At the Lab School, we have found that even straight academic content—mathematical functions, grammar, syntax, spelling—can be taught effectively to learning disabled children through the arts. A vowel can dance between two consonants. Computing methods can be "invented" to save a flock of sheep in a make-believe encampment of ancient Assyria. The whole social science curriculum of the Lab School is carried on through an academic club method that I designed in 1965 and that employs all of the arts.

The Academic Club Method

When Tom first came to the Lab School, he joined the youngest children in the Caveman Club, never thinking of it as a social science class. He and his classmates met for fifty minutes every day in the dramatic setting of the "cave" (a basement storeroom where simple decorations and props made the make-believe come alive). The children wore their "wild animal skins" (lengths of leopard-print cloth), and they threw themselves with gusto into their roles, calling each other by their cave names. It was a perfect place for Tom (who was quite prehistoric himself, in many ways!).

The Cavemen whispered a secret password to their teacher, the Cave Lady, as they crept in order through the narrow entrance of the cave. (The vocabulary-building password might be *fossil* for a couple of weeks, until every child learned it.) The stylized entry warded off distractions and brought the children around the "fire" (flashlights covered with red material) fully focused and ready to begin. The Cavemen soaked up knowledge of archeology, paleontology, toolmaking, and the formation of early societies through their own experience and involvement. For most of them, it was the best period of the day.

The following year, Tom's group was placed in the next developmental sequence in the Gods Club, where they were steeped in the mythology, history, lawmaking, and governing principles of ancient Egypt, Greece, and Rome. Pictures and symbols were beginning to have some meaning for Tom. He could enjoy studying hieroglyphics and practiced his own on papyrus. Developmentally he was ready for more work in symbols, patterns, and relationships. He liked being an all-powerful god, symbolizing wisdom or immortality or one of the elements of nature. In the third year, Tom's club tallied with his own love of adventure, mystery, miracles, and rituals. The Knights and Ladies of the Middle Ages Club was centered in a period when magic was truth; this was the time of chivalry, alchemy, feudalism, Beowulf, and King Arthur. Tom was so taken with the story of Beowulf that he and the rest of the group made a Super-8 film of the story, a combination of animation and acting set to rock 'n' roll music.

A Judgment on History

Tom liked the Renaissance Club best, when he was around eleven, because that age of discovery and enlightenment matched the stage of his own development. Truth was the magic of the Renaissance. He relished learning how the council in Florence made decisions about ownership of property or declarations of war; Tom and his classmates examined the problem before the council, decided on the best course of action, and then compared their own judgments with the verdict of history. For example, centuries ago near the village of Voltera, ruled by Lorenzo de Medici, then only nineteen years old, discovery was made of a metal called alum. When mined and processed, this metal could be used to keep dyes from washing out of wool cloth. But there developed a conflict over how to exploit the valuable new metal. Lorenzo wanted to run the mines himself and collect the profits directly. The villagers preferred to mine, process, and sell the alum themselves and send the revenues to Lorenzo. When the question was presented to Tom and his fellow council members, they debated it and voted to let the villagers run the mines. Then Tom and his classmates consulted the history books to see what had actually happened. Their teacher read the text to them. They found, much to their delight, that the real Council of Florence had voted just as they had, but Lorenzo took over the mines anyway. The children were furious, as no doubt the villagers of Voltera had been too. But delving further into history, they were somewhat mollified to find that Lorenzo learned from his youthful mistakes and in later life did not so easily defy the will of the council.

My son, a classmate of Tom, went to the National Gallery and told his father as they were leaving that he had just seen a painting by Lippi. "You know, Dad—Lippi, the Renaissance painter. One of the first guys to use perspective." His father asked him how he knew about perspective. "Oh, Mrs. Medici [as the children called the artist who taught the Renaissance Club] has us line up on the street and look at street lamps. When you're farther away the lamp is tiny and it's large when you're close and that's perspective. And we've seen it in pictures. Tom and I had a ball on that street." The Renaissance so profoundly affected him that he used his understanding as a basis for judgment on other matters. When we were off to a showing of Matisse paintings, he asked, "Would Lorenzo de Medici have sponsored him? Then he must be a great artist!"

The fifth year, Tom was Galileo in the Philosophical Society in a room decorated to represent a timeless tavern. Great philosophers, such as Socrates, Newton, Locke, Diderot, Rousseau, and Voltaire, joined Galileo around the beat-up circular picnic table; each had a concrete object representing his main theme as a way to trigger memory. Voltaire carried a paper chain as a reminder of his belief that people had the right to break the chains of their own mental and political bondage; Galileo carried a pendulum as a reminder of his experimental investigations of natural laws that enlarged man's vision and conception of the universe. There was a pictorial time line on the wall, with each philosopher's period clearly represented. Each philosopher also had his geographical place marked with a flag on a large wall map. Each had his main ideas listed on a colorful poster, and each one gave a birthday party for himself, featuring food from his country. Galileo brought pizza on his day, and Voltaire (and his mother) produced a chocolate mousse for his.

The philosophers took great interest and enjoyment in learning how each one of them had influenced the founding fathers of America, seeing which of their ideas appeared in the thinking of Jefferson, Adams, Franklin, Madison, and Hamilton. Had Tom been in the Lab School this year, he would have been a museum curator. We replaced the Philosophical Society with the Living Museum of History that reviews the work of the previous four years, from the Old Stone Age up through the Renaissance to 1492, and prepares the way for the study of modern history. Our current student body has more severe language problems than previously, and the Museum Club is a better vehicle for teaching them social studies and developing their language skills.

American history is always introduced in the sixth year, and its theme is derived from the special interests of the group. In different years, the children have been American Pioneers, American Explorers, American Revolutionaries, and American Immigrants. Tom and his buddies were fascinated with money, so I set up the American Industrialists Club. They studied how America's wealth was built up, who benefited and who lost out in the process, and how the accumulation of wealth affected the westward development of America. Tom, Mr. Du Pont, sat in the parlor car of a train moving across America with Rockefeller, Carnegie, Guggenheim, J. P. Morgan, and others. They not only counted their millions but studied the map to decide on investments and probed the life of early America to see how they had changed it. A historical period was evoked, as it was in the other academic clubs, painting a picture in Tom's mind.

In the junior high the next year, Tom was one of the orphans in the Charles Dickens Club, one day forced to eat "pretend" gruel and obey every command; another day he examined Victorian life and compared it to modern life. Oliver Twist, David Copperfield, Pip, and Scrooge became familiar friends because Tom heard these wondrous tales and experienced them.

In the junior high, clubs must adapt to teenage interests and take on new forms. Tom was in the Restaurant Program, the Commercial Enterprise Group, and the Corporation, where organization and life skills—such as cooking, keeping inventories, filling out forms, using the telephone, learning to be interviewed, and learning the different rights of employers and employees—were stressed.

When he was in the elementary school, Tom had been Agent 007 in the Secret Agents Club in the Lab School's six-week summer sessions. He learned reading readiness skills by detecting sounds, pairing fingerprints, discriminating among disguises, and learning codes. He also enjoyed similar activities that made exciting use of distances, directions, and maps in the Pirates Club, and variants of both detective work and use of space in the Keystone Cops Club. He learned math skills in the Storekeepers Club and the Carnival Club, and worked on expressive language in the Broadcasters Club.

Each summer club had twelve youngsters, who had some choice of which to join (usually they were given a choice of two). The clubs met daily for an hour. In the winter curriculum, Tom had no choice of program. He followed a developmental sequence in history. His clubs met four times a week. Now they meet daily at the Lab School for fifty minutes per session throughout the school year. Usually there are no more than eight students per club.

The club approach is designed to lure the child, to capture his imagination and enthusiasm, to build on his love of imaginary play, and to offer him fun and success in learning by immersing him in the atmosphere of a given historical period or plunging him into the situation of a real-life experience.

The Development of the Club Method

I designed the academic club method based on the theory that we can teach children what they need to know through the very things that interest them most, what they like to do and want to do. The first question to ask is: What *do* they need to know? What, specifically, am I aiming to teach them? The answer depends on the children being taught, but it can cover the entire range of academic subject matter and all forms of remedial work, including readiness and academic skills. The second question is: What dramatic framework, what theme, will serve as a vehicle to convey what I want to teach? What will act as an enticing dramatic theme? This means searching out the special interests and concerns of the children I hope to teach. What do they do when they play? What do they talk about? What television programs do they watch?

I first recognized the power of this approach by watching one child who was intelligent but failing at school. This child was not unique; there were many others like him who didn't seem to learn at school. Yet all of them were learning in one way or another at home. I asked what was going on at home, in their backyards, and on the streets. How were they learning there? From keen observation, it became evident that they were learning a great deal through play, through making things, by pretending, reenacting what they saw, heard, and touched. They were learning through the arts, although nobody called it that, using the arts to make sense out of all the things that interested them, learning ways to organize their world and function in it. The arts were serving as supreme teaching tools. Children's play is, in fact, serious learning, demanding their total involvement.

The idea of clubs grew out of a series of my three children's birthday parties, all revolving around a main theme, such as secret agents, pirates, Civil War heroes, or moon men, that created a marvelous environment for learning a whole world of academic skills. One year we had an Indian party. All guests wore appropriate costumes, and all decorations conveyed American Indian life. Drumbeats accompanied Indian games, such as "Follow the Tracks," table favors were homemade Indian drums and feathered hats, and the birthday cake I made was a recognizable tepee. My children and I spent weeks preparing and planning for the party: reading about American Indians, listening to records, visiting museums, and looking at films, slides, and photographs of Indian life. Our explorations covered history, geography, government, science, art, music, dance, literature, and drama. Choices for the celebration had to be made constantly so decision making was an important part of the experience.

When I designed a teaching approach of this sort, I chose the word *club* carefully. It implies membership, belonging, ownership. Clubs are groups where each person has a recognized place. There is much room for individualization built into group activities in a club. By its very nature, a club is noncompartmentalized; the arts, the subject matter, the concepts, and the ideas all bear on one another, reinforce one another, and funnel toward the same objectives while the children are immersed in the dimensions of their play. Schools need to pick up on the ingenuity that children use in their play on the streets, in the backyards, and bring it into the classroom for serious academic purpose. Unfortunately, our Calvinist background seems to resist the idea that children can have fun while learning. When they have fun at school, parents—and sometimes teachers—worry that they are not learning. Parents of children who have been in academic clubs at the Lab School and elsewhere are converts; they are overwhelmed by how much their children learn. The club approach was first tried out in summer projects with children who were failing at school. It was then made the core of the Lab School social science curriculum. In the summer program, the academic clubs teach reading readiness, expressive language, and math skills. Other schools have seen the method work and have followed suit. The clubs can be developed with twenty-five youngsters in a club. Obviously learning disabled children need smaller groups for maximum impact.

Planning the Clubs

Any subject can be taught through a club. It is gently woven into a dramatic framework and approached through all the arts, literature, science, logic, history, geography, and civics. All the senses, the body, and the mind come alive in a club; creative problem solving is demanded from both teacher and students. Although the teaching may look very informal, academic objectives for a club are carefully programmed and continually reviewed. Club leaders plan their club activities with the greatest of care and keep files for future club leaders on available resources—museums, book lists, reference works—that they have discovered. They outline the basic concepts and objectives and plan precisely for the details of special projects. They build the necessary limits into their ingenious curricula so that the experience can be handled by these over-stimulated children. The academic step-by-step teaching is reflected in the ongoing reporting that is part of the club record-keeping procedure. The objectives, activities, materials used, and concepts and vocabulary presented, as well as comments on individual and group behavior, are also documented by the teacher in daily reports that are used constantly for reference.

An artist or teacher who becomes a club leader begins by immersing herself in the topic—the literature that exists on an adult level, the artifacts of a historical period, the art, architecture, music, dance, drama, poetry. She follows her own interests and builds on her own strengths, be they the graphic arts, music, or political science. She studies in depth the history, geography, and civics of the topic and as much as possible includes some knowledge of the scientific discoveries, inventions, and innovations of the period. The club leader's experience, and thus her presentation, needs to be multisensory so she can better convey the information through means other than speech. It is important that club leaders feel an excitement in this new learning experience for themselves, for this feeling is contagious and children respond with enthusiasm.

Every facet of a club is highly structured, which is just what a learning disabled child needs. The club's use of space, its setting, costumes, seating arrangements, its routines, rituals, badges, passwords, and "coming in and going out" behavior, predetermined by the dramatic framework, are designed to meet a child's need for order. Discipline is handled within the same framework; the Secret Agents Club would have "agent rules," run by the captain; an Indian tribe would respect "its elders"; the Storekeepers, with their employee cards, are hired by the manager. The Renaissance Councillors Club would use "council" discipline. Cavemen have rules for survival; Knights have a strict code of chivalry. Dramatic cover is provided not only for the teacher, the subject matter, and discipline but also for the child. As a Caveman or Zeus or Galileo or Mr. Du Pont, Tom could dare to experiment and risk failure with a courage that he was unable to muster in the regular classroom because it is not he who might fail but his character. (Children often do this with puppets too.)

The academic club method is designed to involve the children fully so that they, who cannot read and have opted out of learning, become full participants in their own education. Drama, which is central to the academic club method, helps to screen out distractions and achieve focus. The entry procedure focuses the child. The props and room decorations give a picture in the mind of the particular subject under study and keep the focus on the topic, triggering memory. For children who need help locating their own bodies in space, arranged seating is a blessing. A Secret Agent sits on the chair with his 007 number marked on it; an Egyptian god sits beside his column, which is decorated with his own hieroglyphics; a Medieval Knight sits on a pillow with his heraldic symbol on it; a Star Trekker mans his control panel; a Disc Jockey sits by his record. Language is developed through immersion in the topic, through being read to, through discussing projects, and always through the password as well as a vocal dismissal procedure.

Deep involvement is attained through the child's experiencing this total environment approach. A club draws on the full range of children's experiences and relates subject matter to their lives, relates the past to today's world, and relates cause to effect and planning to action. For the ordinary child without learning disabilities, the academic club method is sheer pleasure in learning, and all kinds of research, reading, and writing activities can be built into it. A club works as well in a regular classroom as in special classes, and it can run for as little as a month or as long as a year.

Clubs can be run by regular staff or by part-time artists and teachers who come in to teach one hour a day. Parents or university students can serve as aides. All children, and especially learning disabled children, can be taught through things that they like to do and want to do, as well as through the exercises they need that require plain hard work. They can learn almost any subject an adult understands in depth. All the time they can be given readiness training. A profound understanding by artists and teachers of the underlying skills needed for reading, writing, spelling, arithmetic, language development, and abstract thinking will lead to success. These foundations must then be programmed systematically into every area of a child's life throughout the day. The whole panoply of art forms can be used as teaching tools for academic readiness. Starting in the preschool and continuing throughout education, the arts can teach skills that are needed in conjunction with the main work of the classroom.

The arts were central to Tom's schooling as they have been to all other Lab School students over the past thirteen years. In the academic clubs, in art, crafts, woodwork, dance, drama, music, and filmmaking, Tom was learning the very readiness and academic skills that he needed to help him forge ahead as a student. For the most part, he was a total participant, actively engaged in each endeavor and having fun. At the same time, he was learning art forms that he could enjoy and appreciate. He was experiencing the sense of mastery that breeds the confidence to move on. All the arts were offering him information and insights that he could carry with him on his journey into knowledge.

10

Parents: Their Concerns and Feelings

Parents of handicapped children often feel helpless and incompetent. There are no simple answers, formulas, or panaceas for them. No one product or one way of behaving for them to follow can fix what's wrong.

> Some people, when they feel very uncertain,
>   give the appearance of being very certain.
> Some people, when they feel helpless,
>   are attacking,
>   angry,
>   defensive,
>   mute,
> and they give the appearance of being uncaring or
>   unhelpful.

A severely learning disabled child can affect husband-wife and a whole host of other family relationships. The following letter from a parent lets us view some of the pain that a family can feel. Professionals need to keep enough in touch with that pain to avoid increasing it; it is important to seek ways to lighten the load and give true support to parents.

July 17

Dearest Joan,

I can't tell you how much I'm looking forward to your visit—it's been eight years since the last one. I'm glad your family is growing well—I wish I could say the same.

Henry is almost nine, and I feel ninety. You remember how sick he was as a baby when you were here last? Well, he kept that up for two years—colds, croup, earaches, bronchitis—never properly getting over one before he came down with another. It seems like he never had time to just plain grow like other children. Bill was an angel—he did extra things with Rosie while I coped with Henry.

Once he walked, Henry always looked battered because he kept falling. I used to carry a silver fifty-cent piece to press on his bumps to keep them from turning black and blue. He walked and talked at the normal age, like Rosie, but he was different. There was a pain deep inside me that just ached for this child—and it still does. Everything seemed so hard for Henry, though he was full of smiles and spark. Too much spark. He was everywhere and into everything—still is. I could lose him in a flash. One time I ran upstairs to get a clean pair of rubber pants, and, when I came down, the front door was open and Henry was in the middle of the street with a police car stopped and a policeman about to pick him up and look for the right house! Now he climbs way up high in trees and can't get down, and it terrifies me.

For eight years, Joanie, I've lived with a pit-of-the-stomach fear that something will happen to him. It's a desperate feeling of "Oh my God—what will go wrong next?" I dread every time the phone rings. Bill's folks say, "A few good spankings will set him straight." Mother says I just need patience. Dad says, "What are you trying to do—turn him into a sissy? He's all boy." I'm trying everything I know how to do. I'm exhausted from trying. But when I take Henry out, people look at me askance and say, "Lady, do something about this child."

His nursery school teacher said I babied him because he couldn't button or zip, and his clothes were forever falling off. His kindergarten teacher said I should discipline him more because he was too lazy to learn his letters and numbers. His first-grade teacher called one parent conference after another. I tried to help Henry sit still and learn his letters. At the same time, Rosie complained that I was never that easy on her, and she hassled Henry half to death, telling him, "Just try, Henry. You're not trying!" Bill and Rosie and the neighbors all told me I spoiled him, so I tried to be tougher. I took away the TV, which was the only thing he enjoyed, but he cried all the time and seemed more babyish than ever. I couldn't make him be more independent because he had so little to be independent with!

The pediatrician says not to worry; he's a "late bloomer." The eye doctor says he sees well. The Hearing Society gave some routine tests at school and tried to tell me he was deaf—and it took three ear specialists and an audiologist to prove that he wasn't. Now we've been sent to a psychiatrist who makes both Bill and me feel like the most inadequate parents in the world. He's asking us if our marriage is OK, and I sometimes wonder if it is! We've stopped going out or seeing friends. Henry is repeating second grade, and Bill has a session with him every night because he says I mollycoddle him. He shuts the door but I hear his voice getting louder and more impatient, then Henry crying and the books being slammed down on the table—and I wonder if our life will ever be good again.

I'm angry. Joanie, I hate the world for doing this to us. I wish we could just pick up Henry, get on a boat, and take him clear away from it all. Do you understand that we love this handsome little boy and we don't know what to do? He doesn't sit still and he can't do his school work. And yet he talks so intelligently (such a big vocabulary!), and he describes things wonderfully. He is intelligent. Do you know he's called "dumb-head," "retard," "spaz" by the other children! I don't know which of us is crying more—Henry or me. Bill is carrying so much responsibility at the office that I try not to burden him with too much of this.

It will be so good to have you to talk to, and I'll try to make your visit a good one. I promise.

Love,
Sue

Henry's mother feels:
DRAINED
BLAMED
GUILTY
HELPLESS
OVERWHELMED
CONFUSED
HURT

ANXIOUS
UNCERTAIN
ATTACKED
AFRAID
Almost all parents hurt when their children
hurt.

Parents of children with learning disabilities are very apt to catch their youngsters' emotions. Feelings are as contagious as a cold. When their child feels depressed, they do too. When their child comes in brimming with anxiety, before they realize it, they too are anxious. Or perhaps they sense the deep injustice their child feels—the rage and the fury. We all tend to overidentify with our children and feel their bruises with them. When the child is failing at school, when he is being teased and bullied, when he is friendless or lonely, the hurt that a parent feels is almost unbearable. Sometimes a parent will take on the child's feelings, mix them with his or her own sense of the world's injustice, and then wildly overreact on his behalf. The parent knows from his child's gestures, the way he walks, the manner in which he enters the car, the way he asks what's for dinner, how school went that day. The parent of the learning disabled child, so worried anyway about his day at school, will attend even more to the youngster's demeanor.

Usually a mother is home far more than a father is. She becomes more involved in the daily ups and downs; she has to cope more with the instant frustrations, the anger, and the sadness. She worries constantly. The learning disabled youngster has so many defeats that he tends to feel bad about himself, and the person on the front line, probably his mother, feels defeated too. Unfortunately a number of the professionals she goes to for help make her feel worse.

A father may not come home until dinnertime, so he doesn't see the child so much. It's usual that at first he feels that his wife is exaggerating the child's difficulties and that she's overconcerned. Then it's typical for a father to feel that stricter controls, more rewards and punishments, and harder work will take care of the situation. When they don't and when the specter of learning disabilities raises its head, the father may have more difficulty than the mother in accepting it—particularly if a son is in trouble. The dreams of achievement, Little League, a better livelihood than his, and all the unmet hopes he had go into a father's pain. The defects of the child overwhelm many fathers (and plenty of mothers too), and they too feel defective.

A significant number of disabled youngsters are adopted. Presumably they were affected by maternal malnutrition, poor maternal care, not enough oxygen at birth, and many other such reasons. Their parents, who have suffered the anguish of not being able to conceive a child themselves, hurt even more when faced with the child's defects; they tend to feel even more inadequate. Sometimes, however, they feel less guilt because they did not give birth to the youngster and do not have to torment themselves looking for causes. When people are hurt, they react in different ways. They may eat a lot, or drink a lot; some work a lot or fight; others pity themselves or withdraw. And, worst, some reject what is hurting them.

Rejection can take many forms when the hurt is caused by a child: too little care, too much care, too little concern, too much concern. Pain makes people anxious and sometimes unreasonable. A whole lifetime of resentments can be dumped on a child. Fear for the future of a child can loom threateningly large and be dumped on him. Most parents of learning disabled children have anxieties that are realistically based on their day-to-day experience. Parents frequently can't anticipate the behavior of their learning disabled child; they can't explain it in the light of their own childhood experience or their understanding of their other children. Since they don't know what to expect, they remain anxious and off balance.

Anxiety and Overreaction

Eleven-year-old Max was late coming home from school one day. Every other time he had been late, something disastrous had happened: he had gotten lost, had fallen down and been hurt, had gotten into a fight, or had been bullied by a group of children. His mother, nervous, was worried that there was an accident because Max didn't always look when he crossed the street. Then she heard an ambulance siren and stood frozen to the spot. A moment later she was running fearfully into the street, only to see Max ambling happily along, tenderly stroking a wounded bird. She exploded at him. Max yelled a bad word at her and stamped off with his bird, while all the neighbors watched. This sort of episode happens to many parents, but with a learning disabled child it happens more often, more intensely, and for a longer period of time.

Parents' anxieties are just as catching as a child's and may cause a youngster who hasn't been particularly worried about himself to become suddenly terrified that something is dreadfully wrong with him. A sudden increase in a child's anxiety may reflect a sudden increase in his parents' anxiety. Professionals need to note not only the child's anxiety and the form it takes but how parental anxiety is expressed. The number of phone calls to the school, the number of requests for appointments, the quality of the voice, and changes in appearance are all signals.

A parent's overreaction to an admittedly uncomfortable or unpleasant situation can increase a child's worry about himself by leaps and bounds. One vacation morning, ten-year-old Patrick woke early and went down to the hotel dining room ahead of his parents. He asked the waitress what was for breakfast.

"Read the menu," she replied, curtly.

"Do you have scrambled eggs?" he pursued.

"What's the matter with you!" she snapped. "Can't you read the menu, a great big boy like you? My, you're lazy! Kids today expect the world to do everything for them. Now, just open your eyes, young man, and read the menu!"

Patrick could not read the menu. His face was pale and tearstained when his mother joined him a few minutes later. He didn't want to tell her what had happened, but when she coaxed the story from him, she was absolutely furious. Over Patrick's protests, she bawled out the waitress and called the manager. Patrick was mortified, and his half-formed doubts about himself were devastatingly confirmed by his mother's overprotective overreaction. Patrick ran to his room, locked the door, and refused to come out.

Another mother might never have given Patrick the freedom to go down to the dining room alone and take his chances with a bad-tempered waitress. She would have made certain that each step of his day was planned, made fully manageable to him, and supervised. By providing the organization and foresight that he lacked himself, by buffering him against the insensitivity of other adults or the cruelty of other children, by taking over, she could easily have created a world for him in which he had no initiative, no privacy, and no opportunity to make his own decisions. Teachers and doctors call this mother "intrusive." With the best of intentions, she leaves no room for a child to develop his own personality; she tries to absorb all of the child's problems and prolongs his infantilism. This damaging kind of emotional overprotection must not be confused with the well-prepared structure and organization that all learning disabled children need. A different mother might simply have said to Patrick, "Well, I wonder what happened to that lady today that made her take it out on you. Next time, tell a cranky lady like that, 'Look, I have reading problems and some day I'll be able to read, but I can't right now.' "

It's hard enough for parents to acknowledge that they have a learning disabled child; for some it becomes an almost overwhelming tragedy. This seems to be particularly true of families who are highly intellectual and whose world is tied up in abstractions—and the child is left out. It is often true of parents who are authors, journalists, or playwrights, whose lives depend on writing, whose pleasure lies in books, and who see their child excluded from the world of literature and words. It is true, frequently, of educators whose lives are devoted to academic excellence, who admire scholarship and value degrees, who feel that fate has slammed the door on their child's fulfillment. It seems especially hard for these families to accept the child at his own level, to nurture the areas of his intellect and imagination that are not defective, and to enjoy him for the qualities that lie outside his mind.

The problem seems especially poignant for the family of twins, where one twin is fine and a constant reminder of what the learning disabled one might have been. Parents suffer in a special way when their learning disabled child is the eldest one, and they find themselves holding the younger children back, trying to instill in them the need for respect for the eldest one, trying to gain time for the learning disabled one before he is inevitably overtaken and surpassed by the brothers and sisters. It is just as hard, in another way, when the learning disabled child is the middle one, the odd man out, surrounded and surpassed academically on both sides. Parents feel a special ache when their last child is learning disabled. In some ways, it is hardest for parents to bear when he is their only child, the repository of all their hopes and dreams. It is almost irresistible to push him a little more, tutor him a little longer, and urge him to try harder. Sometimes parents try consciously to avoid putting pressure on the child without realizing that the shape, the pace, and the tension of their lives are themselves a form of pressure.

The Feelings of Brothers and Sisters

A learning disabled child can provoke intense emotions in his brothers and sisters and complicate their lives in ways that they will inevitably resent at times. They had wanted a perfect brother or sister whom they could be proud of and stand with, shoulder to shoulder, against the world. Instead they are in the position of always having to explain the invisibly disabled child to other children. Just as parents are blamed for the unacceptable behavior of their learning disabled child by neighbors and shopkeepers, so brothers and sisters are often held responsible by their peers. A youngster may feel very resentful at being labeled "Weirdo's sister," or at having a child she scarcely knows come up and say, "Hey, do you know what your brother did?" or "Is your sister dumb or something? She can't read!"

Professionals need to know that the other children in a family may feel neglected, and they may envy the learning disabled child for the extra time and attention he gets from their parents. His illnesses, his school problems, his messiness, and his incompetence may appear to brothers and sisters as an unfair source of privilege. They don't see that their mother makes concessions to the learning disabled child at certain times so that frustrations and commotion can be avoided, so their father can unwind from a hard day, dinner can be enjoyed, and the whole family can be at peace together.

They may feel put upon when they are urged to include the learning disabled sibling in their play and their free-time activities. He has few friends of his own, and it is natural for parents to seek occasional relief, to expect cooperation and a sharing of responsibility from their other children. But he can be such a burden! They have to watch him every minute to see he doesn't hurt himself, destroy someone else's possessions, or disappear. He wrecks any hope of making new friends that day. They can't go far or move fast. Or little sister may be perfectly behaved, but she doesn't understand the simplest things and they have to spend so much time explaining.

They may feel mean and guilty for feeling this way because they really do love their brother or sister. They care deeply about him underneath the irritations. It's a rare family where the siblings are not extraordinarily understanding at times and where they don't act appropriately in emergencies. We can't expect more. They must come to terms with the problem in much the same way their parents do.

Parents go through stages with their normal looking, intelligent child who doesn't learn or behave as other children his age do.

It's a shock to see things going wrong.

It's a shock to hear that all is not well.

It's a shock to have to face up to these difficulties.

It's easier to deny the problem, and it's normal to begin with that reaction. Professionals must be aware that parents must face a whole gamut of emotions before they can grapple effectively with the stark truth that their child has learning disabilities. There is no set order to these feelings. Usually they start with denial and, most often, end with acceptance and hope.

Denial

My child doesn't really have anything
   wrong with him.
He only needs more time, more under-
   standing neighbors, a better teacher,
   a better school.
These people don't understand him.
He's just the way I was.
There's nothing basically wrong.

        Flight
        These doctors jump to conclusions.
        We're going to see another specialist.
        They're only out to make money with
           more tests and more examinations.
        They probably get a kickback from the
           other doctors they recommend.
        We have to fly to the East [or the West].
        There's a new specialist with a good
           reputation.

Isolation

Why doesn't anyone care?
Nobody seems to understand.
Why can't they make allowances?
He's much more interesting and unique
than most other children.

Guilt

Why me?
What did I do to him?
Why is God punishing me?
How could I have made life better for
him?
If only I hadn't let him bump his head.
If only I had kept him from catching
measles.
If only I had played with him more.
If only I had been more strict.
If only I had talked with him more.

Anger

Doctors don't know anything! They
should have caught it earlier!
That teacher is out of her mind!
These psychologists are for the birds!
I hate this neighborhood!
That child makes a monkey out of me!

Blame

You baby him.
You're the one who spoils him.
You don't make him take responsibility.
We never had anything like this on my
side of the family!
This child is just perverse.

Fear

Maybe it's worse than they say.
Is he retarded and they won't tell me?
Is it a progressive disease?
Will he ever be able to marry? Have
children? Hold a job?

Envy

Look at those other kids.
They don't know how lucky they are.
Everything comes easy to them.

How did they become so popular?
We're better parents.
It's not fair!

Bargaining

Maybe he'll be OK if we move.
Maybe he'll do fine in third grade.
Maybe if we stay home more he'll be OK.
Maybe if we send him to camp he'll shape up.
Maybe if I work with him every night he'll be OK.
Maybe if he goes to visit his grandparents he'll pick up.
Maybe if . . .
I'll do anything to help him.
Oh God, what can I do?
Maybe if . . .

Depression

I've failed him.
I'm no good.
No wonder he can't make it.
I can't either.
The world's no good.
I'm no good.
There's no hope.

Mourning

Think what could have been.
He might have . . .

Acceptance and hope

OK.
So he's got learning disabilities.
What can I do to help?
How can I make him feel better about himself?
What are his strengths?
What are his interests?
We'll make it!
It will just take time and some concerted efforts.

When parents recognize that their child has learning disabilities, they have the same choices as the child: to pity themselves or to do the best with what he has and work hard at it.

Most learning disabled youngsters grow up to be achievers. Many other youngsters never excel in reading, and a huge number are poor spellers, but they still become successful in business, mechanical fields, architecture, the arts, and many other occupations. Some are lawyers. A number of them become teachers. Some become exceptionally creative, imaginative problem solvers (while others, of course, do not). Some have become doctors, scientists, inventors, or generals. Harvey Cushing, brain surgeon; Paul Ehrlich, bacteriologist; William James, psychologist; President Woodrow Wilson; Vice-President Nelson Rockefeller; General George S. Patton—all these famous men are known to have suffered from one or more learning disabilities that they overcame, compensated for, or learned to live with in adulthood.

Diagnosing Learning Disabilities

Today there is great hope that a learning disabled child will be able to function effectively in our society. More parents, as well as professionals, are becoming alert to the problems of the learning disabled child earlier in his life. In the past, a youngster's problems would not be recognized until the sixth grade unless they were very severe or unless they were mixed up with disruptive behavior. Now they are likely to draw attention in the second or third grade, and it certainly should be no later. Most services are becoming available to both the children and their families.

There are pockets of ignorance all over the country, and, in those cases, the first place to encourage parents to seek help is the Association for Children with Learning Disabilities (ACLD) which has branches all over the nation. In Washington, D.C., Closer Look, an organization funded by the Department of Health, Education and Welfare, has been supported by the federal government to help parents find the help they need for their children. Other organizations also help parents.

Association for Children with Learning Disabilities (ACLD)

For parents, teachers, and other professionals.

Purpose: To provide needed information and support, to follow the latest educational and medical research, and to support legislation for special classes and trained teachers in the field.

Location: Find the organization nearest to where you live by writing to ACLD, 4156 Library Road, Pittsburgh, Pennsylvania 15234.

Closer Look

A national information center for parents and professionals, operated by the Parents' Campaign for Handicapped Children and Youth.

Purpose: To provide practical advice on how to find educational programs and other kinds of special services for handicapped children and youth.

Location: Closer Look, Box 1492, Washington, D.C. 20013.

National Easter Seal Society

For parents, teachers, and other professionals.

Purpose: To be a source of information on publications concerning the learning disabled child, to provide clinics, and to sponsor research and workshops.

Location: National Easter Seal Society, 2023 West Ogden Avenue, Chicago, Illinois 60612.

The Council for Exceptional Children (CEC)

For administrators, teachers, therapists, clinicians, students, and other interested persons.

Purpose: To provide an information center for general and specific information on learning disabilities and to publish information.

Location: CEC, 1920 Association Drive, Reston, Virginia 22091.

The Orton Society

For teachers, other professionals, and parents.

Purpose: To study preventive measures and treatment for children with specific language disability, and to sponsor research and share their findings.

Location: The Orton Society, Inc., 8415 Bellona Lane, Towson, Maryland 21204.

Parents need information, as well as assurance, on learning disabilities. A few good books can go far toward clarifying the complicated problems of this child who is so deceptive in terms of what he can and cannot do. See appendix 2 to this book.

If a child is not doing well by second grade and he shows many of the traits I have described, it may be worthwhile to seek help from the school system. Under the new Public Law 94-142, the states are mandated to provide the proper education for each handicapped child, and this includes locating them ("child find"). The schools will have psychologists do the testing. If parents are dissatisfied, they should be encouraged to find a second opinion. Sometimes it helps to hear the same opinion twice or have it explained more in depth; occasionally there is a difference in opinion. If parents are still not satisfied, they need help in finding the diagnostic center near them that knows the most about learning disabilities and have the child tested there. Help in finding such a service might come from their nearest ACLD chapter or by writing to Closer Look.

If no diagnostic center is close enough, they should try to find a psychologist whose specialty is testing and who knows the manifestations of learning disabilities. The results must be interpreted to them in detail. Here are some of the questions they might be encouraged to ask:

> What are my child's strengths?
> What are my child's weaknesses?
> How much disparity is there between the two?
> Is any further testing by medical specialists needed?
> Is a neurological examination advised?
> Will educational treatment alone be enough?
> Does my child need a special class or special school?
> Does my child need a tutor?
> Does he need an occupational therapist?
> Does he need a speech therapist?
> Does he, or do we as a total family, need psychological counseling?
> Does he need medication?
> Which suggestion has top priority? And why?
> What can the school do? And how can we tell them what to do?
> What can we, as parents, do?

Organizing the Child's Life

Professionals need to give to parents of learning disabled children advice about home management so they can provide structure in the child's life—order in his space and sequencing in his time. Everything in his room needs a place. If there are not too many things, it is easier to have a clear place where each thing can be put away. Shelves are often preferable to drawers because he can see his things in their proper place rather than having to visualize what is in a drawer. Parents need to know that structure can be introduced into his time by making him fully familiar with the parts of each of his usual routines—what comes first, next, and last. Less common events, like excursions, are explained by steps: "First we'll go to the store in the car; we'll buy the groceries at the store; then we'll stop at Aunt Ruth's house to say hello; then we will drive home again."

Parents need to know that it helps the child if the usual routines of the day occur at regular times, without too much deviation. It is worth the effort to keep mealtimes and bedtime as consistent as possible. Yet parents must not feel guilty for the occasional changes that have to take place in terms of the rhythm of the total family, outside demands, and emergencies.

Parents must learn that they not only have to take over the organization of space and time for the child until he has the tools to do it himself, but they also have to be aware of how impossible democratic choices are for this child. "But I want him to think for himself!" is the typical response. "I don't want to run an autocratic family. That's against my principles." They must realize that just as structure gives the child a sense of security and safety in his disordered world, organizing his choices for him is allowing him to function. Only slowly is the child prepared for being a participant in a democracy and for taking the risks entailed.

The child's choices are best kept at a minimum, since his indiscriminate reactions prevent him from sorting out alternatives. At first a parent has to make all the choices, but the child can learn to handle limited choices even though many alternatives may still confuse him. If, when he is getting dressed, he is asked, "Would you prefer to wear your red soccer shirt or your blue T-shirt today?" he will probably be able to make a clear decision, whereas the question, "What shirt do you want to wear today?" may produce total inaction or a tantrum.

Getting dressed is a struggle for many learning disabled children not only because of the choices involved but because of a need for sequencing and order. Here professionals need to help parents to place themselves in the place of the child who is trying to do the task. What steps are involved in putting on a pair of socks? In what order do the steps have to take place? What is involved in threading a belt through the loops on a pair of pants? What skills are needed?

Structuring the Child's Behavior

Everyday behavior also requires structure. A learning disabled child needs to know more precisely than other children exactly what is expected of him. His parents have to set clear limits for him and let him know what is acceptable and what is not, patiently but firmly, over and over again. Parents must learn that they have to structure the way they talk to him, using few words rather than many, being very specific when they give him instructions. "Put your puzzle back on the shelf now" will bring better results than "It's time to put your things away." Instructions that are given step by step are easier to follow than several instructions given all at once. "Go wash your face," followed by, "And now brush your teeth," followed by, "Now go get your pajamas on," will succeed, whereas "Run along and get your face washed and your teeth brushed and come back down when you have your pajamas on" will result only in confusion.

Normally parents watch a child go from solo play to parallel play to playing with one friend to playing with others and becoming part of a group. It is a natural process that we all take for granted, with occasional reminders: "You don't treat your friend like that. You let him go first in your house. You go first in his house. You serve your guest first." Professionals need to help parents recognize that with the learning disabled child, the way to play with another youngster must often be explicitly taught. Because of immaturity, a learning disabled child often cannot play in groups until he is much older than other children. In this case, parents need to provide imaginative and unusual playthings to entice other youngsters to come over and play and then structure the games that the children play together.

With careful forethought, parents need to plan for their learning disabled child to experience success. Sometimes they have to step in and save face for him when defeat or humiliation seem unavoidable. When he starts a project, it is important for his parents to hold his attention span through each step long enough to get him to finish the job and once more demonstrate to him that he can succeed. Leisure time, homework, and long-term projects are particularly demanding of a parent's imagination and patience. Professionals need to give parents as much assistance as possible in talking about these problems and brainstorming on how each particular family can best meet the child's needs.

Planning, foreseeing outcomes, avoiding debacles, applying a child's emotional brakes for him, providing structure in all areas—these take great stamina and perseverance. Parents of learning disabled children often find that they need more sleep than normal in order to keep their energy and equilibrium at a high level of efficiency. They need as much praise, as little unconstructive criticism, as many helpful hints as possible.

Medication

Sometimes structuring does not seem to be enough, particularly if the child is hyperactive and so distractible that he can't focus on anything for more than a few minutes at a time. Then it is often a help if a physician—a pediatrician, neurologist, or psychiatrist—treats the child with medication. A common reaction of parents to this suggestion is, "I'll be darned if I'll let anyone drug my child." But experience has shown that certain stimulant drugs such as Ritalin and Dexedrine make these children calmer and less active and consequently better able to concentrate. It appears that stimulant drugs help the child to blot out many of the unfiltered messages that come from his senses and his body and habitually overstimulate him; in so doing they calm him down.

The aim of stimulant drugs is to improve a child's concentration and self-control. The person who can best tell if a certain drug is achieving this effect is the child's teacher. It is common practice for parents and doctors to tell the principal of a child's school, but not his classroom teacher, that the experiment is going on. Within a day or two usually, the teacher will mention to the parents or the principal that the child has greatly improved. The teacher is not told ahead of time because her fresh reaction, uncolored by any expectations, is needed to tell if the drug is truly working.

Medication is not the right treatment for every child. Drugs have been badly abused in some places in America, especially where schools, not doctors, have prescribed medication for hyperactive youngsters. In many cases, however, medication has made previously impossible children available for learning, able to listen, concentrate, learn, and start up the ladder of success rather than remain on the treadmill of failure.

Seeking Professional Help

All children need as much positive reinforcement for their good efforts as they can get. They need to be rewarded with praise, a gesture, or some other form of approval whenever they succeed. But even the best parents cannot salvage the ego of a child who has failed again and again in school, in the neighborhood, and on the athletic field. Often a tutor, a special class, or a special school is necessary to provide the therapy needed to make this child feel competent, to show him that he is capable of doing something about himself, that he is the master of his own destiny.

The defeat that is so often met by a learning disabled child can make it hard for him to develop a strong sense of self, and sometimes it is necessary for parents to consult a psychologist or psychiatrist. These professionals can help build the ego strength so vitally needed for every child's development. Sometimes play therapy, sometimes an individual therapist who talks with the child, sometimes group therapy can help. These methods can help his parents, too, to cope with the reality of living with learning disabilities. The fears, anger, guilt, and anxiety suffered by both the child and his parents can become better understood and thereby eased. When a child feels victimized by his learning disabilities, or seems totally unmanageable or very depressed, it is frequently necessary to consult a professional counselor. To locate this person, one might begin by checking with the local Association for Children with Learning Disabilities.

Many psychologists and psychiatrists, even today, do not know much about learning disabilities. Parents need to be made aware of this situation because a learning disabled child needs structure in his therapy just as much as he needs it in other areas of his life. Parents can find out if a therapist understands the unique problems of learning disabled youngsters by asking questions like the following ones:

What do you look for to decide whether a learning disabled child needs therapy?

How would you explain the purpose of therapy to a learning disabled child?

How do you work with the child who has trouble expressing himself in words?

What can you do with a child who can't focus his attention?

Is it effective to work with a child without working with his parents?

How do you see the relationship of his low self-esteem to a child's learning disabilities?

Under what conditions do you recommend medication?

Can you explain to me the relationship of learning disabilities to my child's social problems?

For an evaluation, the therapist meets with the parents once or twice to take down the history and to understand their concerns, has one or two sessions with the child, and then sets up an interpretive session with the parents. After the diagnostic evaluation, parents have a right to ask the therapist or counselor some questions that will give them an impression of how he or she views their child and to see if the evaluation meshes with their own observations. Some new information should be provided from the evaluation, but they should also be able to recognize their own child. Here are some questions they might ask at this time:

Can you tell us what you see as our child's strengths and weaknesses?

What would be realistic goals for our child at this time?

How can therapy help achieve the goals you describe?

How would you explain this to our child? How would you help him understand what's wrong and why he needs help?

A therapist qualified to work with a learning disabled child must be able to answer questions like these in clear, simple terms because he will be dealing with a child who has difficulty in processing language. If the therapist is vague, obscure, or full of technical jargon not understandable to the parents, quite likely he will not be effective with the child either. Like teachers, parents often feel that they are not supposed to understand readily what a therapist is aiming to do, the process he's using, and how he feels the therapy is going. Therapy involves the art of communication; feelings must be communicated and relationships established. Therefore the quality of the relationship established with the parents is crucial in order to gain their trust. If the therapist does not have their trust, he will not be able to give them the kind of support that they need. If parents do not feel reassured by the answers they receive or do not feel positive toward the therapist, they should be encouraged to find another therapist in whom they can place their confidence.

If the parents are not sure of their own feelings, they should not hesitate to talk over the situation with the prospective therapist once more. A positive, supportive relationship is needed to proceed with the difficult work ahead. Helping the learning disabled youngster is a joint effort; trust in the therapist is necessary. The trust must be established *before* starting the child's treatment because it is crucial not to interrupt an ongoing therapeutic relationship. The therapist who understands learning disabilities can make an enormous impact on the child's behavior at home and at school, and he can have a marked effect on the parents' attitudes and their ability to manage the child. The therapist can affect the comfort and well-being of the whole family. But parents must begin by feeling some comfort with the therapist.

Parents' Own Problems

Great resourcefulness and planning are required from the parents of a learning disabled child, yet they are only human. Family life puts the same pressures on them as on anyone else, and there is no way they can do all they would like to do. Perhaps the most important place they can start work is in the area of their own attitudes.

Parents need to be helped to hold on to optimism regarding the child's strengths, building on whatever he likes to do best and using the momentum of his enthusiasm—even if the only thing he likes is television. That, too, offers possibilities. (See chapter 8.) He must know that his abilities are much more important to his parents than his failings.

It is vital for parents to develop their sense of humor in every way they know how. Laughter helps surmount many hurdles, and it gives the child an important unspoken message: that life is basically sunny despite all his difficulties. Comical elements can be found in many situations, even though they are sometimes hard to see. When the whole family can see the humor in some of the experiences they go through together, the result is worth the effort.

Parents should try not to dwell on the future in their own minds. They can plan realistically for today, tomorrow, next week, even a few months ahead. But it is unrealistic to become preoccupied with the long-range future of a young child. There is not yet enough knowledge, there are too many variables, and there are too many unknown factors for this kind of worrying to be useful in any way. Instead of worrying if their seven-year-old will make it to college, they need to grab hold of the present and deal with it step by step, just as their child must. They need to know the problems and both the short-term and long-term objectives. False hopes will help no more than feelings of doom, and, in due time, the college potential of their child can be discussed. Sometimes, however, a child may reach the age of sixteen or eighteen before this becomes entirely clear. In other cases, an experienced person who has worked with learning disabled children over many years can be fairly sure how the child will be able to handle adolescence.

If parents can face their problems truthfully, they will be able to talk to their child truthfully about his. They can emphasize that he is smart but that he has problems. People can and will help him. They can acknowledge that progress will take time, that he will have to work harder than most other people, that there are no easy answers, and that both they and he know it feels unfair. Clearly they don't talk to a teen-

ager the way they do to a seven-year-old, but the quality of
honesty has to be the same.

The lack of talent in the learning disabled child can be
recognized in the same way parents would recognize lack of
artistic or musical talent or mechanical prowess in any other
youngster. They can point out to him that they too have areas
of incompetence. They would like to be talented, but lack of
a certain ability does not make them any less whole persons.

Parents should be encouraged to give themselves permission to make mistakes and learn from them. This gives the
child permission to make mistakes, too, and survive. He
must be shown that amends can be made for the mistake and
things can be restored—perhaps not quite the same as before, perhaps better. When something gets broken—
particularly by the child—it must be mended. (It must not be
thrown out. The child himself feels broken and incompetent
and needs to see broken things put back together. He has
trouble seeing the parts that make up a whole. He needs as
much help as possible in putting together his whole world.)

Parents must be helped to identify their own feelings and
those of their child, so they know when they are absorbing
and expressing the child's feelings. Parents can be more
help to the child when they isolate what his feelings are. If
they follow his ups and downs in their own moods, their
lives will be a veritable seesaw. They need their own attitudes and feelings intact in order to give the child the support he needs. And let's hope that these parents have caring
families and friends who give them the support they need.
They need all the emotional nourishment and sustenance
that is available to them.

Parents need to trust themselves. Professionals working
with parents of learning disabled children need to tap their
own ingenuity to find as many ways as possible to help parents feel better about themselves, feel competent, and trust
their own observations and judgment. Usually parents know
their own child better than anyone else does. Usually they
love their children very much. They need information, practical suggestions, and solid support.

11

Parents and Teachers and Public Law 94–142

Gilbert is not doing well at school. He's in the third grade and can barely read, write, or spell. He is quick to figure out math problems in his head but he can't do them on paper. He doesn't pay attention to instructions and rarely follows them properly. He can't sit still and tends to wander around the classroom. Gilbert is confused about how to get started on projects, yet he asks excellent questions. His parents are not surprised to hear from his teacher that Gilbert is very sloppy, forgets where he's supposed to be, leaves a trail of belongings behind him, trips over his untied shoelaces, and talks incessantly.

Gilbert's parents are typical in that they hope whatever it is that's wrong will disappear—and quickly! They offer rewards to entice him to put out extra effort. Then they use admonitions and punishment. They don't allow him to watch TV during the week. They don't permit him to play outdoors with his friends. Gilbert's father starts working with him, then turns the task over to his older brother and sister so there will be fewer tears. All kinds of homemade remedies are tried—more sleep, a nutritious diet (with extra vitamin supplements), fewer sweets, no sweets, no soft drinks, then more exercise, extra hugs. But, unfortunately, Gilbert's problems do not go away; in fact, they get worse. He is taken to a pediatrician who proclaims that he is in good shape and should not be pressured, then to the eye doctor and hearing specialist who also say he is fine.

Meanwhile, the third grade teacher, Miss Porter, is very confused by Gilbert. He can talk to her about the presidential elections, what it means to be a nonreader, the relation-

ship between Greek myths and the Navaho Indians Rain
Dance (i.e., in both cases "people believed in them"). She
decides that if he can think like that, he can certainly learn to
read. She vacillates between feeling he isn't trying hard
enough and feeling that something is drastically wrong. Gilbert can't even recognize all the alphabet letters no matter
how often and in how many clever ways she tries to teach
him. He can't keep his mind on his work.

Finally, Miss Porter and Gilbert's parents have a conference. There it is agreed that Gilbert is bright and that they
obviously need more information as to why Gilbert can't
read, write, or pay attention in class. Under Public Law 94–
142, Gilbert, his parents, and his teacher may be able to
receive appropriate help.

Public Law 94–142

The 94th Congress adopted PL 94–142, Education for All
Handicapped Children Act, in November 1975. It became
effective in October 1977, with the final phase to take effect
in September 1980, to assure free and appropriate education
for all handicapped persons aged 3 to 21. Learning disabilities were recognized by Congress as one of the handicapping conditions requiring appropriate education.

The legislation is very exciting because it is truly child-
centered. In the best tradition of American humanism, it
aims to give each handicapped child every opportunity to
achieve his potential. It has resulted in regulations published by the U.S. Office of Education outlining a comprehensive system of special education procedures to be
implemented by state and local education agencies throughout the nation. These regulations are available to the public.

   The spirit of the law
      dictates that the unique needs
         of each handicapped child are to be served
            by providing him with the appropriate education.
   Unfortunately, the practice of the law
      frequently reflects the budgetary constraints
         of local and state agencies.

Although Congress passed the law to provide incentives to
the states to integrate the quiet minority of the handicapped
into our school systems, the monetary incentives are small,
the responsibilities are huge, and the drain on state and local

budgets is monstrous. The generosity of spirit shown by Congress in this fine piece of legislation has not been matched by generosity of appropriation.

Nonetheless, as the desperate needs of handicapped children emerge, as it becomes evident that a proper education can make the difference in the quality of lives lived, new hopes have been raised and new pathways charted. School systems have attempted to tackle for the first time the individualized needs of youngsters who cannot learn in traditional ways. Because of this legislation, schools are spending far more than ever before on their handicapped students. At the same time, however, school budgets are being drastically reduced due to dropping school enrollments, skyrocketing inflation, energy costs, and a myriad of local concerns. As a result, school systems and parents find themselves increasingly pitted against one another.

Parents cannot assume that the very existence of PL 94–142 is going to mean that their child's needs will be served appropriately. However, as parents become acquainted with the law, they see that it gives them the right to challenge the school system at every point to make sure that their child receives the education he needs for his handicapping condition. Parents of learning disabled youngsters have to be even more aware of their rights, not only because of the shortage of funds but because of the vast number of students who give evidence of some form of learning disability.

What is a learning disability? Unfortunately, even now, in 1980, there is no agreement among specialists as to exactly what constitutes a learning disability, which battery or batteries of tests can properly diagnose neurological dysfunction, and how learning disabilities can best be treated. We do know that the learning disabled child needs to be taught in a special way: he needs to learn how to learn. Parents like Gilbert's parents have to find ways to use PL 94–142 to make sure this happens.

Teachers like Miss Porter need to know the provisions of the law in order to advise parents about their child's right to a proper evaluation and an individualized educational program. Just as for a parent, there is nothing more frustrating to a teacher than to see a child's needs and not be able to meet them. Because the teacher is an employee of the school system, there is only so much he or she can do under PL 94–142.

Teachers can voice their concerns and become advocates for the child up to a certain point. But it is the learning disabled child's parents or guardian who must be the permanent advocates for the child, and who must translate the humane intent of the law into concrete, practical action.

Eight important aspects of this law are interrelated and need to be understood: (1) eligibility for all, (2) individualized evaluation, (3) a child's records, (4) individualized educational program (IEP), (5) least restrictive environment, (6) personnel development, (7) due process, and (8) parent participation.

Eligibility for All

Eligibility for all means that every child with a handicap is entitled to a free and appropriate education. This concept grew out of the civil rights movement of the 1960s in which unfair discrimination against minorities was challenged at every point. In this case, the minority is the handicapped child!

Under PL 94–142, no child is "uneducable." The beauty of the legislation is that it is committed to the belief that all children can learn, that it is up to educators to figure out how to teach them, and that education must be viewed not simply as an academic process, but as one that includes instruction in basic living and vocational skills.

For some handicapped youngsters, special programs must be provided, and if they do not exist in the public schools, then school systems must pay private facilities to do the job. However, for other handicapped youngsters special programs are not necessary.

For too long there has been a prejudice against the obviously handicapped child. Often because of the way he looks and/or his problems in mobility, he has been excluded from regular public education when, in fact, he could learn in a regular classroom if he could get his wheelchair into the room or if he received some limited, but specific, aids. That child can no longer be excluded from the regular classroom. The eligibility-for-all concept is for the handicapped child what the 1954 Supreme Court decision was for the black child. And where equal educational opportunity is denied, each has redress under the law.

Whereas the wheelchair child with his very visible handicap, but no learning problem, does not need to be taught in a special way, the learning disabled child, who is usually invisibly handicapped, needs very special teaching techniques in order to survive in school. But the learning disabled youngster often falls between the cracks. "A little off, but he's not handicapped; he'll make it," said one school administrator, echoing many others. Often the invisibly handicapped child is not served even though he is as entitled to a free and appropriate education as is the child with obvious handicaps. Federal funding for the handicapped will cover not more than 12 percent of local school enrollment. Local and state funds must be used for any handicapped students above that number. The visibly handicapped are readily included, but too often the parents of a learning disabled child are forced to fight for their child's inclusion. Gilbert's parents may well be faced with this problem because he doesn't look handicapped, and because testing by itself may not reveal the severity of his disability.

Individualized Evaluation

Gilbert can receive an evaluation through the public school system at no cost to his parents. In his case, because Miss Porter and his parents have had a conference and agreed that more information is needed, it is likely that Miss Porter will suggest a meeting with the school principal. At this conference, Gilbert's parents will request that their son be evaluated for possible special education placement. PL 94–142 specifically states that a school may not formally evaluate a child without parental permission. Gilbert's parents must sign the appropriate evaluation request forms and a separate form giving permission to the school system to test and evaluate their son. Copies of any previous assessments done privately or by other school districts are to be submitted with the forms. Miss Porter will also submit a statement describing Gilbert's problems in her classroom.

Parents who are unable to work through their child's teacher should call the school and ask to meet directly with the principal to request an assessment of their child. Parents of children who do not attend public schools and have had no previous assessment by the public school system need to telephone the office of the Superintendent of Schools to make arrangements.

Parents and teachers must monitor what happens to their request. In many school districts there are delays of several months to a year until the testing is done. PL 94–142 places a huge burden on local school districts to identify all handicapped children aged 3 to 21. They must locate children never previously identified—those in the public schools, as well as children in other public agencies, institutions, and private schools. Ultimately, school systems will be charged with identifying all handicapped children from birth on, and every one of them will have to be evaluated. The number of necessary evaluations is staggering. Often there is a shortage of trained personnel to do the job. Some states cannot afford to hire additional personnel, and others feel they are already over-committed. Some local school boards resist reallocating funds from their athletic or regular academic programs to special education when they see a disproportionate per-pupil expenditure already going to the handicapped. Nevertheless, the child who is not evaluated within a reasonable period of time suffers unnecessarily. The teacher cannot give him the special help he needs; thus, not only is he confronted by failure for an inordinate amount of time, but his reaction to that defeat can also affect the entire tone of the classroom. Gilbert's parents, it turns out, must wait two months and might have had to wait even longer had Miss Porter not joined them in applying pressure to the school system to speed up the date for evaluation.

PL 94–142 mandates that a full individual evaluation must be administered by trained personnel. An individual intelligence test is crucial to determine a child's true academic potential. However, no single test can be used as the sole criterion; the evaluation has to be tailored to assess the child's specific educational needs. Once the child's academic potential has been established through the IQ test, diagnostic testing should continue to determine specific areas in which he cannot function. Group tests are not appropriate because they strike at the deficit areas of the learning disabled child—the inability to follow instructions in a group, to work at grade level, to work within specific time limits.

The tests selected may not be racially or culturally biased;

and if English is a second language, tests must be provided and administered in the child's native language, unless clearly it is not feasible to do so.

PL 94–142 requires that the evaluation team must be multidisciplinary and must include at least one teacher or other specialist in learning disabilities. The information coming from parents, teachers, and other sources about the child—his physical condition, cultural, or social background and adaptive behavior—must be documented and carefully considered by the team. At least one member of the team other than the child's teacher is required to observe the child in his classroom setting. Parents need to make sure that as many members of the team as possible see their child personally and get a feel for what the child can and cannot do.

Parents have the right and the need to ask the evaluation team or the team member they see such questions as:

What tests are being given to my child?

Why have these specific tests been chosen?

What can be learned from them?

Will you be looking for the strong points as well as weak areas?

Will you be able to tell me how my child seems to learn best?

How will the test information be used to help teach my child?

The present system for identifying learning disabilities is complicated because professionals do not agree on what constitutes a proper battery of tests, or even on which tests can best evaluate specific disabilities in areas such as language or visual perception. (See Appendix 6 for a list and descriptions of the most frequently used tests.)

Under PL 94–142 a child may be identified as learning disabled if the evaluation team finds a "severe discrepancy" between his achievement and his age and ability levels in one or more of the following seven areas:

1. oral expression
2. listening comprehension
3. written expression

4. basic reading skills
5. reading comprehension
6. mathematics calculation
7. mathematics reasoning

The term "severe discrepancy" was not defined by Congress because, again, there was no agreement among the expert advisors. Various school districts use their own criteria and diagnostic tools. The result is that in one district 50 percent of the children were found to have severe discrepancies and, therefore, were considered learning disabled, while another district claimed that only three percent of the children showed discrepancies severe enough to be judged learning disabled.

The evaluation team may not identify a child as learning disabled if the severe discrepancy between ability and achievement is primarily the result of blindness, deafness, motor handicap, mental retardation, emotional disturbance, or "environmental, cultural, or economic disadvantage." There are some children, however, who have both cerebral palsy *and* learning disabilities; the same is true of the blind, the deaf, the emotionally disturbed. The child who is economically disadvantaged is not automatically learning disabled; however, a high incidence of learning disability can be expected because of the poor prenatal care, malnutrition, and a host of other factors that may contribute to the delayed development of the child's central nervous system.

Furthermore, there are some youngsters who show some discrepancies in all or many areas, but do not have a severe discrepancy in one or more of these areas; they may, or may not, be learning disabled. So much depends upon the diagnostician's depth of experience with learning disabled youngsters, upon his or her ability to recognize the subtle constellation of difficulties and characteristics that point to a learning disability. The score differentials on tests are often not as meaningful as the quality of errors and/or mistakes made in academic work, the erratic quality of the work, and the behavioral manifestations of learning disabilities. What the law doesn't deal with are the intangibles: the learning disabled child's immaturity, the developmental lag that produces his inability to sustain selective attention. Hyperactive, hypoactive, and normally active learning disabled youngsters may all have attention span difficulties. All may lack the tools to organize the information bombarding them through their senses, to make life more understandable and meaningful.

The daily challenge to teachers and principals is this: these are intelligent children *who are unable to cope adequately with classroom routine.* As noted in earlier chapters, learning disabled youngsters are often disorganized, distractible, impulsive, perseverative, and emotionally labile, over-reacting to the least little thing. They may be egocentric and unable to work in a group. They may be able to pass a test working alone with one adult but may not be able to do work in a group. And what about the child who cannot find his way around a building, who takes weeks to learn where his classroom is? Or the child who has no sense of time and is late to every class? Every teacher knows the child who can't deal with the slightest change in routine, who falls apart when confronted with unfamiliar material such as a new workbook, who takes months to adjust to a new teacher. Learning disabled youngsters cannot follow a simple set of directions, particularly in the classroom setting. Many of them are so awkward and clumsy that they cannot follow classroom routines within the proper time limits, and they misinterpret social interactions. Recess and lunch are troubled times because they involve so many choices, so much decision-making, so much organizing of time and space. How are these subtle behavioral manifestations of learning disabilities to be measured so that these children can receive the special education they need?

The inability to cope adequately with regular classroom academic work is the other area that the law does not touch unless the child shows a severe discrepancy between his potential and achievement. Many do display this discrepancy, but there are learning disabled students who don't show it on tests. Their oral expression may be immature and disorganized, but adequate in a testing situation; however, in a classroom, they can't organize information to ask a question, are unable to communicate what they have learned, and miss the main point of a discussion. They miss a great deal because they are very concrete and literal, do not pick up on nuances, inuendoes, and multiple meanings of words. The children who are unable to begin work without a teacher standing over them every moment, who can't sustain work without constant teacher monitoring, and who don't know how to finish a task are in trouble in a regular classroom; they need to be taught the approach to a task while the other students simply need to be taught the material. It's exceedingly difficult to cope adequately with regular classroom work if you have attentional difficulties, cannot process directions easily, and require repetition and/or interpretation of all instructions; the challenge is even greater if you are "the one-way kid" who has only one way of doing things, one answer, and cannot consider alternatives. The child who impulsively plunges into work, never proofreads, and needs slowing down may be considered just careless, but the patterns of his behavior spell out a form of learning disability to specialists in this field. The student who never finishes his work in the allotted time, who processes information slowly and works at a snail's pace, needs special teaching to learn to increase his speed. The youngster for whom the act of writing is a form of medieval torture may be able to write enough to pass a test but cannot keep up with written work in the classroom. Children who are overwhelmed by being introduced to too much information at once and cannot tolerate too much going on at once cannot function in a regular classroom. They need to have information and work broken down into small increments; they need to learn in very small groups. Many of the youngsters described here show enough discrepancies in test scores to qualify for special help, but some with the hidden handicap, who desperately need help, do not. The problems are even more complex when evaluating children under six and with young adults. Learning disability specialists need to go back to the drawing board to describe these many needs and what can be done about them.

Once the multidisciplinary evaluation team has concluded its assessment, the team is required to produce a written report of the results and a copy must be sent to the parents. Fortunately, PL 94–142 demands that the report be written in understandable language. If it is not, parents should insist upon clarity and feel free to ask for explanations. The report must include a statement as to whether or not the child has a learning disability and what tools and processes were used to make this determination. The problem areas of the learning disabled child are to be clearly identified and related to the test results and behavior observed. Finally, each team member has to certify in writing that the report reflects his or her conclusions. If not, a separate statement must be prepared by any dissenting members.

Some parents who do not want their child to have to wait for an evaluation will opt for an alternative route: testing by an independent agency, hospital, university diagnostic clinic, or private diagnostician trained in learning disabilities. Some parents do not trust "the system" to take an objective look at their child. Others want a second opinion. Parents who are dissatisfied with the public school evaluation and recommendations can secure a private, independent evaluation at public expense unless the school system successfully demonstrates that its evaluation is appropriate. If the school system proves, before an impartial hearing officer, that its report is appropriate, the parents can still obtain a private evaluation, but at their own expense. In any case, PL 94–142 requires the school system to consider and comment in writing on whatever outside evaluations are submitted.

Some diagnostic centers provide free services, others charge on a sliding scale, some provide full or partial scholarship, and others may charge anywhere from $200 to $600 for an evaluation that includes: a parent interview, a fully battery of tests, a conference interpreting the results, and a detailed written report. Some clinics or collaborative groups also agree to act as a liaison between parents and the schools. Parents must ask private facilities in advance what the total cost will be, how soon the process can begin, how long the child will be tested (one morning, two mornings, a whole day, two whole days?), how many different professionals will be seeing their child, what their specialties are (i.e., educational diagnostician, psychologist, speech and language therapist, occupational therapist). Parents have a right to expect a good diagnostic report outlining the child's strengths, areas of difficulty, questions to explore further, ways in which the child seems to learn best and, thus, the most effective channels for teaching. A well-trained diagnostician is a keen observer and an astute listener. He or she notes how a child approaches a task, holds a pencil, sits in a chair, what questions he asks, as well as when a child becomes frustrated, with what kind of material, and how he deals with the frustration. All of the child's test behavior is treated as important diagnostic information to be stirred into the same pot with test scores, school reports, medical reports, and information given in parent interviews, to produce a comprehensive picture of a child's learning profile with very clear and specific recommendations for action. A diagnostician should be able to report to parents in as much detail as necessary the information gleaned, the way in which it was discovered, and its significance for the child's schooling and his life at home. Most diagnosticians will guide parents on how to interpret the information to their youngsters. And often the diagnosticians themselves will interpret the test information directly to an older child.

It is important for parents to sit down with their child before the child goes for testing and say something like:

> "We know you're smart. We know you are having trouble learning certain things at school. We need, and *you* need, more information on how you learn best, how your teachers can help you the most. That's why tomorrow you will be seeing —————."

The learning disabled child needs to know that his parents are convinced he will learn, that they understand the problem is one of detecting the best ways to teach him, and that they have found a specialist who knows how to achieve this goal. The emphasis must be put on ways to help the child succeed, rather than concentrating on what's wrong with him. From the youngster, parents may still hear: "So you think I'm dumb?" "So you think I'm crazy?" The child's fears cannot be totally allayed, but they can be alleviated if parents make it vividly clear that they are seeking ways to help him learn better and will share what they discover with the child.

If a child is sent directly for diagnostic evaluation from his classroom at school, it helps if the teacher will take the time to reinforce what the parents have said at home and tell the child that he will be taking some tests so that "we can learn how you learn best. It will help all of us."

A Child's Records

Parents have the right to see all the accumulated information concerning their child and to have a representative of their choosing inspect and review the records. Test materials, reports, teacher comments, correspondence with professionals, conferences held about the child are all to be made available. Students aged 18 and over have the same rights with regard to their records as do their parents, including the right to an explanation of anything they don't understand.

PL 94–142 continually confirms that parents are a working part of the team that is to educate a handicapped child. The law guarantees parents the right to ask that misleading or inaccurate information be removed from their child's file or, at the very least, be amended with an explanatory statement. The records of a learning disabled child must be studied closely because his behavior and reactions can be misinterpreted by those who are not familiar with learning disabilities. For example, the learning disabled child's slow processing may mean that he responds in a very delayed fashion to a previous conversation. And it could be in his file that this behavior "had a schizoid quality." The social inappropriateness of the learning disabled child might have been labelled as emotional disturbance when it wasn't. A learning disabled teenager may have been called retarded because of being unable to count change. A parent would want to make sure that this is called "an area of retarded development" rather than a statement about the child. Many parents have discovered that the records are full of reports characterizing their child as lazy and unmotivated, when in fact it is the child's lack of focus and sense of defeat that are really being described. However, parents also need to know that there will always be things in a child's file that they may not like, but that may be true. No one except for the child's teachers and other legitimate school personnel has access to a child's records. Confidentiality is to be protected to such an extent that schools must write down the names of anyone who has looked at a child's file, why they did, and when. Before anyone else is given access to the records, a written consent form detailing the purpose and the name of the person must be signed and dated by the parents. The child's and the parents' rights are protected at every point.

Within 45 days of their request, parents must be allowed to study their child's record. Becoming familiar with all of the information helps parents prepare for the meeting to design an individualized educational program and placement for their child.

Individualized Educational Program (IEP)

> Any *individual*, aged 3 to 21,
> identified as handicapped
> is unique
> and
> must have
> an *individualized* educational program (IEP).

An IEP is a written plan setting forth the specially designed instruction that the student needs for learning and the reasonable expectations for him that can be monitored.

Within 30 days after a child like Gilbert has been identified as handicapped, an IEP meeting must take place. The IEP is the mechanism by which a child receives the special services and instruction he needs; without it, he cannot receive special help. To write Gilbert's IEP his learning problems have to be known, as well as his strengths, and the ways he seems to learn best. The skills he needs to learn and their prerequisites have to be outlined in order to establish very specific goals for him to achieve in the areas that are handicapping him. Based on how he seems to learn best, certain methods and techniques of instruction are recommended. Every IEP must include the following minimum components:

1. statement of the child's present levels of educational performance,
2. statement of annual goals or achievements expected by the end of the school year,
3. short-term objectives stated in instructional terms which are the steps leading to the mastery of annual goals,
4. statement of the specific special education and support services to be provided to the child,
5. statement of the extent to which a child will be able to participate in regular educational programs and justification for any special placement that is recommended,
6. projected dates for initiation of services and the anticipated duration of the services, and
7. statement of criteria and evaluation procedures to be used for determining, on at least an annual basis, whether short-term objectives are being achieved.

Gilbert's parents are an important part of the IEP development, as is Miss Porter. They meet with a representative of the public school system who is qualified to provide or to supervise special education. Since Gilbert has just been identified as learning disabled, a member of his multidisciplinary evaluation team would join the meeting too. If Gilbert were older, it might be appropriate for him to join this meeting, although this rarely happens except in secondary schools. Other individuals may participate in the IEP meeting at the request of the parents or the school system. Clearly, the results of Gilbert's assessment are central to the IEP meeting, because it is through the work of the evaluation team that a child's academic potential, performance, special needs, and best learning style are detailed.

Prior to the meeting, Gilbert had been tested by a psychologist, an educational specialist, and a social worker. The results showed that Gilbert gave evidence of average intelligence and, in some areas such as reasoning and vocabulary, he was in the superior range of his age group. His math ability proved to be extraordinary, although he could not do written math, and the examiners were impressed with his advanced knowledge of history and science. The evaluation demonstrated that he had some visual motor difficulties, and visual discrimination and visual memory problems. He showed a large discrepancy between his achievement and his age and ability level in two areas—written expression and basic reading skills. The report noted that he learned best through his auditory channel. Although they identified Gilbert as mildly handicapped, the evaluation team concluded that Gilbert had so much talent that he could learn to compensate for many of his deficits and, therefore, could remain in the regular classroom. The team thought he could benefit from some tutoring and the use of special aids such as a tape recorder. These recommendations were discussed at the IEP meeting.

The school system representative on Gilbert's IEP team recommended that Gilbert remain in his regular classroom, but that he receive special services, including reading and handwriting tutoring one hour a day and the use of a tape recorder instead of having to write. Miss Porter said that Gilbert's gross motor skills also needed special services and that his short attention span was of concern to her. They agreed to add an adaptive physical education program twice a week.

Gilbert's parents were uncomfortable with these program suggestions. They didn't want to challenge the school system representatives, for they didn't think they knew enough. But, on the other hand, the degree of Gilbert's distractibility and disorganization didn't seem to come out as serious problems needing specially designed instruction.

If the IEP meeting was uncomfortable for Gilbert's parents, who were somewhat sophisticated, imagine what it must feel like for an unsophisticated parent or a parent from a foreign country for whom the whole educational process is often awesome and threatening. Many of these parents need convincing that their child is not bad but has some learning problems, that the school system is not bad and can provide some new kinds of teaching to help their child learn. Frequently, once they are calmed and can feel some trust that someone really wants to help their child, parents can offer important diagnostic information and clues as to how their child succeeds best at home. This information can be translated into effective teaching techniques for use at school.

It took some time for Gilbert's parents to realize that they had lived with him the most, probably knew him the best, and that the evaluation team's report did not describe his needs as thoroughly as they felt was necessary.

PL 94–142 clearly states that every opportunity must be provided to allow parents to have an active involvement in making decisions regarding their child's IEP. Public school systems are required to encourage parent participation, to provide detailed documentation of all their efforts (including telephone calls, corespondence, home visits), and to arrange a mutually convenient IEP meeting time. Only if parents have rejected all attempts of the school to involve them may an IEP meeting take place without them. Parents cannot be pressured to give their consent to the IEP. They should sign the IEP document only after they are genuinely satisfied that it represents the best individually designed program for their child.

Parents need to ask for explanations of any educational terms they don't understand and seek a description of the functions of the various support service personnel that might be working with their child such as an occupational therapist or speech and language specialist. Parents need to feel free to ask a number of questions, such as:

1. Do you base your long-range goals on just test scores or on what he does in the classroom, or both?
2. What are my child's main problems? What would be the next layer of problems that are not as severe but for which he needs help? Are any of these problems included in the short-term objectives?
3. What approaches do you plan to use with my child, and why?
4. Will you use different approaches in different subjects? If so, what and why?
5. Can you explain to me why the approaches that you have selected are the best ones to teach my child? How much exposure do your teachers have to a wide variety of techniques and materials effective with learning disabled students? Do they have enough access to different methods and materials?
6. How large a class will he be in? If he's in a regular classroom, how can you assure that his IEP is carried out?
7. What training in learning disabilities has his teacher received? What about the special teachers who see him?
8. Are there aides in the class; if so, what are their duties and what is their training?
9. What special support services does my child need? Will they be provided in his school building or must my child go to another facility for them?
10. How many times per week will my child receive service? (This is usually based on the next question.) What is the present caseload of the personnel giving the support services?
11. When can we meet during the year to discuss my child's progress on his IEP?

Most school personnel genuinely want to clarify for parents the intent of their program. However, there are all kinds of ways these questions can be asked from either genuinely wanting information and assurance about a child's program to wanting to unload years of pent-up frustration and anger on a school. The focus must be kept on the best interests of the child at the present time. At least in the beginning, it helps if each party is receptive to the questions and comments of the other.

Ordinarily, most parents are satisfied with the answers to their questions and sign the IEP. Gilbert's parents were different in that they felt that their child's learning problem was more severe than the evaluation had demonstrated. On the advice of their local Association for Children with Learning Disabilities (ACLD), they asked for a second evaluation, an independent private assessment, which can be secured at public expense unless the school system initiates a due process hearing where it successfully demonstrates that its evaluation is adequate. In Gilbert's case, the school system agreed to a second evaluation.

Within a few weeks Gilbert was evaluated again by a private agency whose report indicated that although he tested within the average range, there was evidence that he had the potential of nearly superior intelligence which was mitigated by his severe perceptual handicaps. The report outlined his severe visual discrimination, visual memory, eye tracking, and visual motor problems; it pointed out his immaturity in organizing any task, in trying to integrate several things at once, and his inability to link visual symbols with specific sounds (decoding). This evaluation found that Gilbert had some fine auditory discrimination problems that affected how he heard the different vowel sounds. The examiners observed that this youngster was clumsy and awkward, demonstrated poor balance and coordination, did not know left from right, could not isolate one part of the body from another or plan his movements. They found that his visual motor skills were similar to those of the average child five years younger than Gilbert.

The second evaluation agreed with the first in terms of Gilbert's extraordinary vocabulary and reasoning, his vast knowledge of history, science, and other topics, but did not accept the finding that he could compensate for all his deficit areas with proper use of these talents. In fact, the second group of examiners indicated that the degree of hyperactivity, distractibility, impulsiveness, and perseveration shown by Gilbert in the testing would make it exceedingly difficult for him to learn in a large class. The judgment of the second set of examiners was that if Gilbert's learning needs were not addressed properly and promptly, it was likely that he would develop emotional problems beyond his existing lack of confidence and poor image of himself. Apparently Gilbert was becoming convinced that he was retarded; he was angry that people weren't telling him "the truth" about himself. The second evaluation recommended that Gilbert be placed in a self-contained classroom in order for him to develop the very elementary competencies he needed for academic work and to feel better about himself.

The IEP Committee met again to review the information from the second evaluation. Gilbert's parents asked that he be placed in a self-contained classroom.

The school system representatives on the IEP Committee felt that Gilbert was not handicapped enough to be taken out of the regular education program completely; that putting him in a special class was tantamount to segregating him and violating his civil rights. Miss Porter took the lead in suggesting that the IEP Committee change the original recommendation and have Gilbert spend part of the day in a resource room learning basic skills, but that he join her class for social studies, science, music, and recess; she also recommended that he receive occupational therapy twice a week.

The hesitancy of the school representatives on the IEP Committee can be understood; this child did present an unusual profile and clearly could function, in some areas, on a high intellectual level. The school representatives made it clear that they had limited financial resources and had to place many children much more severely disabled than Gilbert in special classes. Special classes cost more than special services. Also, state systems are cautious because they have been flooded with requests by parents in many suburban communities seeking special education services for their bright and *not* learning disabled youngsters to help them in the race for better grades.

Most parents don't want their youngsters to be labelled as severely handicapped, or placed in a special class or special school, for they want their children to feel as normal as possible. However, Gilbert's parents and an advisor that they brought with them to the second IEP meeting contended that by keeping Gilbert in a regular classroom even part of the day the system would be convincing him during that part of the day that he was inadequate and incompetent. They believed that with the new IEP there was still no way Gilbert could succeed academically, socially, or emotionally, so they refused to sign the IEP. Gilbert's parents used their rights of due process (to be discussed later in the chapter) to challenge the school system's recommended placement, and a third IEP meeting took place following the hearing. In Appendix 7 is the IEP that Gilbert's parents and the school system finally agreed upon and signed. Just as all parents are to receive a copy of the signed IEP, so, too, did Gilbert's parents.

An IEP must not contain general goals—e.g., "Gilbert will learn to read," but, rather, very specific objectives—e.g., "Gilbert will identify letters of the alphabet in sequence from a written model with 80 percent accuracy within the time period of 9/80 to 11/80." Teachers and parents of learning disabled students do tend to chortle when they have to put a percentage figure on the consistency with which a task will be performed, since a prime characteristic of the learning disabled child is inconsistency.

Frequently parents ask for school advice on how they can most help their learning disabled children at home. Some parents like to design a very informal IEP for the home because it helps them to target very specific areas to help their child. Clearly all parents need to help promote any latent talents and the child's socialization needs and generally to help him feel better about himself. Just as there are disputes in many areas among specialists in learning disability, so there is no meeting of minds as to whether or not parents should work with their children in the very areas where the child is hurting. It really depends on the personalities of the parents, the personality of the child, the atmosphere in the home. A good rule of thumb would be that a parent should ask himself or herself, how much extra anxiety, confusion, frustration, or anger is my working with my child adding to our home life? Usually it is best for parents to work with a child on what he can do well, where he feels competency and can associate parental help with success and pleasure. Home should remain a safety zone where competencies are built and enjoyed since school too often treads on dangerous vulnerabilities.

The IEP is a commitment to the individualization of education. It forces adults to look at the whole child, target the areas in which he needs the most help, set goals for him to achieve, and teach him in the ways he learns best. This is a superb idea. In fact, every child in our school system would benefit from an IEP! Certainly, attention to individual learning styles is central to special education. All the techniques that work with learning disabled children work even faster and more effectively with younger children with no problems. *Standardization is the danger* to education in general and to learning disabled children in particular. In some communities the IEP is being handled by standardized means. Teachers and specialists are pressing some buttons on a computer or looking in a book for the level at which the child is performing at reading (i.e., pre-primer) and are copying down the goals, objectives, and techniques contained therein. Computers and other aids can help as long as the child's individualized needs, interests, and styles come first.

There is no question that to do an IEP properly takes an enormous amount of time, energy, and thought—an effort for which teachers receive no extra pay. The task can be overwhelming to many special education teachers (who are primarily responsible for developing and implementing the IEP once the child has been placed in their class). The sequential nature of academic programming has to be understood by the writer of the IEP in order to outline in detail which skills a child must master in order to reach a certain goal. The act of having to write an IEP can promote the best kind of diagnostic-prescriptive teaching. Many teachers feel a pride in the IEPs they draft, in the systematic way they are going about helping a youngster, and this leads to their feeling more positive about their work. And the learning disabled youngster can only benefit from those feelings!

If a learning disabled child does not show any measurable progress within the projected dates on an IEP, the IEP challenges the adults to seek out new ways, try different methods, and go back and look at the severity of the child's problems. The quality of the treatment plans varies according to the teacher's background, training, and exposure to a wide variety of techniques and materials. For the severely learning disabled, however, progress may be recorded in many areas, but the reading or spelling scores may not rise in a very significant manner for two or three years. *PL 94-142 does not hold teachers accountable for achieving every annual goal, but it does hold schools responsible for offering the services written down on the IEP.*

What PL 94-142 does not provide, and what seems to be needed, is a Case Manager from the IEP conference on—one person responsible to protect and preserve the child's IEP—who keeps in touch with all the parties involved, who visits the school placement, checks on special services, raises appropriate questions, acts as the child's advocate within the system. Although expensive, such a system would mean that one person in the vast bureaucracy, where everything tends to become so impersonal, would be fully acquainted with the child and would thoroughly know his needs and the techniques that have been tried. Hopefully, the Case Manager could be a person to whom parents could turn with trust rather than treat as an adversary.

Least Restrictive Environment

The intent of PL 94–142 is to insure the maximum growth of every student with a handicapping condition by providing him with an appropriate education in the least restrictive environment. It is at the IEP conference that the appropriate education is detailed along with the locale where special services are to take place. The least restrictive environment concept does not, as is frequently feared, lead automatically to the inclusion of all handicapped children into the regular program. If it did, it would have another name.

Much of the public has given PL 94–142 another name because the United States has been flooded with articles calling it the "Mainstreaming Act." *Yet the word "mainstreaming" never appears* in any part of the legislation. However, the clear intent of Congress in using the three words "least restrictive environment" was to assure that to the greatest extent possible and appropriate handicapped children should be educated side-by-side with children who are not handicapped.

The impetus for this emanated from the fact that for too many years students with problems were dumped into catch-up classes where expectations for achievement were so low that poor performance was a natural result. Also, black students and children for whom English was a second or third language often were mistakenly classified as retarded. Racial segregation was supported by this misuse of separate classes and facilities. So there was mounting pressure to end such practices. Then it surfaced that handicapped children had been lumped together as a group that could not function in regular classrooms and had been segregated into special classes or facilities, often apart from regular school buildings so that nobody would have to be reminded of their existence. Again, there was usually little expectation of achievement. Many of these students did not need special teaching techniques as much as they needed access to the regular classroom, and with a few special aids they could master the work.

School is a place where a child ordinarily experiences a sense of mastery and competence. If a child can be in a regular classroom with a minimum of services that are enough to help his handicapping condition, and if he can experience mastery in that situation, then that child is served appropriately. There are a number of learning disabled students who have mild handicaps who simply require special kinds of aids such as being allowed more time to do their work, more specific structure to help them organize their work, and the breaking down of instructions into smaller increments. Others can succeed in the regular classroom with the help of typewriters, tape recorders, and other such materials. There are other learning disabled youngsters who need one-to-one tutoring daily, but can feel competent in many activities of the regular classroom. Some learning disabled students need to spend part of the day in a resource room where they are to receive special help in such areas as reading, spelling, and oral and written language, but join the regular classroom for all nonacademic programs and as many other academic programs as possible. Other learning disabled youngsters with greater difficulty may be in a special class in their neighborhood school for every period except lunch and sports. The severely learning disabled need to be in a self-contained classroom or learning center for the entire day or may need placement in a special school. For a very few, a residential school will best serve their needs. There exists this continuum of services that school systems must provide. An important facet of PL 94–142 is that the least restrictive environment can change according to the needs of the child. Previously, once a child was in a special class or special school, he rarely got out. PL 94–142 provides for continual reevaluation by the annual reviews and interim reviews.

The greatest controversies regarding the least restrictive environment center around a child like Gilbert. There are some classroom teachers who can help mildly to moderately learning disabled students find ways of functioning that minimize their disabilities and enable them to feel enough success each day to continue to believe that they can learn. However, students like Gilbert usually feel more inadequate and frustrated by remaining in classrooms with children who are not handicapped. For Gilbert to be placed in a regular classroom when his needs cannot be met there is in fact a more restrictive environment than to be placed in a self-contained classroom where he is helped to learn and succeed. It was not the intent of Congress to plunge Gilbert into an environment where he feels more inadequate and more frustrated and is subject to teasing and social isolation because of his deficits. Since Gilbert is bright enough to see that others can easily do what he, with massive effort cannot do, how can he feel better about himself as a person in a regular classroom? In that situation, Gilbert can feel so defeated that he may turn inward or he may become the class clown, the negative influence, the vandal, the disrupter who keeps everyone from learning.

By placing a child in a self-contained classroom, he does not have to be denied normal experiences. He can be introduced to exciting materials, challenged intellectually and creatively, taken on trips, and given opportunities to interact with the community. The self-contained classroom can allow the child to absorb the materials and the experiences by structuring them in ways so he *can* learn. Normal experiences belong in the self-contained classroom.

Many students like Gilbert belong in a self-contained classroom of 9 or 10 severely learning disabled youngsters until they are ready to move into a resource room and finally, with the proper support services, into a regular classroom. We would never think of throwing a pre-schooler who doesn't know how to swim into a large pool telling him to swim. Yet every day we are throwing children who do not know how to learn into regular classrooms and often we watch them begin to drown. Parents need to be vigilant in regard to what is best for their child. This means looking closely at the child's needs and being able to face the handicap courageously. There are some parents who lose sight of the needs of their own child and become involved in the stigma that they feel will taint them with their child's special placement. All parents want to see their child "make it" and not be isolated as "different," but the emotional complications that occur from a child failing day after day can become more severe than the learning disabilities themselves.

The severely learning disabled child is multihandicapped. As one teacher cogently said, "He's a little bit blind in that his eyes don't make sense out of what they see on a page; he's a little deaf in that he can't organize the information coming in from his ears. Frequently, he has touches of what could be called cerebral palsy in that his movement is disjointed and clumsy. Sometimes his speech is halting and he can't find the words that he needs. Emotionally, he tends to overreact or to act inappropriately. And yet he has many areas of competence. He's the hardest to teach."

Can Miss Porter, who has 34 third-graders in her class, among them one blind and one deaf child, give hyperactive, severely learning disabled Gilbert and two other moderately learning disabled students the help they need in focusing, the monitoring they need to control themselves, the step by step teaching of the prerequisites in order for them to learn the alphabet? Miss Porter might be able to serve Gilbert's needs systematically if she had only 15 students in her class, a trained aide, and many support services available; even then it would be difficult.

A fallacy in all of our schooling at the moment is the belief that large classes serve children's needs. All over the United States we have evidence that test scores are going down, discipline problems are soaring, children are not learning to read and write properly, yet not one school district is reducing class sizes drastically in order to give children and teachers a fighting chance to succeed. Why? Because citizens and their representatives decide that money must be allotted elsewhere. Yet we continue to wring our hands in despair at the poor quality of our schooling and too often blame the teachers.

Teachers are rarely given the support and training they need to work with handicapped youngsters.

Personnel Development

There are extensive provisions in PL 94–142 for states to develop comprehensive systems of personnel development with ongoing pre-service and in-service training programs to be made available to all personnel who are engaged in the education of handicapped children.

Some states have indeed tried to carry this out, but most teachers complain that they have not received comprehensive or any special training to work in a regular classroom setting with the handicapped; they say they have at most attended one workshop or lecture or seen some films. In particular, most teachers have not been trained in the special techniques that help learning disabled students. There is not enough special education included in the undergraduate programs training elementary and secondary school teachers, even though the Bureau of Education for the Handicapped of the Office of Education has given "Dean's Grants" to heads of a number of Schools of Education to inspire them to work with university faculties on the problems of the handicapped. It is hoped that as a result of the "Dean's Grants," when the university faculties teach courses to future teachers in reading, language arts, mathematics, science, and social studies, they will bring in the special needs of the learning disabled child in these areas. All teachers in training need to be made aware of children's different learning styles. Not enough universities require courses on learning disabilities as part of the degree program for elementary and secondary school teachers.

In some states the self-contained classrooms for learning disabled youngsters have been run by teachers who have had minimal or no training in learning disabilities, whether or not they were certified by their state school systems!

The training of teachers of the learning disabled must begin with an understanding of normal perceptual and cognitive development in young children. They need this information in order to understand the prerequisites involved in learning language, reading, handwriting, spelling, and arithmetic. This is necessary not only to understand the learning disabled child and the developmental stage he is at, but also in order to write a proper IEP to meet his special needs.

Teachers who will be in charge of self-contained classrooms or who will be resource teachers, must study the world of the learning disabled child, the means of teaching him how to learn and basic principles of remediation. They need to have a year's practicum working under a Master Teacher with the learning disabled. Their individualized needs must be recognized and cared for if we want them to meet the individualized needs of the learning disabled children they will teach. Exposure to a wide diversity of materials and techniques is mandatory as part of their education. Intensive training in diagnostic and remedial reading, language, perceptual-motor development, and arithmetic must be required for teachers of the learning disabled along with courses on behavior management and psycho-educational assessment. It is important that their creativity is tapped so they will learn to use all their own personal resources; teachers in training need to be taught to make individualized materials and teaching games so that they will not rely solely on commercial materials to teach children.

Furthermore, all special education teachers need to learn to do Task Analysis. They have to analyze a task and understand all the steps a child must master in order to complete the task successfully. Task analysis is not only a key to good remedial teaching but it is the precise technique that helps teachers develop sequential objectives on a child's IEP. Developing IEPs must become part of every teacher's training.

University graduate programs have to accommodate the needs of special education teachers in order for them to provide appropriate education for a child like Gilbert. Teachers like Miss Porter, through their professional organizations, must demand the training and support services they need.

Due Process

Extensive due process provisions are contained in Section 615 of PL 94–142. Essentially this part of the law provides parents with the ways and means for challenging decisions or inactions of the school system with regard to:

1. notice of actions to be taken or refusals to act,
2. identification of their child as handicapped,
3. evaluation of their child,
4. educational placement of their child,
5. specially designed instruction (appropriate education) being offered their child.

The school system also has its rights of due process. For example, the school can request a due process hearing on a parental refusal to consent to an evaluation or to placement. There are some parents who cannot tolerate or do not wish to accept the handicaps of their learning disabled children.

These are the people who say there's nothing wrong with the child, that it is simply poor teaching and lack of discipline in the schools. If parents refuse help for their child, the school can and must take on an advocacy role for the student to allow him to learn.

Gilbert's parents did not know what to do after they had signed the forms to have an evaluation and no action was taken over a two-month period. It was only because they attended a meeting of the local chapter of the Association for Children with Learning Disabilities (ACLD) that they learned what legal steps could be taken on Gilbert's behalf. To begin with, the advocacy group advised the parents to buy a notebook to write down every phone call they made to the school system, the date of the call, and the person to whom they spoke. Gilbert's parents learned to request that all responses be made in writing and to write letters themselves to the school system confirming what had been said on the phone and in person.

Gilbert was evaluated within a two-month period not only because the parents applied pressure to the school system, but because Miss Porter also continued to request that the child be evaluated. When Gilbert's parents were dissatisfied with the results, they studied PL 94–142 enough to know that they had the right to have an independent education evaluation and the right to be told where it could be obtained at no expense or low expense. The tricky part was whether the school system would pay for the evaluation or ask for a hearing in hopes of demonstrating that its evaluation was adequate. Had it gone to a hearing, the Hearing Officer, who must not be a part of the school system and must be impartial, might have ruled that Gilbert's parents had to raise the money independently.

If the school system had challenged Gilbert's parents' request for another evaluation, there was still another step for the school system to suggest short of going to a hearing. While not in the law, mediation is being used by many states to resolve differences. The advantage is that it is not a formal confrontation; the disadvantage is that it has been used by some states to delay for an interminable period the taking of any action.

After Gilbert's parents did have the second evaluation, they returned to an IEP meeting to discuss how the school system could provide the most appropriate education for their child. They disagreed with the school system's interpretation of the least restrictive environment, so they refused to sign the IEP and requested a hearing. At this point they turned for help to one of a number of possible advocacy groups. See Appendix 5 for suggestions on how parents can obtain free and low cost assistance. Law Schools often have clinic programs; also, the federal government has given each state funds for protection and advocacy systems to protect the legal rights of developmentally disabled children. ACLD chapters can help obtain legal help through this means. The school system is required to inform parents in writing of any free or low cost legal services available in their area.

Gilbert's parents were advised that although they didn't have to, it would be best for them to be represented by an attorney. They sought out a lawyer and these are the kinds of questions they asked him:

1. Are you familiar with PL 94-142 and relevant statutes?
2. Have you defended other parents in hearings?
3. Is there anything that can be done short of a hearing?
4. As a parent, what is my role in a hearing?
5. What are the possible repercussions for my child in having a due process hearing?
6. What sort of preparation must I do?
7. What kind of witnesses do we need?
8. What are the guidelines used by a Hearing Officer in making his decision?
9. How much will all of this cost?
10. What is our first step?

Most attorneys will study all the records relevant to identification, evaluation, and placement and then try to work out a reasonable agreement with school officials to avoid taking the case to a hearing or to court. Negotiations broke down in Gilbert's case. The school system adamantly insisted that it had many children who appeared to be more severely disabled than Gilbert, who were more in need of a self-contained classroom, and the school administration argued that the least restrictive environment for Gilbert was the regular classroom. If Gilbert's parents had been fighting for placement in a private school for the severely learning disabled, the same arguments would have applied, plus the cost factor. And the parents would have had to prove that the local public school facilities could not meet their child's special needs.

After the formal request for a hearing has been filed, both the hearing and the decision of the Hearing Officer must occur within 45 days. Documents have to be submitted at least five days in advance by both sides or they cannot be used, unless both sides agree to waive the rule. The list of witnesses (usually professionals with expertise in learning disabilities) also has to be presented at least five days in advance of the hearing. Parents have the right to obtain a written record or tape recording of the hearing. Hearings are closed to the public unless the parents ask for them to be open. If the parent wishes, the child may be present. As with most parents, Gilbert's parents decided that Gilbert should not have to undergo such a procedure. Until his parents and the school system agreed on a placement, Gilbert was required to remain in Miss Porter's classroom.

There is no question that the wear and tear on parents can be emotionally draining, but Gilbert's parents figured the cost was worthwhile because his future was at stake. In Gilbert's hearing there was a minimum of unpleasantness, accusation, or pettiness. In some hearings, particularly when parents are attempting to win approval of private school or residential placement, the parents have been vilified by the school system's legal counsel who must advocate for the school system's budget.

Gilbert's parents were at his hearing for a few hours. Some hearings go on for a number of hours or many days. The Hearing Officer gives both parties the chance to present evidence, allows cross-examination and usually he has a number of questions himself. The Hearing Officer has to provide a written decision within the 45 day limit of the initiation of the request and in his decision outline the facts upon which it was based.

In Gilbert's case, the Hearing Officer ruled that the school system's proposed placement was inappropriate and he gave the administration 20 days to come up with a new IEP and the appropriate placement. Within days Gilbert was placed in a self-contained classrooom and one year later he was doing well; although still below grade level, he was reading, doing some written math and his writing skills, though improving, remained very immature. All in all, he was becoming convinced that he would be able to be a good student eventually. Gilbert's parents felt that their efforts had been worthwhile.

If Gilbert's parents had lost the hearing, they would have had the right to appeal to a state agency composed of impartial examiners whose review of the hearing and subsequent decision must be made within 30 days of the appeal. The public school system has the same right of appeal for review of the hearing. Gilbert's parents can go on to appeal through civil action in a court if the state agency upholds the decision of the Hearing Officer.

There has been a rash of hearings, court suits, and class action suits, primarily concerning the placement of severely learning disabled students whose parents feel that state and local systems are not offering adequate facilities with well-trained teachers to educate their multihandicapped children appropriately. For the most part the federal courts have been ruling for the children. The backlash, however, is growing among state and local officials and among citizens in general who deplore the outlay of so much public money and the administrative time that is involved in such litigation. Even more, a private school education at public school expense is deeply resented by some. School systems must have better facilities and trained teachers to meet the needs of severely learning disabled students, and advocacy groups need to help the public gain a better understanding of the serious issues involved.

Parent Participation

Parent participation permeates all aspects of PL 94–142. The law acknowledges the importance of parents every step of the way and encourages their involvement in the development and approval of educational policy. Participation at public hearings and parent membership on local and state advisory panels on the education of handicapped children allow parents not only to affect educational policy but also to influence procedural guidelines and ways of monitoring them.

The intent of PL 94–142 is to best serve the individualized needs of each child with a handicapping condition by providing an appropriate education. Parents and teachers of learning disabled youngsters need to work together as much as possible to achieve this goal. If it could be possible for local systems to have a Case Manager who follows each handicapped child through his education, then parents, teachers, and school administrators might all feel heard, supported, and, as a result, might be able to work more closely together. Learning disabled youngsters need all the support they can get. Basically, it is in the child's best interests not to have schools and parents as adversaries, but as team members.

What we all share in common
   is a concern
      for a child who is disabled in learning.

What we all know
   is that the quality of teaching received
      can make a crucial difference
         in the quality of a learning disabled child's life.

What we all need to do
   is to use PL 94–142
      to give a learning disabled youngster
         the most appropriate and finest education possible.

12

Adolescence: Socialization and Organization

The parents of a teenager with learning disabilities are older and more tired than they were when he was a child. *Tomorrow has come.* Not only is he not cured, he is more difficult than ever to manage. He is still very dependent, while becoming harder to control and guide. He is bigger, stronger, more withdrawn yet more defiant, and his parents find that now, more than ever before, they need

more energy,
more stamina,
more patience,
more tolerance,
more hope that he will be able
to manage effectively in the world.

It is normal for the parents of learning disabled adolescents to want to give up sometimes. Their frustration and anxiety have increased. The future has to be reckoned with, and they are deeply concerned about it. Schooling, vocational possibilities, and social opportunities have to be studied carefully. They have to devise ways to help the learning disabled adolescent be able to learn to be self-sufficient. When the child was younger, his parents could use their ingenuity and problem-solving resources effectively, programming ways for their child to succeed and have fun, tempting other children to join in and be his friends. But teenagers are rarely lured by parental endeavors except in the form of tickets to football games or other exciting events, and not always by these.

Teenagers live by the rule of the pack. They band together against or, at least, apart from the adult world. This is a normal process, separating themselves temporarily into their own society, integrating the past—their childhood—with the present, getting ready to deal with the future. It is a time when peer relationships are crucial, and they are most often guided by one another through communications that may appear incomprehensible to adults.

Some learning disabled teenagers have the social maturity to keep up with the pack; they may feel defeated at school but not in the neighborhood. However, the majority of learning disabled adolescents do not have either the social maturity or the communications skills to gain solid membership in teenage groups, and they feel increasingly isolated. As Ms. Anthony put it, "I used to cry because Jim couldn't read and he and I had to watch his younger brothers and sisters surpass him at school. Now I am filled with tears because he is so alone, so isolated, hanging around the house more and more, glued to the TV."

Often the learning disabled adolescent doesn't know what to do with himself. His constant proximity to his parents increases the friction between them, increases his feeling of being picked on, and heightens everybody's unhappiness as all the people involved come to feel more and more inadequate. It is common for parents (and teachers) to say:

It's time for you to shape up.

You're too old for that!

When will you start growing up?

How long are you going to keep this up?

Won't you ever learn?

When will you stop acting like a two-year-old?

When will this end?

Professionals need to realize that most of the time these things are not said to hurt the youngster, to be mean, or to get even. They are expressions of helplessness, frustration, fear, guilt, or anxiety. These words come spontaneously out of pain, out of not knowing what else to do. Yet while parents are struggling with these realities, the other children in the family may criticize them for not being tough enough, or kind enough, or helpful enough with the learning disabled brother. Often they scream at their parents, "Do something about him!" Almost every parent tries to do his or her best for a child, and when the best is not good enough to make things change, the parent may feel desperate.

The learning disabled adolescent feels the same desperation. He absorbs all the angry, guilty, frightened feelings that make him feel unworthy. He learned during his most formative and impressionable years that he couldn't do things, couldn't understand, and couldn't perform like other children, and the cumulative effect of repeated failure firmly established his poor self-image. His perception of his home is frequently that his parents nag him all the time because he can do nothing right. His perception of school is often one of nagging teachers. He feels he is being told he is "no good" all the time.

> I can't do anything right.
> I'm no good.
> I'm dumb.
> I'm a retard.
> Nobody likes me.
> Everybody's picking on me.

These are some of the feelings that the learning disabled child shoulders as he grows up. He doesn't understand or he misunderstands many aspects of his life, and he receives correction or criticism, which he translates into "everybody's picking on me." It probably reflects his very real view of the situation because he doesn't interpret the correction or criticism as being helpful. Often he sees his world as a series of mistakes, one after another, all totaling personal disaster. It's hard to grow up feeling good about himself under these conditions. If he has special skills, a learning disabled child can feel good about his success in sports, his artistic talent, or his popularity with a group, but still has a gnawing feeling that something is wrong with him.

This is why straight talk is so important. It is vital that the child hear over and over again from different sources that he is intelligent but that he needs more time to learn than others and that he will make it in the world. He needs as much information about himself as he can handle, and he needs it frequently. He may still feel dumb. But at least he knows he is not retarded and does not have any progressive brain disease or whatever else he may secretly dread.

Feelings of Guilt, Anxiety, and Incompetence

In many ways, life seems very unfair to the learning disabled child. He perceives the world in the only way he can, albeit incorrectly, and he meets rebuff or ridicule as a result of what he says or does based on that perception. This youngster is often brought into child guidance clinics because someone thinks he is an angry, willful, unmotivated, or spoiled child who is purposely not performing well at school. This very frightened child cannot, rather than will not, perform well at school.

If you are awkward and you are faced with the task of rewiring a delicate stereo set, the job has to be done by you and you alone, and you know you are not up to it, how do you feel? Suppose you don't know how to draw. You have tried drawing many times, and you know you are terrible at it, but you have been told by an implacable authority that you must draw a picture for public display. How do you feel?

When you feel incompetent, you can easily feel imposed upon, and this can lead to anger. "Why me?!" is a frequent rejoinder of a learning disabled child when he is asked to do something. Some say of this child, "He has a chip on his shoulder," or, "He has a mad on the world." To an extent, he does.

He's angry at the world's demands on him, demands he cannot meet. He's angry at himself for not being able to do what he wants to do. He's angry at his parents, teachers, brothers, sisters, neighbors, and classmates for seeing him in the act of not being able to do. He's angry at God or God's representatives in church or synagogue. He's angry at being what he is.

When a child is angry, he does a lot in excess by acting out or withdrawing. He frequently makes others into scapegoats. A learning disabled child, seeing his own inadequacies reflected in others, can be a terrible tease, picking on the flaws of his companions and then perseverating. A beautiful, blond boy of thirteen, who was very intelligent, had severe learning disabilities. He followed a pattern—in school, on the playground, and at camp—of finding the least attractive youngster in the crowd and asking, "How does it feel to be ugly?" This child did not feel attractive himself; he felt ugly, worthless, and inadequate, and he projected his feelings on others. As soon as he overcame his handicaps to a point where he felt better about himself, he no longer displayed this need. The amount of teasing, provoking, and bullying that goes on in special classes for the learning disabled can be overwhelming, and it is one of the biggest management problems for teachers. "Mary is always calling me stupid!" complains Alison. Why? Because Mary feels stupid. "Harry's called me *dumb fool* all week!" says Jerry. Why? Because Harry feels like a dumb fool.

Along with the anger is the accompanying helpless guilt. Placing blame on things undone and constant self-castigation are familiar ways of acting when one feels guilty for not meeting standards. Rituals are important to the learning disabled child not only because his inflexibility craves what is familiar and safe but also because of a primitive belief that wearing a certain sweater, sitting in a special seat, or using a red pen will make everything work. "If only I had worn my good luck ring and the blue ribbon which I had in my hair the last time I got a good mark on the test, I could have done well today," mused Connie. It is typical of a very young child to count on magic to solve problems. The more profound the guilt a child feels, the more disparaging he feels about himself, the more he makes the people around him feel guilty and bad about themselves.

If a young person's nervous system has matured and if he has received sufficient remedial help to overcome the worst of his learning disabilities by the time he reaches adolescence, he will probably suffer no more than the normal stresses and strains of that period of life. Adolescence is the pathway from childhood to adulthood with much backward and forward movement. It's a time of identity crisis. Who am I? What do I believe in? Am I child? Am I a grown-up? If the turbulence of this period is combined with the profound self-doubt and confusion stemming from severe learning disabilities, the youngster faces a very painful and difficult time.

All children become less cute and endearing as they grow up, but this is normally offset by their developing sense of independence and responsibility. The learning disabled child, however, does not become much more independent as he grows older. His delayed maturation keeps him from acquiring the skills needed for independence. He has become a teenager by his number of years; he may have the physical size and puberty development of a teenager, but his neural development and his behavior are like those of a much younger child. Yet the world expects his behavior to fit with his appearance. The bigger the child, the more grown-up he looks, the harder it is for people to tolerate his immature behavior. The sixteen-year-old who is still small and baby-faced can get away with more than a gangly six-footer whose stubby beard has begun to show.

No Substitutes for Organization

The learning disabled adolescent's disorganization infuriates his parents and teachers for he is careless, untidy, messy, clumsy, forgetful, unthinking, and egocentric. Hank begins each day by sleeping through the clatter of his alarm clock; only his mother's strong will and strong arm finally get him up. He skids out of the house many minutes too late, leaving a trail of chaos in his wake—unmade bed, dumped-out drawers, forgotten books, spilled milk, and the front door standing open behind him. By the time he reaches school, he has missed the bell, and classes have started. He is angry, defensive, miserable, and embarrassed; he hates the way the day has begun, and he hates himself for being the way he is. To cover these feelings, he makes a grand entrance into his classroom: "Tadaaa! Superman is here!" He interrupts an interesting discussion, nobody thinks he is funny, and his teacher, thoroughly irritated, reprimands him sharply. Hank slinks to his seat, making an obscene gesture at an athletic classmate who clearly scorns him. He hears nothing that is said during the rest of the period, for he is preoccupied with his own inner turmoil, hurt feelings, helplessness, rage, and the firm conviction that nobody likes him—and never will—and that he cannot do anything right—and never will.

And so Hank's life goes. Untidy and disorganized, he forgets to take a bath, brush his teeth, and comb his hair. His bedroom smells awful, and he would never change his clothes if his mother did not take full responsibility for doing his laundry and laying out clean clothes. When other kids tell him his feet stink, he does not draw the conclusion that he should wash his feet and his socks; instead he thinks they are picking on him again because they don't like him. Instead of reforming, it is likely that he becomes even more disorganized plowing through the morass of homework papers, dirty clothes, and unfinished projects all scattered around him. Most teenagers have a problem with messiness in varying degrees, but the learning disabled youngster has them more pronouncedly, in more areas, and they last longer. Usually they are combined with poor planning, a lack of punctuality, poor study habits, poor follow-through, and unproductive uses of his time.

A college developing a program for intelligent students with learning disabilities concentrated heavily on audiovisual equipment and other academic props for these young people who had difficulty with reading and writing. After spending great amounts of time and money planning for these academic problems, the directors found that the students couldn't get up in the morning, couldn't organize their homework, lost their belongings, couldn't find their classrooms, forgot their assignments, and in general were so hampered by their pervasive disorder that they could not benefit properly from the academic program. The college finally instituted a buddy system whereby a well-organized student was teamed up with each learning disabled one, and they began to work explicitly on the organizational problem so that the students could learn successfully.

The three Rs are not substitutes for organization. Organization needs to be taught, taught again, and reinforced by every available means until habits and procedures become routine or, if possible, automatic. The learning disabled adolescent must consciously program himself to stop, think, figure out what comes first, next, last, and then go back and check to make sure he did it. This process is very demanding and exhausting. The tendency of the learning disabled youngster to react indiscriminately and to have his attention all over the map uses up enormous amounts of energy. He fatigues easily, making every task that much harder. Frequently learning disabled people who are successful adults stress their fatigue. They will tell you that, even today, the hardest thing for them to combat is this fatigue that comes from the constant overloading of their senses, the ever-present clamor of stimuli on their attention, which they must consciously work to keep under control. They need to develop systems to help themselves with organization. They need to program for the fatigue by allowing more time and more intervals of rest or by obtaining extra help on certain aspects of their jobs. They must be more conscious than the average person of the slow processing in their brain and the resulting inefficiency that demands so much of them. They have to come to recognize their own patterns of fatigue (as they must know their deficit areas) and find ways to compensate.

From the time a child enters adolescence, school, parents, recreation centers, and all other adults who come in contact with the learning disabled need to center attention on the organizational skills that he will employ for his adult life. The youngster has to be taught explicitly how to gather up what he needs to work with, how to begin a project, and follow through to the end. Adolescence is the age when checklists have to be made up with the help of the child, outlining every stage of each task and each household chore. He has to be in on the planning to get an overall view of how to accomplish a task and to see what all the stages are, to check off what has been done, step by step, and eventually internalize the process so that it can be performed automatically. This system applies to mopping the floor, emptying the garbage, delivering newspapers, and making a project for school. It is hoped that this method of breaking down a task, systematically finishing each stage in order, and checking off a list will, with sufficient repetition, become a habit, transferable to all other areas of activity.

Learning disabled young people are delayed in development, often by two, three, or even as many as five years in certain areas. They are immature. Some parents realize this, and offer a great deal of protection and the guidance appropriate to a much younger child. Other parents take into account only the actual age and demand that their children act appropriately. One may encourage infantile behavior, while the other makes unrealistic demands. A fine line is needed, to encourage independence at every step while giving necessary support—this is no easy task.

Independence usually relies on organizational skills. Self-sufficiency means taking responsibility for oneself. In areas where a learning disabled adolescent needs to learn specific, everyday skills to enhance his self-reliance, he can be taught to do many of these things, and the feelings of competence he derives from mastery set him up for more accomplishment. The following list taps some of the daily living skills the adolescent must master. They may cause great difficulty to many learning disabled teenagers for they involve organization, planning, memory, and a sense of time and place.

Use the Bus
Learn to go around town.
Know the bus insignias.
Know their destinations.

Do Simple Cooking
Feed self.
Cook eggs and toast.
Heat soup.
Make hamburgers, hot dogs, frozen dinners.

Set the Table
Lay out correct place settings.
Clear the table.
Wash and dry dishes.

Make a Bed
Know sequence of sheets, blankets, bed covers.
Learn tucking-in techniques.

Use Newspapers
Know the organization.
Learn where to find the sports, amusements, want ads, etc.

Eat at Restaurants
Learn how a menu is organized.
Understand the check.
Learn to order.
Calculate the tip.

Use Money
Learn to count change.
Keep money in a systematic way.
Make simple accounts.

Deal with Time
Learn to read the clock.
Make approximate schedules.
Learn the "feel" of intervals of time: how long is fifteen minutes? Half an hour? Two hours?

Do Shopping
Plan purchases.
Find the right store and department.
Make choices.

Use the Telephone
Know how to dial numbers.
Learn emergency numbers.
Learn how to ask clear questions.
Give and receive pertinent information.
Make an appointment.

Fill Out Forms
Learn to fill out job applications and questionnaires.
Understand bank forms (use enlarged forms and go slowly, step by step, from simple forms to more complex ones).

Coping with daily life demands developing strategies. Learning to live effectively with certain handicaps employs strategic thinking. Educators as well as parents need to teach strategies to teenagers.

Games are important for learning disabled adolescents for

more reasons than the social know-how of playing chess, checkers, bingo, backgammon, Monopoly, Ping-Pong, pool, or pinball. Games also develop nonverbal reasoning and logic. They demand strategies just as life does, and these are of vital importance to the learning disabled teenager.

Because of his good intelligence, this child learns the strategies of con men at an early age, plus all kinds of strategies of avoidance and denial. The adults around him can provide the learning disabled teenager with the experience he needs to invent strategies as he needs them, ways to get through situations when he does not know what to do. Using games of confrontation can help him to confront his own battles and talk about them. There are ways to win, and he needs to know them.

Developing Survival Strategies

The important educational job for both teachers and parents is to help teenagers and young adults develop survival strategies. These young people have to recognize their needs and develop their own survival techniques, for school in the short run, for adult life and job holding in the long run. They need tricks to help them to stick with a problem until it can be solved or successfully bypassed. They need conscious devices to trigger memory. Whether it's by using magnetic letters or simply magnets holding notes on a refrigerator, or their own bulletin boards, or a special hook near the door where they can hang notes to themselves, they need concrete help in remembering what they have to do. A special place has to be found for homework to be put in order to help them remember to take it back to school. Name tapes on all clothes, book bags, eyeglasses, and notebooks help the disorganized to hold on to his or her belongings. A special place or container for keys must be provided in order to prevent their loss. Poor memories demand smart, practical strategies. Seymour learned to control his habit of speaking impulsively and thoughtlessly by chewing gum. Another student achieved the same result by keeping his finger pressed to his chin. Mildly learning disabled youngsters who cannot take fast dictation, for instance, might learn to use a tape recorder or work out an arrangement with another student to take the notes in exchange for typing them. Professionals may need to provide some of the strategies, but it is more important for a youngster to learn to devise his own.

When the nervous system is overstimulated, both the brain and the body work inefficiently, wasting energy on indiscriminate matter. This is compounded by, or produces, slow processing. The result is fatigue. Strategies to deal with that fatigue must be invented by the student and by the parents and professionals who advise him. To begin with, he must recognize when the fatigue sets in so that he can do something about it. Leota found that by moving her body position frequently and by breaking her assignments into short periods, she could minimize the effects of fatigue. She found ways to maintain her focus when her mind wandered by moving small objects about on her desk. And she found it essential, from time to time, to retreat to a place where she could find silence and solitude as a relief from the perpetual overload on her senses. What worked for Leota did not for her friend Vanessa, who had to find other ways of dealing with fatigue.

Concentration on Language Skills

No system can compensate for a dearth of basic language skills that make for easy communication. Solid language training has to take place for the adolescent who has poor language skills. These skills need special concentration not only to help him get along with people but as preparation for finding a job. In a job interview, he has to be able to answer questions on demand, and performance on demand may be his nemesis. He must know how to listen carefully to questions and stick to the point in answering them. He has to remember to have eye contact with the interviewer, to be appealing as a person, to be attractive and clean in appearance, and to give indications of his reliability and sense of responsibility. Talking about these things is not nearly as effective as role playing, in which the teenager can play the role of both the interviewer and the job hunter while an adult takes the other part.

Socialization Problems

The learning disabled adolescent frequently finds himself shut off from young people his own age, not only because of his appearance (which advertises his own opinion, "I am not worth knowing") or his inappropriate behavior, but because he really can't share with other youngsters. He isn't yet capable of sharing ideas or feelings or even belongings with any degree of give and take. Often he has difficulty with communication. His language does not flow. Words are not useful tools for him at an age when young people like to talk about themselves a great deal. Words become a burden to him because they create confusion rather than clarity and understanding. When he tries to take part in group activities, he feels himself to be odd man out, and this feeling invites others to reject him. His personality, the total of his behavior, which was tolerated when he was younger or excused because he was just a child, now turns people off. They are made edgy by his unreliability and impulsiveness. They get fed up when he perseverates, going on and on about his favorite subject. They become bored by his gullibility, impatient with his inability to do two things at once, threatened by his disorderliness, and exasperated by his self-centeredness and stereotyped responses. Furthermore a young person like Hank does not make people feel good about themselves when he is with them. He, like his classmates Bea and Arthur, frequently make people feel harassed and overwhelmed which, unfortunately, is the way Hank, Bea, and Arthur feel.

Bea doesn't look at the person who is shaking her hand effusively. Arthur pushes right between two adults who are actively engaged in conversation. Bea demonstrates her social ineptitude by barging into a private office without an "excuse me"; so do Hank by throwing his books on the table where the guest is drinking coffee and Betty by pulling at the teacher's sleeve and talking to her a mile a minute while the teacher is settling down the class.

Bea, Arthur, Hank, and Betty are not stopping to look, listen, and feel what's going on. Not one of them takes a look at a person's face to see if the expression is one of sadness, anger, fear, or embarrassment. Not one looks to see if people are involved with one another. Not one listens to what's going on. It is extremely hard to size up a situation under these conditions, yet we know that the learning disabled child is a poor judge of size, shape, and direction and doesn't perceive more than his own wants and goals as of that moment. The learning disabled child is immature and egocentric; he is not intentionally unconcerned about others, but he is not yet ready to focus on their needs.

Bea, Arthur, Hank, or Betty might demonstrate social clumsiness at the dinner table or in a school discussion by interrupting constantly and usually with inappropriate remarks. Without a good sense of timing, conversation is virtually impossible, and the tendency to monopolize the conversation is far too easy. This is an immature pattern, understood when it occurs with the very young child but unacceptable to society in the older child.

Most children learn decorum and polite behavior not only by being taught rules but by copying their parents and others. The learning disabled child has trouble copying and does not absorb the family's behavior. Furthermore there are several ways of behaving in a given situation, and our One Way Kid cannot deal with alternatives. When he sticks to one stereotyped way, his social clumsiness makes others feel uncomfortable and irritated.

He often feels picked on and bullied, and he often is because of his awkwardness and disruptive effect on others. He can wreck a group activity that depends on teamwork and cooperation. He can't wait, can't take turns, doesn't understand rules, misses the point. He may dampen the group's enthusiasm, convinced that any deviation from a familiar method won't work. He may try too hard, injecting discomfort into the group by his loud laughter at jokes he doesn't understand, his overeagerness, his tenseness. He is forever doing too much or too little. His problem is not misbehavior but miscalculation. He is clumsy and makes inappropriate responses. Later in life, he finds out he can't keep a job because his behavior is inappropriate. Or perhaps he loses his job and never recognizes that the real cause was his own behavior.

Teaching Social Behavior

Professionals working with learning disabled teenagers and adults need to teach them how to pay attention to feedback, how to recognize it, and then how to use it. Socialization for many severely learning disabled youngsters has to be taught step by step, just as the tasks in reading and math are broken down and accomplished one step at a time.

Tina was thought to be a most unfriendly young lady. She brusquely pushed past adults she met in the hallway at school, and she was barely civil to her parents' friends at home. She felt as unliked by grown-ups as she did by her classmates. Her parents wondered why Tina couldn't see what she was doing and observe what impact her behavior had on other people. They talked to her endlessly about this, but to no avail. Fortunately she was one of a small group of teenaged girls at school who were invited to take a grooming class. In fact, the class was designed explicitly to teach teenagers like Tina how to behave appropriately.

The teacher of the class asked one of the students to play the role of the hostess. The teacher then played the part of a guest. She barged into this imaginary situation, not looking at the girl playing hostess and brushing right past her. The teacher then entered again, this time offering her hand, looking the hostess in the eye, and saying, "Hi! It's so nice of you to invite me." She then discussed with the girls which of these two entries they preferred. Clearly it was the latter, and the students analyzed why. They each took a turn playing both hostess and guest in a variety of similar situations, and talked over the effects together.

Parents can reenact situations like this with younger children, but for teenagers, the schools, recreation groups, and church groups are needed to do this kind of teaching. Learning disabled youngsters cannot fathom these very simple ways to make people enjoy being with them. Eye contact, a smile, a reassuring pat, a firm handshake, a pleasant greeting, a gently phrased question, a polite interruption, a thoughtful inquiry, and sometimes a needed silence—all these are social skills that must be taught, each for its own place, one by one. Videotape machines can be enormously helpful for a young person to help him see himself as others do. The use of the absurd can also be an effective way to begin this kind of training, with the adult doing some most inappropriate and comical things. The exaggeration begins to define what is inappropriate, and from there the adult and the adolescent can move together toward understanding subtler behaviors.

The art of socialization is highly complex. Many learning disabled children have mastered it. Some have not, but they can, in time. No child has all the problems listed below, but even a few of them impede socialization.

What works against learning disabled youngsters using good judgment in social situations?

Disorder, disorganization, scatter.

Lack of impulse control (acting without thinking).

Low tolerance of frustration and need for immediate gratification.

Body and spatial problems (difficulties in judging size, shape, distance, direction).

Poor concepts of time and timing.

Perserveration (repeating an action or phrase or topic over and over again).

Difficulty in shifting from one situation to another.

Emotional lability (overreacting, moodiness, change-ability).

Poor listening skills, poor memory, poor grasp of sequence (forgetting what they are doing and what they are supposed to do next).

Inability to look at what is going on and to visualize.

Giving as much weight to the most minute detail as to the key point.

Difficulty in making choices of any kind.

Concrete, literal comprehension, missing subtleties and nuances.

Egocentric outlook (the inability to put themselves in others' shoes).

Inability to relate cause and effect, and to generalize from social experiences (the inability to predict).

How do learning disabled youngsters demonstrate poor judgment in social situations?

Barging thoughtlessly into situations and interrupting without looking.

Having trouble taking turns.

Acting belligerent (when in reality they do not comprehend directions).

Making inappropriate remarks, gestures, actions, poorly timed responses.

Misreading the social signals given by others (not understanding facial expressions, posture of symbolic movements that indicate fear, anger, guilt, complicity, irritation, sadness, etc.).

Missing the point of what other people are doing, off target.

Letting others take advantage of them; carrying out destructive acts for others.

Blowing up at the slightest hint of criticism, tiny mistakes, postponements, or delays; overreacting to mild teasing.

Telling jokes that are not funny; not understanding the jokes, puns, riddles of others.

Picking on everything that is different from last time (appearing uncooperative and intransigent by seeing only one way to do things).

Being bossy (the need to organize others stemming from their own internal disorganization).

Planning poorly.

Quitting, running away, or making fools of themselves when they cannot explain their failure to perform competently.

Placing blame on others (denial of their own role in a situation that has gone wrong).

Needing to win at all costs (this can lead to lying, cheating, destroying the game).

A Need for Acceptance

Lester is desperately lonely; he would do almost anything to feel accepted and liked by other youngsters. Because of his loneliness, he is in greater danger of being led astray by others than is his fourteen-year-old neighbor, a boy who is fortunate enough to have developed normally, with good judgment, self-confidence, and a clear understanding of right and wrong. When Les was little, other children found it was easy to take his toys. Now they find they can get his money. Where he used to give them cookies in exchange for "friendship" now he gives them money. Or he may give them alcohol or drugs, which can lead to stealing if he hasn't money of his own with which to buy them. He'll cheat, lie, tattle, take on a new friend's values and prejudices (which may be alien to his own), or he may become a "slave" to a person, following any command in order to gain friendship. He'll do anything to make a friend and to belong. Because he feels unwanted, he may be drawn to fringe groups that harbor other lonely, alienated people—religious cults or groups embracing bizarre food fads and diets. He may be drawn into vandalism or other delinquent behavior that he did not think up but for which he will invariably get caught. He may be lured into trying hard drugs, alcohol, or sex in all forms as a social route. The activity itself is not important. The warding away of loneliness and the embracing of companionship in any form is what matters.

He tends to be off balance here as in physical activities: overdoing, timing badly, judging incorrectly. Once more, he falls flat on his face and has to learn, one step at a time, how to cope with these situations. Too often he tends to retreat to the television, to become glued . . . or to the icebox, to become fat . . . to the bar, to become drunk . . . to the motorcycle or car, to race away . . . or to playing with the mother and baby next door, because he has become weary. Social clumsiness isolates the learning disabled youngster even more than his physical clumsiness. "It's not fair" is a frequent rejoinder of the learning disabled adolescent—and it isn't.

This same isolation, the lonely longing to belong, if channeled and trained, can draw a learning disabled adolescent into groups that can greatly help him. These can range from chess clubs to bowling teams to amateur theatrical groups. Where such groups don't exist, parents, teachers, or community organizations can *and must* create them. There is a need for group activities where learning disabled teenagers can learn the skills of daily life and acquire the know-how and the social "passports" to allow them to move confidently in the grown-up world of everyday living. There are many young Americans who do not know how to make constructive use of leisure time. Imagine what it is like for the learning disabled teenager! He must be taught explicitly the resources in his neighborhood and in his community, and needs help to discover what he likes to do and how to go about doing it. He has to be taught how to organize himself to engage in satisfying activities, or he may opt for the TV because it is there, safe, and does not require any organized action. In order to learn that his voice counts and that our democracy depends upon involvement and active participation, an adolescent needs to be taught how to vote, learn about candidates and the positions they stand for, and how to form opinions and chose one candidate over another—an exceedingly difficult task for all of us, but particularly for the young person who has trouble assigning priorities. They need to be shown the value of asking questions, perhaps by supplying them with the questions at first and then helping them form their own. These are life skills that help them feel they can better their own lives and validate their stake in the world.

Teen clubs need to be a top priority among parents and teachers of learning disabled youngsters, where the emphasis is on success in socialization accomplished step by step. How to make friends, keep friends, and be a part of a group are lifetime skills that need to be taught. They are the skills that comprise socialization, which means survival.

Learning disabled adults also need clubs and groups where they can share experiences and learn from each other. Time Out to Enjoy, Inc., is a national, nonprofit, self-help network for learning disabled people eighteen years of age or older. Local chapters concentrate on solving problems of mutual concern, sharing resources, and providing speakers to organizations or facilities that are interested in learning disabled adults. The headquarters is: Time Out to Enjoy, Inc., 113 Garfield Street, Oak Park, Illinois 60304. Another group that young adults can write or send a cassette tape to is ALDA, Association for Learning Disabled Adults, Post Office Box 9722, Friendship Station, Washington, D.C. 20016. LAUNCH, Inc., The Coalition of LD Adults, another self-help group, can be reached through the Department of Special Education, East Texas State University, Commerce, Texas 75428. The Association for Children with Learning Disabilities now has an organization of learning disabled adults all over the country. The ACLD Adult Committee, 4156 Library Road, Pittsburgh, Pennsylvania 15234, also has a list of college programs that will accommodate the learning disabled. There is a monthly newsletter that is specifically directed to learning disabled young adults describing secondary schools, colleges, and services. This is Partners in Publishing, College "HELPS" Newsletter, Post Office Box 50347, Tulsa, Oklahoma 74150. A comprehensive bibliography on learning disabled adults has been prepared by Dr. Samuel D. Clements, Executive Director, Child Study Center, University of Arkansas, Little Rock, Arkansas 72211. A clearinghouse for groups of and for disabled adults in every part of the country who need help facing problems in employment or social acceptance is the American Coalition of Citizens with Disabilities, 1200 15th Street N.W., Suite 201, Washington, D.C. 20005. (See Appendix 5.)

Some learning disabled adults continue to need support systems. A number of professionals in this young field feel that lifetime counseling for the learning disabled adult is a top priority and should be available in every junior or community college for learning disabled adults whenever they need it.

Developing a Special Talent

Many successful learning disabled adults have had one area of special competence that allowed them to shine, to have a goal, and to build confidence. It is crucial for a learning disabled youngster to find one talent or one skill on which he can concentrate, if at all possible. Once such an interest is identified, it can be encouraged and trained by parents, teachers, and all other professionals who work with this child. If the youngster learns well by demonstration, he should have a chance to become apprenticed to somebody who is already skilled. Suppose a boy has a knack with machines; find a mechanic who will let the boy work in his garage as an assistant or pay the mechanic as you would any other tutor. Senior citizens are a great untapped resource in our society. Through church groups and interest clubs, they have a great deal that they could offer in working individually with learning disabled teenagers. Their calm manner and organization, their experience with life, and their available time can make a difference in the life of a learning disabled adolescent.

Sports can open up a whole world, even to an unathletic boy or girl. By dint of hard work with their learning disabled child, parents can bring alive sports that they love themselves. Step by step, they can build up an understanding and appreciation of football, baseball, basketball, golf, or almost any spectator sport. The ritual and procedure of stadium behavior can be learned and enjoyed. A learning disabled youngster with a keen interest in a sport may find purpose and satisfaction as a manager's assistant on a team—taking care of many routine but vital details, like towels and jackets, and earning the right to wear the team's uniform. He might become an expert on facts and figures concerning his favorite sport or simply have fun attending games with his father.

The learning disabled person needs a realistic view of his strengths and capabilities as well as his weaknesses and disabilities, to make the most of what he has. Nothing is more pathetic than the person who pretends to be what he is not, who chases after impossible goals, destroying himself along the way. This is not to say that the learning disabled adolescent should settle for the lowest practical opportunities, without aiming higher. For many, a college education is possible and attainable. Junior colleges and community colleges are becoming a haven for young learning disabled adults after they leave high school. The time they gain there often gives them the opportunity to mature, to find a specialty, to develop organization, discipline, and study habits that will enable them to succeed in a competitive four-year college or to hold a job. Vocational schools are the answer for others who have no particular, visible bent but who are especially good with their hands.

Some learning disabled children, through neural maturation and systematic special education, grow out of their learning disabilities. Many grow out of most of their disabilities and learn to compensate for the rest. Others carry the baggage of many learning disabilities with them through life, grappling with them, using strategies to overcome or get around the deficit areas. Given a good bit of extra time and skilled teaching they can learn to function independently in adult life. Unfortunately, many of them do not receive the help they need to become productive. They need the same kind of highly individualized instructional programming for success in vocational areas that they needed in special education. Profiles of their strengths and areas of deficit need to be matched to job categories. What's required on a particular job demands task analysis—the sequence of steps needed to be learned to perform the tasks effectively. The learning disabled require step-by-step teaching through their strengths to achieve mastery. Parents and teachers need to insist that severely learning disabled adolescents receive an IWRP (Individual Written Rehabilitation Plan) in coordination with special education provisions under PL 94-142. The highly individualized specialized attention needed to be given to the severely learning disabled adolescent (as incredibly expensive as it is) is less expensive than paying for welfare because of joblessness, psychiatric clinics, courts, and prisons. And what about the devastation of the entire family unit when an intelligent young person with potential falls by the wayside because of lack of necessary support services?

Rehabilitation counselors find the severely learning disabled adult especially difficult to help. They say, "Give me any other handicap but L.D." because the learning disabled are such a jumble of inexplicable behaviors marked by extremes of competencies and incompetencies. "They are bright so they get bored with repetitive tasks, but they are inefficient and can't do the simplest of things. They oversleep, don't allow enough time to arrive at work on time, have no time sense." Another counselor says, "He loses his way everywhere, even within a building and he would forget where his head was if it wasn't attached to his body." Another vocational rehabilitation counselor stated, "They are messy, unmotivated, don't care!"

The learning disabled adolescent usually *does* care. In fact, he is often trying his heart out! He breaks 52 dishes at the restaurant because his motor skills are so poor. It's not for lack of trying but for lack of coordination and organization. A very perspicacious young adult with learning disabilities stated that parents and teachers must *instruct learning disabled adolescents to show that they are trying*. They need to gain the support of their fellow workers, supervisors and, also, customers, by being able to talk about their difficulties, and to be savvy as was the learning disabled adolescent who, each day, told her customers "It's my first day and I'm nervous." For some, it is an impossible task to be a waiter and finding more suitable employment is necessary.

We know from talking with learning disabled students and

young adults that they put in double or quadruple the time that others do to learn something and master it. Their effort is massive. It is courageous. *But their hidden handicap prevents them from receiving positive feedback for their determination and stamina.* How can they be helped to let the world know what they are going through, without asking for pity?

Originality, ingenuity, a fresh eye, and an unconventional approach have led many learning disabled youngsters into the arts. Not held back by their learning disabilities, many thrive creatively in fields like montage, cartooning, window display, filmmaking, architecture, interior decorating, ceramics, and landscaping. Tony made a flute and learned to play it in a special class when he was fourteen, and something inside him caught fire. By sheer perseverance, he graduated from college, majoring in music. He became a first-rate musician, and today he plays in an orchestra. Tom was a hyperactive boy who annoyed his teachers by drumming his fingers on the desk. He took up drums seriously in high school and, after he graduated, joined a band, which is now touring the country. Boats have been a source of great satisfaction and employment to some—the building of boats, sailing, and teaching these skills. To others, marine biology, oceanography, or the environmental sciences become a passion.

Too often in the past, an intelligent young person who doesn't spell well, who may be disorganized, reads with difficulty, and who does not make it to college has ended up as a short-order cook, or a grocery sacker in a supermarket, or has been relegated to some other unimaginative job that he does not do well and where he is wasted. His abilities would qualify him for many useful challenging occupations if suitable training programs existed. There is a need for systematic work-study programs in the helping professions such as hospital work, as nurses' aides or physical and recreational therapists; in day care centers and childrens' recreation programs; for work with growing plants in nurseries, plant farms, and with landscape architects; for jobs in hotels, stores, and banks.

Even if a learning disabled young adult is fortunate enough to find the appropriate job, he may still have difficulty socializing and taking care of himself. Independent living skills must be fostered with learning disabled young people. Parents and teachers have to program tasks so young people can perform them independently and feel self-reliant. Situations need to be set up where constant peer interaction is a normal experience. For the severely learning disabled, neighborhood halfway houses and group homes are taking over where parents and teachers leave off. In the states of California, Washington, and Oregon, group homes established for no more than 6 to 10 learning disabled young adults have been effective in helping provide the transition from home to independent living. Their aim is to help young adults learn to take care of themselves, share responsibility, and function effectively in the community as well as at work. Unfortunately, because these homes with qualified personnel are so expensive to run, there are very few of them meeting the needs of thousands upon thousands of learning disabled young adults. The investment somehow must be made. More of these are desperately needed throughout the country with the necessary components of mental health workers, vocational counselors and special educators as staff providing the life lines to the flourishing of healthy relationships and satisfying living.

Human Qualities

In the end, what counts are human qualities. A person's sense of himself, his feeling of comfort with himself, and thus his ease with others are what matters. How many adults do you know whose knowledge of spelling or trigonometry makes any difference to you? Does it matter how good your friend's handwriting is or how many historical facts he can recite? Is it important that your friends be very athletic plus very scholarly, as well as talented in some artistic field? The chances are that you want to be with a person you enjoy, someone with whom you have easy communication to share interests and concerns, someone who is fun and caring. You want a friend who laughs with you, not at you, who can share your worries as well as your pleasures. A friend does not have to be fashionable, but a certain amount of cleanliness, neatness, and attractiveness matter. You want someone you can count on, whose word is good, who comes through on promises, who doesn't keep score on favors given and received.

To be a good friend, to be a fine mate, to become a good parent—these are crucial goals in our society, yet we do not educate any of our young people to fulfill them. We study, we plan, and we prepare for almost everything in life except our relationships. And what do we spend our whole lives doing except relating to other human beings? Most of us pick up enough clues, by tuning into what is going on around us, to get along well with other people. But there are many among us—and a number of them are hampered by learning disabilities—who do not unconsciously absorb what happens around them and apply it to their own lives. They need to be taught these skills explicitly.

So socialization joins organization as top priorities for the learning disabled adolescent. As much as the learning disabled child needs systematic instruction in reading, spelling, math, and other academic areas, whether he will be a successful adult really revolves around socialization and organization. This is the great challenge to parents and professionals working with the learning disabled adolescent.

13

The Key Is Organization

There is order in the universe.

There is order in life.

There is order in growth, from one step to the other.

The body develops its own order.

The mind develops its own order.

Ordered movement of the body brings ordered growth of the mind.

When the nervous system matures naturally, it orders the messages coming into the brain from all the senses and prepares the way for the master organizational job: developing groupings, patterns, and systems of thought. The organizing system within us lets us relate one person, one object, one situation, one set of feelings to another. If ideas are not related, then each experience is unique, unrelated to everything else, with the result of fragmentation. When every single thing has to be dealt with separately, energy is used inefficiently and wastefully. Part of growth is the making of connections producing patterns and systems for faster, more efficient performance.

The toddler flails his arms and screws up his face as he tries to run. He grows up to be a twelve-year-old who runs gracefully and fast, relating his movements to each other, using his body as a unified, coordinated whole. The learning disabled youngster, because of his immaturity, makes life much more difficult for himself and others. Teachers and parents are often heard to say:

Why can't he make life simple for himself?

She makes a mountain out of a molehill.

He does everything the hard way.

She makes easy things complicated.

He always finds a roundabout way to do things.

The learning disabled schoolboy who brings one six-pack of Coke at a time from the kitchen to the living room and the learning disabled teenager who loads the car one item at a time are inefficient; they use an excess amount of energy for a simple task. They have not organized themselves to look at the job, picture in their mind what it demands, and develop a system to get the work done effectively in as short a time as possible. The same is true with remembering a series of numbers, facts, or ideas. They have to be grouped to facilitate memory. To remember important American explorers, a student has to have learned the facts, isolated the prime characteristics of explorers, grouped these together with names and dates, and stored them in his mind to be pulled out as a category when necessary.

Humphrey, who became sidetracked by details when looking at a picture, studying a lesson, or exploring great ideas, could not make sense of the statement, "Aristotle, Plato, and Socrates all had one thing in common. They were searching for the _____." He did not see how Aristotle's way of logically categorizing reality, Plato's approach to unity through ideals, and Socrates' method of asking questions could all be ways of seeking the truth. Humphrey's teacher gave him three pieces of paper and asked him to fold them in three different ways. She then asked him to look at the ways they were similar. From his seeing that all three were of the same color, shape, size, and texture, she slowly extracted from him that Aristotle, Plato, and Socrates were all searching for the truth although they went about it very differently.

> As we mature,
> we relate more and more ideas,
> on higher and higher levels,
> adding, substituting, refining, regrouping,
> boiling things down to their simplest elements.

Organization and reorganization produce simplicity. Formulation and reformulation produce clarity. We continue to order our existence as long as we live, simplifying it through increased organization. The difference between adults and children lies in the amount and degree of planning, preparing, and setting of priorities that adults do. Adults have to build organization into every aspect of a learning disabled youngster's life until he can take it over for himself. They have to set the boundaries, carefully establish limits, and provide order for the child with disorder until he can begin to establish his own borders and simplify his existence.

Sort, sort, sort. The child has to be given every possible opportunity to sort things—from buttons to toy cars to pictures to lotto cards, eventually to symbols, to words, to ideas. He needs training in groupings, categorizing, and systematizing numbers, facts, and ideas. Even with the best provisions, neural maturation cannot be hastened. A youngster's growth can be encouraged by the systematic learning of readiness skills rather than impeded by the pressure of unfair demands to learn at his age level. He can be given the undergirdings so that when neural maturation does take place, he has the foundations to leap ahead academically. He has to be helped to create an inner voice to order him. Strategies to help him build on his strengths and to help him get around some of his areas of weakness can be taught to him. Learning tricks to trigger memory, aids to help him focus, and ways to keep himself on a task until it is completed are a necessary part of schooling for the learning disabled child.

Everything he does well is a jewel to be treasured.

Every sense of accomplishment he feels is a deposit to success.

Every adult he trusts is an investment that will pay off.

Every opportunity he has to enjoy himself, to have fun, to feel good about himself, is a form of savings bond.

Lives have been saved and made productive by people's feeling good about themselves. This comes about through the mastering of tasks and through the establishing and maintaining of relationships. It comes about through very hard work on the part of the learning disabled youngster and all the important adults who share his life.

The needs of learning disabled youngsters are at last beginning to be recognized. The child who was previously incorrectly labeled as retarded or emotionally disturbed can now receive the help he needs. There is greater hope today than ever before. We know more. Public Law 94–142 is forcing states and counties to do their job. Parents and teachers are more on the alert so the child with difficulties is spotted earlier. There are many resources. More can be done.

Still the major responsibility sits squarely on the shoulders of the parents of each learning disabled youngster, followed by his teachers. The job is immense; the demands are constant.

> The continual providing of order,
>   the continual planning ahead,
>   the continual programming for a child's pleasure
>   and success,
>   the continuing training for independence
>   mean
>   continually putting a child's needs first,
>   and
>   that is not always possible or
>   always desirable.

Adults have needs. Adults have pressures put upon them not only by their children but by other adults, their employers, neighbors, co-workers, community, church, and their own parents. Adults have their ups and downs. They are only human.

One cannot serve the needs of even the most needy youngster every single moment. One can do only his or her best. A teacher cannot give all her attention to one or two learning disabled youngsters in her class to meet their needs, while neglecting twenty-eight others.

She can give as much structure as possible. She can attempt to obtain the best education for each child and to unearth the needed services. She can join parent and community groups to apply pressure on officials to help with the job. This much must be done for these intelligent young people who have so much potential.

Whether it is at home, in the church or synagogue, at the recreation center, in youth groups or in school, we know there will be times when the learning disabled child inevitably becomes frustrated, despairing, angry, anxious, guilty, and fearful. Big ups and huge downs—rarely a middle ground—characterize this child. The adults around him are very susceptible to the same feelings, and, if they allow themselves to take part in his ups and downs, their life can become a seesaw.

It is normal to feel angry with a learning disabled child. What is important is to find the cause of the anger and analyze it. See what can be done to prevent the situation or the set of circumstances from happening again next time. Sometimes simple exhaustion from the ever-present demands causes anger, and a good night's sleep takes care of it. Sometimes the anger is deeper. The frustration of helplessness, of being unable by any human power to "make it all be all right" for a child can produce many varieties of anger.

All teachers and parents share the experience of failing at times, particularly when they are surrounded by uncertainty, unpredictability, inconsistency—the climate of the learning disabled child. Any adult who is intensively involved with this child is unavoidably going to make many mistakes. Jean Piaget points out that a child's misunderstandings and his mistakes are the most revealing source of information about his progress and development. Perhaps the same principle can be applied to adults.

We can learn from our mistakes and our confusions, not only about the child himself but about where we, the adults, stand in relation to him. The more we know about the nature of the learning disabled child and the more we know about ourselves, the better we will be able to separate our feelings and reactions from his. There are times when this is very difficult. We are affected because we care deeply about him, and that makes us vulnerable. Yet it is clearly in the child's best interest that we not identify too closely with him.

A toughness, as well as a sensitivity, is required of adults who work with learning disabled youngsters. The child must be kept to standards, held to finish each reasonable task he begins, and helped to learn to monitor himself to be sure he is picking up the feedback from materials and people that will tell him whether he is doing a task correctly and appropriately. The learning disabled child must be helped all along the way to know as much as possible about how he learns, the aids he must have, and the strategies he must use to help himself. Along with sympathy and understanding, the adult must resolutely help the learning disabled young-ster to establish attainable goals for himself and stick to them.

The teacher has the crucial task of teaching the three Rs to this child—systematically, doggedly, imaginatively—until he has learned them. Into this curriculum, at every point, must be incorporated the teaching of socialization. The key to both is teaching organization. The child needs to be taught how to organize himself for learning. When he can finally hold this key in his own hands, he will have the means to open the doors to new worlds of learning and living.

Appendix 1

Glossary

Abstract Thinking

The ability to use categories and classifications; to grasp relationships such as cause-effect, part-whole; to generalize; to see similarities and differences; to analyze and synthesize; to deal with words and concepts that have no concrete referents, that can't be known directly through the senses (for example, *democracy*). The opposite of concrete and literal thinking.

Apraxia

The inability to motor plan, to make an appropriate body response.

Auditory Discrimination

The ability to perceive the difference between sounds or sequences of sounds. Example: hearing the difference in the final consonant of *can* and *cat*.

Auditory Perception

The ability to understand and put meaning to sound; the brain organizes what is heard into something meaningful.

Body Awareness, Body Schema

The awareness of one's own body and the parts that make up the whole.

Body Image

Feelings and perceptions about one's own body, including body schema; feelings of attractiveness or ugliness, or fatness or thinness, for example.

Catastrophic Reaction

A sudden loss of control, an overflow emotional response to a relatively minor frustration or demand; it is out of proportion and seemingly unwarranted.

Concreteness

The need to see or touch in order to understand, plus the tendency to treat every

233

situation as unique, unrelated to previous experience.

Constancy	The ability to perceive the essential quality of an object regardless of its presentation, such as changes of size, color, or position. Example: the letter *a* is always the same no matter what its color, typeface, or position on the page.
Decoding Problems	Problems of associating sound with symbol.
Developmental Lag	Delayed maturity in one or several areas of development.
Developmental Tasks	A series of tasks (or skills) related to mastery, normally accomplished by a growing child in a predictable sequence. Often the learning disabled child needs to be taught these tasks explicitly because his deficits prevent him from acquiring them automatically.
Directionality	The ability to perceive and label directions, such as up-down, in-out, front-back, left-right, north-south.
Distractibility	Easily sidetracked, often unable to focus and concentrate on a given task. It happens usually because the nervous system is unable to screen out extraneous sensory stimuli. The distractible child is unable to select certain stimuli and exclude others.
Emotional Lability	A tendency to sudden swings of mood. Related to organic difficulties in inhibiting behavior and manifested by quick changes of emotional behavior, from laughing to crying, gaiety to sadness, tranquility to temper tantrum.
Encoding Problems	Problems in converting oral language into written symbols.
Expressive Language	The ability to communicate with others. The opposite of receptive language.
Eye-Hand Coordination	Coordinated movements of eye and hand in which the eye guides the hand to the accurate completion of a task.
Eye Tracking Difficulty	The inability of the eye to maintain focus and move smoothly, as in reading a line left to

right across a page or following a moving object.

Faulty Body Image The inability to integrate the various perceptions within one concerning one's body and its relationship to the world. Makes one unsure of where various parts of the body are; the shape and size of parts of the body are confused in one's mind, and all of this affects the way one moves. A child may be unable to imitate a simple posture of movement because of faulty body image.

Faulty Checking Mechanism The inability to refrain from acting on an impulse (see *impulsivity*).

Figure-Ground Perception The ability to focus on one thing (figure), allowing all else to drop into the background (ground).

Fine Motor Difficulty Problems with the use and coordination of small muscles for activities such as writing or sewing.

Gross Motor Difficulty Trouble with movement through space in which large muscles are used and in which balance is important, for activities such as running, walking, chalkboard writing.

Hyperactivity, Hyperkinesis Unorganized purposeless action, excess, random movement, inappropriate motor response, stemming from immaturity of the central nervous system.

Hypoactivity Underactivity, sluggishness, failure to respond when response is appropriate. Like hyperactivity, it stems from immaturity of the central nervous system.

Impulsivity The inability to inhibit, control, check, or even delay inner impulses for organic reasons; the child is driven to act on impulse without stopping to think through the consequences. The child's difficulty in postponing pleasure or gratification, waiting in line, and waiting to speak is related to this.

Kinesthetic Perception The perception of movement that comes through the sensations of muscular activity.

Laterality The awareness within the body of the difference between right and left; it is the conscious awareness that one side differs from the other, correctly labeled as the right side and the left side.

Low Frustration Tolerance The inability to withstand much frustration without either blowing up or withdrawing.

Maturation Lag A delay in the development of the central nervous system. A child's behavior, perceptions, and cognitive development resemble those of a much younger child.

Midline Difficulty A tendency to avoid moving any one part of the body (arm, for instance) across the midline of the body.

Motor Plan The ability to control the body in order to make an appropriate and efficient movement. The ability to motor plan depends on accurate body awareness, balance, and coordination.

Overload The result of too many sensations bombarding the nervous system at once. Results in the inability to respond to one stimulus and exclude the others, as though three people were talking to you at once; you cannot hear any one of them clearly, and you are not able to respond appropriately to any of them.

Part-Whole Difficulty The inability to perceive the parts that make up a whole or to break down the whole into its components.

Perception The process by which the brain organizes, integrates, and makes sense out of the stimuli coming from the eyes, ears, nose, and taste buds and from sensations in the muscles and the skin.

Perceptual Deficits, Perceptual Handicaps An inability of the brain to order correctly or use effectively the data one perceives. These difficulties stem from damage to the parts of the brain which control movements, vision, audition, and impulses. Often doctors can find no evidence of damage to the central nervous system, so they cannot say that it is damage or injury, but the constellation of difficulties that the child shows tells the doctor that there are perceptual deficits. When the child cannot perceive effectively, he cannot sort out and screen the stimuli he is receiving, so he has a hard time making sense out of his environment.

Perseveration The persistent repetition or seemingly senseless continuance of an activity that the child cannot stop when he wants to because he's not able to put on the brakes and/or does not realize what he's doing. Also manifested in the child's problems of shifting from one activity to another, accepting changes in routine, and postponing activities.

Processing Difficulty The inability to integrate, organize, and make sense out of sensory information. It is organizational rather than interpretational breakdown.

Receptive Language The ability to comprehend the spoken word.

Scatter Performance Uneven development, which produces strong abilities and high performance in certain areas, failures or poor performance in others. One's total performance appears erratic, unpredictable, and inconsistent, known as *scatter* or *scattered achievement*.

Sequencing Difficulty The inability to remember a series in its proper order; for instance, letters in a word, days of the week, months of the year, following directions involving more than one action.

Soft Signs In neurological terms, a lack of evidence of brain damage in a child, but specific learning disabilities seem to exist because of the constellation of difficulties the child experiences (poor attention span, uneven performance, distractibility, poor coordination, time and space problems, impulsivity, and perseveration).

Structure Carefully planned, guided, sequenced space or activity. Not synonymous with rigidity, it encourages growth.

Tactile Perception The ability and the process by which the brain organizes the data perceived through touch and makes effective use of it. When a child has tactile perceptual difficulties, he

	cannot tactually discriminate textures and shapes and therefore cannot identify what he touches.
Task Analysis	The ability to analyze a task, break it into its components, down to the smallest steps, and know the sequences so a task may be learned step by step.
Vestibular System	The balancing system of the inner ear that regulates the adjustment of body movement to gravity.
Visual Discrimination	The ability to perceive visual differences accurately. The learning disabled child frequently confuses *b*, *d*, *p*, and *q*.
Visual Perception	The ability to understand and put meaning to what one sees.

Appendix 2

Recommended Books

Learning Disabilities

*Alley, Gordon, and Deshler, Donald. *Teaching the Learning Disabled Adolescent: Strategies and Methods*. Denver, Colorado: Love Publishing Company, 1979.

Anderson, Camilla. *Jan, My Brain-damaged Daughter*. Portland, Oregon: Durham Press, 1963. Story of a psychiatrist's daughter, her unusually severe health and learning problems, her problems relating to others, overreactions, and frustrations.

Anderson, L. E. *Helping the Adolescent with a Hidden Handicap*. San Rafael, California: Academic Therapy Publications, 1970.

Banas, Norma, and Willis, I. H. *Success Begins with Understanding*. San Rafael, California: Academic Therapy Publications, 1972. A guide to prescriptive teaching programs illustrated with the Wechsler Intelligence Scale for Children and the Detroit Test of Learning Aptitude.

Benton, Arthur L., and Pearl, David. *Dyslexia An Appraisal of Current Knowledge*. New York: Oxford University Press, 1978.

Brutten, Milton; Richardson, Sylvia; and Mangel, Charles. *Something's Wrong with My Child*. New York: Harcourt Brace Jovanovich, 1973. For parents, about children with learning disabilities; mentions the social problems stemming from learning disabilities.

Bush, Wilma Jo, and Waugh, Kenneth W. *Diagnosing Learning Disabilities*, 2d ed. Columbus, Ohio: Charles E. Merrill, 1976. Excellent introduction to diagnosis.

Clements, Sam D. *Some Aspects of the Characteristics, Management and Education of the Child with Learning Disabilities (Minimal Brain Dysfunction)*, 2d. ed. Little Rock, Arkansas: Arkansas Association for Children with Learning Disabilities, 1969.

Cratty, Bryant J. *Active Learning: Games to Enhance Academic Abilities*. Englewood Cliffs, New Jersey: Prentice-Hall, 1971.

*Critchley, Macdonald. *The Dyslexic Child*. London: William Heinemann Medical Books, Ltd., 1969.

*Asterisked entries are especially recommended.

239

Critchley, Macdonald and Eileen. *Dyslexia Defined*. Sussex: Charles Thomas, 1978.

*Crosby, R. M. N. *The Waysiders*. New York: Delacorte Press, 1968. Excellent for the lay reader, describing problems of learning disabled children. Crosby is a neurologist and is excellent on diagnosis, not remediation.

Cruickshank, W. M. *Brain-Injured Child in Home, School, and Community*. Syracuse: Syracuse University Press, 1967.

*Cruickshank, William M. *A Teaching Method for Brain-injured and Hyperactive Children*. New York: Syracuse University Press, 1965. Classic text. One of the first, most helpful, descriptive books.

Cruickshank, W. M. and Hallahan, D. P., eds. *Perceptual and Learning Disabilities in Children*. Vol. 1, *Psychoeducational Practices*. Syracuse: Syracuse University Press, 1975.

Ellingson, Careth. *The Shadow Children*. Chicago: Professional Press, 1967. A good beginning for lay reader. Describes learning disabled children and reviews their problems.

Frierson, E. D., and Barbe, W. B., eds. *Educating Children with Learning Disabilities*. New York: Appleton-Century-Crofts, 1967. Comprehensive textbook including articles by Clements, Strauss, Myklebust, Eisenberg, and others.

*Gearheart, William R. *Learning Disabilities: Educational Strategies*, 2d. ed. St. Louis: C. V. Mosby Co., 1977.

_____. *Teaching the Learning Disabled*. St. Louis: C. V. Mosby Co., 1976.

Gearheart, William R. and Weishahn, Mel W. *The Handicapped Student in the Regular Classroom*, 2d ed. St. Louis: C. V. Mosby Co., 1980.

Goldberg, Herman K., and Schiffman, Albert B. *Dyslexia—Problems of Reading Disabilities*. New York: Grune & Stratton, 1972.

Gordon, Sol. *Living Fully: A Guide for Young People with a Handicap, Their Parents, Their Teachers and Professionals*. New York: John Day Publishing Co., 1975.

Hallahan, D. P., and Kauffman, J. M. *Introduction to Learning Disabilities: A Psycho-Behavioral Approach*. Englewood Cliffs, N.J.: Prentice-Hall, 1976.

*Hammill, Donald, and Bartel, Nettie. *Teaching Children with Learning and Behavior Problems*, 2nd ed. Boston: Allyn & Bacon, 1978. A good handbook for teachers of learning disabled children.

Johnson, Doris, and Mykelbust, Helmer. *Learning Disabilities: Educational Principles and Practices*. New York: Grune & Stratton, 1967.

*Jones, Beverly, and Hart, Jane. *Where's Hannah? A Handbook for Parents and Teachers of Children with Learning Disorders*. New York: Hart Publishing Co., 1968.

*Kephart, Newell. *The Slow Learner in the Classroom*, 2nd ed. Columbus, Ohio: Charles E. Merrill, 1971. Classic textbook.

*Kronick, Doreen. *A Word or Two About Learning Disabilities*. San

Rafael, California: Academic Therapy Publications, 1973. Social-psychological implications of learning disabilities for child and family. Discusses the socialization process, the family in the community, and recreation and camping for learning disabled children.

_____, ed. *Learning Disabilities: Its Implication to a Responsible Society*. Chicago: Developmental Learning Materials, 1969. A fine, broad view of learning disabilities for laymen and professionals with an outstanding chapter by Sol Gordon on the psychological problems of adolescents and a comprehensive look at learning problems associated with time-space.

*Lerner, Janet W. *Children with Learning Disabilities: Theories, Diagnosis and Teaching Strategies*, 2d ed. Boston: Houghton Mifflin, 1976. Excellent presentation of theoretical approaches to learning disabilities: sensory-motor, perceptual-motor, perceptual-linguistic-cognitive; also stresses role of maturation.

*Levy, Harold B. *Square Pegs, Round Holes: The Learning Disabled Child in the Classroom and at Home*. Boston: Little, Brown, 1973. Excellent beginning book for parents, as well as professionals to read; gives solid understanding of the many facets of learning disabilities.

Lewis, Richard S. *The Other Child Grows Up*. New York: Times Books, 1977.

*Lewis, Richard S.; Strauss, Alfred A.; and Lehtinen, Laura E. *The Other Child: The Brain-injured Child*. New York: Grune & Stratton, 1969. Outstanding book for laymen details some of the conceptual confusions of learning disabled youngsters and describes fully their learning problems.

*Lynn, Roa, *Learning Disabilities: An Overview of Theories, Approaches, and Politics*. New York: The Free Press, 1979.

McCarthy, James, and McCarthy, Joan. *Learning Disabilities*. Boston: Allyn & Bacon, 1969. A good guide for understanding the broader field of learning disabilities.

Mercer, Cecil D. *Children and Adolescents with Learning Disabilities*. Columbus, Ohio: Charles E. Merrill Publishing Co., 1979.

Money, John. *The Disabled Reader—Education for the Dyslexic Child*. Baltimore: Johns Hopkins Press, 1966. A comprehensive look at reading disorders; the last section details specific remedial techniques.

Monroe, George E. *Understanding Perceptual Differences*. Champaign, Illinois: Stripes Publishing Co., 1967.

Myklebust, Helmer R., ed. *Progress in Learning Disabilities*. 2 vols. New York: Grune & Stratton, 1968, 1971. An in-depth exploration of learning disabilities, including neurological foundations, diagnostic approaches, and early childhood education.

Orton, Samuel Torrey. *Reading, Writing and Speech Problems in Children*. New York: W. W. Norton, 1937. One of the earliest books in the field.

*Osman, Betty R. *Learning Disabilities: A Family Affair*. New York: Random House, 1979.

*Siegel, Ernest. *The Exceptional Child Grows Up*. New York: E. P. Dutton, 1974. Outstanding book gives guidelines for understanding and helping the brain-injured adolescent and young adult.

_____. *Helping the Brain-injured Child*. New York: Association for Brain Injured Children, 1962. Outstanding book for the lay reader and the professional, giving very concrete aids and practical advice on helping the children educationally and behaviorally.

_____; Siegel, Rita; and Siegel, Paul. *Help for the Lonely Child*. New York: E. P. Dutton, 1978.

Simpson, Eileen. *A Personal Account of Victory Over Dyslexia*. Boston: Houghton Mifflin, 1979.

Smith, Sally L. *No Easy Answers—The Learning Disabled Child*. Washington, D.C.: National Institute for Mental Health, 1978. Introduction to the world of the learning disabled youngster for a lay audience.

Stock, Claudette. *Minimal Brain Dysfunction Child: Some Clinical Manifestations, Definitions, Descriptions and Redmediation Approaches*. Boulder, Colorado: Pruett Press, 1969. Excellent concrete descriptions of learning and behavior problems of learning disabled children and remedial procedures.

U.S. Department of Health, Education and Welfare. *Learning Disabilities Due to Minimal Brain Dysfunction*. Publication 1646. Washington, D.C.: Government Printing Office, 1977. Pamphlet clearly describes problems of the learning disabled. Available for forty-five cents from the Superintendent of Documents at the GPO.

*Vallett, Robert D. *Remediation of Learning Disabilities*. Belmont, California: Fearon Publications, 1967. Looseleaf notebook of activities for teachers.

Wallace, G., and Kauffman, J. M. *Teaching Children with Learning Problems*, 2d ed. Columbus, Ohio: Charles E. Merrill, 1978.

Warner, Joan Marie. *Learning Disabilities: Activities for Remediation*. Danville, Illinois: Inter-State Printers & Publishers, 1973.

Weiss, Helen, and Weiss, Martin. *Home Is a Learning Place: A Parent's Guide to Learning Disabilities*. Boston: Little, Brown, 1976.

*Wender, Paul H. *The Hyperactive Child*. New York: Crown Publishers, 1973. An excellent introduction for parents.

_____. *Minimal Brain Dysfunction in Children*. New York: John Wiley & Sons, 1971. Discussion of causes of minimal brain dysfunction covers medical and biochemical aspects; includes a good section on management and usefulness of medication for certain children.

Wiederholt, J. Lee, Hammill, Donald D., and Brown, Virginia. *The Resource Teacher: A Guide to Effective Practices*. Boston: Allyn and Bacon, 1978.

Reading

Auckerman, Robert C. *Approaches to Beginning Reading*. New York: John Wiley & Sons, 1971. Annotated compendium of methods, materials, background history, and related research.

*Bloomfield, Leonard, and Barnhart, Clarence. *Let's Read: A Linguist's Approach*. Bronxville, New York: Clarence L. Barnhart, 1961. A structured way to teach reading to learning disabled children.

Bond, Guy, and Tinker, Miles A. *Reading Difficulties: Their Diagnosis and Correction*. New York: Appleton-Century-Crofts, 1967.

Chall, Jeanne. *Learning to Read, the Great Debate*. New York: McGraw-Hill, 1967. An excellent introduction that provides an analysis of all previous research on reading methods.

Dawson, Mildred A., comp. *Teaching Word Recognition Skills*. Newark, Delaware: International Reading Association, 1971. Collection of articles about approaches to word recognition skills: the use of phonics, generalizations, sight vocabulary, word analysis, and visual discrimination.

Dechant, Emerald, ed. *Detection and Correction of Reading Difficulties*. New York: Appleton-Century-Crofts, 1971.

de Hirsch, Katrina. *Predicting Reading Failure*. New York: Harper & Row, 1966. Excellent presentation of screening procedures and reading readiness prerequisites.

Durkin, Dolores. *Strategies for Identifying Words: A Workbook for Teachers and Those Preparing to Teach*. Boston: Allyn & Bacon, 1976.

Earle, Richard A. *Teaching Reading and Mathematics*. Newark, Delaware: International Reading Association, 1976.

Engelmann, Siegfried. *Preventing Failure in the Primary Grades*. Chicago: Science Research Associates, 1969.

Herber, Harold. *Teaching Reading in Content Areas*. Englewood Cliffs, New Jersey: Prentice-Hall, 1970. Guidebook for elementary and secondary school teachers of basic subjects. Discusses methods of teaching learning skills along with content.

Kaluger, George, and Kolson, Clifford J. *Reading and Learning Disabilities*, 2d ed. Columbus, Ohio: Charles E. Merrill, 1978.

Language and Learning to Read: What Teachers Should Know About Language. Edited by Richard E. Hodges and E. Hugh Rudorf. Boston: Houghton Mifflin, 1972. Report of conference held in conjunction with the annual meeting of the International Reading Association.

Language by Ear and by Eye: The Relationships Between Speech and Reading. Edited by James F. Kavanagh and Ignatius G. Mattingly. Cambridge, Massachusetts: The MIT Press, 1972. Conference proceedings.

*Rawson, Margaret B. *Developmental Language Disability: Adult Accomplishments of Dyslexic Boys.* Baltimore: Johns Hopkins Press, 1968.

Robinson, H. Alan. *Teaching Reading and Study Strategies: The Content Areas.* Boston: Allyn & Bacon, 1975.

Roswell, Florence, and Natchez, Gladys. *Reading Disability: Diagnosis and Treatment.* New York: Basic Books, 1964. Textbook.

Russell, David H. *Children Learn to Read.* New York: Ginn & Co., 1949.

Spache, George D. *Toward Better Reading.* Champaign, Illinois: Garrard, 1963.

Stauffer, Russell G.; Abrams, Jules C.; and Pikulski, John J. *Diagnosis, Correction and Prevention of Reading Disabilities.* New York: Harper & Row, 1978.

_____ . *Directing Reading Maturity as a Cognitive Process.* New York: Harper & Row, 1969.

_____ . *Teaching Reading as a Thinking Process.* New York: Harper & Row, 1969.

Stern, Catherine, and Gould, Toni. *Children Discover Reading.* New York: Singer and Co., 1963.

Vogel, Susan Ann. *Syntactic Abilities in Normal and Dyslexic Children.* Baltimore: University Park Press, 1975.

Wilson, Robert M. *Diagnostic and Remedial Reading for Classroom and Clinic.* Columbus, Ohio: Charles E. Merrill, 1972.

Math

Ashlock, Robert. *Error Patterns in Computation.* Columbus, Ohio: Charles E. Merrill, 1972.

Collier, Calhoun C., and Leech, Harold H. *Teaching Mathematics in the Modern Elementary School.* London: The Macmillan Company, 1969.

Copeland, Richard. *How Children Learn Mathematics: Teaching Implications of Piaget's Research,* 2d ed. London: The Macmillan Company, 1974.

Ginsberg, Herbert. *Children's Arithmetic: The Learning Process.* New York: Van Nostrand, 1977.

Golick, Margie. *Deal Me In!* New York: Jeffrey Norton Publishers Inc., 1973.

*Herold, Persis J. *Math Teaching Handbook.* Newton, Massachusetts: Selective Educational Equipment, 1978. An extremely practical guide for teaching mathematics to learning disabled children with "hands-on" materials.

Lovell, Kennedy. *The Growth of Understanding in Mathematics: Kindergarten Through Grade Three.* New York: Holt, Rinehart and Winston, 1971.

Payne, Joseph N., ed. *Mathematics Learning in Early Childhood,* (37th Yearbook). Reston, Virginia: National Council of Teachers of Mathematics, 1975. A collection of papers on teaching math to slow learners; a useful reference.

Piaget, Jean. *A Child's Conception of Number.* New York: W. W. Norton and Co., 1965.

Piaget, Jean, and Inhelder, B. *The Child's Conception of Space.* New York: W. W. Norton and Co., 1967.

Reisman, Frederika. *A Guide to the Diagnostic Teaching of Arithmetic.* Columbus, Ohio: Charles E. Merrill, 1972.

Stern, Catherine, and Stern, Margaret. *Children Discover Arithmetic,* 2d ed. New York: Harper & Row, 1971. A detailed discussion of the use of the Stern materials.

General Development

*Beadle, Muriel. *A Child's Mind: How Children Learn During the Critical Years from Birth to Age Five.* New York: Doubleday, 1971. A good introduction to normal stages of learning in the early years.

*Beery, Keith E., ed. The Dimensions in Early Learning Series. San Rafael, California: Dimensions Publishing Co., 1968. Fifteen outstanding pamphlets, fairly technical, for professionals: *The Essentials of Teaching; Motor and Haptic Learning; Writing; Creativity; Aesthetics; Citizenship; Temporal Learning; Concepts; Reading; Verbal Learning; Visual Learning; Auditory Learning; Attending and Responding; Arithmetic; Humanity.*

*Fraiberg, Selma H. *The Magic Years: Understanding and Handling the Problems of Early Childhood.* New York: Charles Scribner's Sons, 1959. Outstanding book that tunes into children's fears and how they learn to cope with the world and themselves.

Smith, Sally Liberman. *Nobody Said It's Easy.* New York: Macmillan, 1965. A practical guide to feelings and relationships for young people and their parents.

Stone, Joseph, and Church, Joseph. *Childhood and Adolescence.* New York: Random House, 1975. The psychology of the growing person.

Sensory-Motor

Arena, John I., ed. *Teaching Through Sensory-Motor Experiences.* San Rafael, California: Academic Therapy Publications, 1969. Excellent resource for teachers.

Ayers, Jean. *Sensory Integration and Learning Disorders.* Los Angeles: Western Psychological Services, 1972. Brilliant but difficult; for persons with intensive background in the field.

Barsch, Ray H. *Enriching Perception and Cognition.* Seattle: Special and Child Publications, 1968. Difficult reading. Barsch is a neurologist and stresses the role of the body in learning.

Bush, Wilma Jo, and Giles, Marion T. *Aids to Psycholinguistic Teaching,* 2d ed. Columbus, Ohio: Charles E. Merrill, 1977.

Keller, Helen. *The Story of My Life.* New York: Doubleday, 1954.

*Van Witsen, Betty. *Perceptual Training Activities Handbook.* New York: Teacher's College Press, 1967. Excellent for teacher or tutor.

Language

Britton, James. *Language and Learning.* Coral Gables, Florida: University of Miami Press, 1970. A general discussion of language and language development in relationship to learning.

Chukovsky, Kornei. *From Two to Five.* Berkeley: University of California Press, 1963. Excellent, warm introduction to normal language development.

Farb, Peter. *Word Play: What Happens When People Talk.* New York: Alfred A. Knopf, 1974. Provocative book analyzes language according to theories of play and games; shows how personalities are shaped by language.

Greene, Harry, and Petty, Walter. *Developing Language Skills in the Elementary Schools.* Boston: Allyn & Bacon, 1971. Good chapters on written expression, handwriting, and spelling with expectations at grade level for development of written expression.

*Hall, Edward T. *The Silent Language.* New York: Doubleday, 1959. The language subtleties and cultural values that affect our daily lives.

_____ . *The Hidden Dimension.* Garden City, New York: Doubleday, 1966.

Hodges, Richard, and Rudolph, Hugh. *Language and Learning to Read: What Teachers Should Know About Language.* Boston: Houghton Mifflin, 1972. A collection of papers on the significance of language to the development of reading skills.

Vygotsky, L. S. *Thought and Language.* Cambridge, Massachusetts: The MIT Press, 1962. Compare with Piaget. Demanding but provocative.

*Wiig, Elisabeth H., and Semel, Eleanor Messing. *Language Disabilities in Children and Adolescents.* Columbus, Ohio: Charles E. Merrill, 1976.

Diagnostic Testing

Anastasia, Anne. *Psychological Testing.* New York: Macmillan, 1968.

Buros, O. K., ed. *Seventh Mental Measurements Yearbook.* Highland Park, New Jersey: Gryphon Press, 1972.

*Bush, Wilma Jo, and Waugh, Kenneth W. *Diagnosing Learning Disabilities,* 2d ed. Columbus, Ohio: Charles E. Merrill, 1976.

Di Leo, Joseph H. *Children's Drawings as Diagnostic Aids.* New York: Brunner/Mazel Publications, 1973.

*Frierson, Edward C., and Barbe, Walter. *Educating Children with

Learning Disabilities. New York: Appleton-Century-Crofts, 1967. Chapter 3, "Diagnosing Learning Disorders," is particularly important.

Hirsch, Ernest. *The Troubled Adolescent As He Emerges on Psychological Tests*. New York: International Universities Press, 1970.

Ingram, Cregg F. *Fundamentals of Educational Assessment*. New York: D. Van Nostrand Company, 1980.

Johnson, Orval G., and Bommarito, James W. *Tests and Measurements in Child Development: A Handbook*. San Francisco: Jossey-Bass, 1971.

Paraskevopoulos, John N., and Kirk, Samuel. *The Development and Psychometric Characteristics of the Revised Illinois Test of Psycholinguistic Abilities*. Urbana: University of Illinois Press, 1969.

Perlman, Suzanne. *Intervention Through Psychological and Educational Evaluation: Progress in Learning Disabilities*. New York: Grune & Stratton, 1975.

Salvia, John, and Ysseldyke, James E. *Assessment in Special and Remedial Education*. Boston: Houghton Mifflin, 1978.

Samuda, Ronald J. *Psychology Testing of American Minorities*. New York: Dodd, Mead, 1975.

Wallace, Gerald, and Larsen, Stephen. *Educational Assessment of Learning Problems: Testing for Teaching*. Boston: Allyn & Bacon, 1978.

Wiig, Elisabeth H., and Semel, Eleanor Messing. *Language Assessment and Intervention for the Learning Disabled*. Columbus, Ohio: Charles E. Merrill, 1980.

Educational Theory

*Bruner, Jerome S. *Toward a Theory of Instruction*. New York: W. W. Norton, 1966. Need for and how to teach structure of school subjects.

*_____ . *The Process of Education*. New York: Random House, 1960. Need for teaching structure.

Furth, Hans G., and Wachs, H. *Thinking Goes to School: Piaget's Theory in Practice*. New York: Oxford University Press, 1974. Examines need for stimulating reason and thinking in depth and gives concrete practical activities.

Ginsburg, Herbert, and Opper, Sylvia. *Piaget's Theory of Intellectual Development: An Introduction*. Englewood Cliffs, New Jersey: Prentice-Hall, 1969. Developmental approach.

Gorman, Richard M. *Discovering Piaget: A Guide for Teachers*. Columbus, Ohio: Charles E. Merrill, 1972.

Montessori, Maria. *The Secret of Childhood*. New York: Ballantine Books, 1972.

*Piaget, Jean. *The Language and Thought of the Child*. London: Routledge and Kegan Paul, 1948.

*Pulaski, Mary Ann Spencer. *Understanding Piaget: An Introduction to Children's Cognitive Development.* New York: Harper & Row, 1971. Very good presentation of Piaget's maturational stages.

Principles of Education

Ashton-Warner, Sylvia. *Teacher.* New York: Simon & Schuster, 1963.

Eble, Kenneth. *A Perfect Education.* New York: Macmillan, 1966.

Glasser, William. *Schools Without Failure.* New York: Harper & Row, 1969.

*Holt, John. *How Children Fail.* New York: Pitman, 1964.

*Lane, Howard. *On Educating Human Beings.* Chicago: Follett Publishing Co., 1964.

*Long, Nicholas; Morse, William; and Newman, Ruth. *Conflict in the Classroom,* 3d ed. Belmont, California: Wadsworth Publishing Co., 1976.

Mok, Paul P. *Pushbutton Parents and the Schools.* New York: Dell, 1964.

Silberman, Charles E. *Crisis in the Classroom.* New York: Random House, 1970.

Public Law 94–142

Common Sense from Closer Look. Washington, D.C.: Parent's Campaign for Handicapped Children and Youth, 1978.

Education for All Handicapped Children: A Study Report. Washington, D.C.: National Education Association, 1978.

Lerner, Janet, Dawson, David, and Horvath, Lester. *Cases in Learning and Behavior Problems—A Guide to Individualized Education Programs.*

Martin, Reed. *Educating Handicapped Children: The Legal Mandate.* Bellevue, Washington: Edmark Association, 1979.

Meade, James G., Ed. *The Rights of Parents and the Responsibilities of Schools.* Cambridge: Educators Publishing Service, 1978.

Moore, Jean J., and Mason, Doris M. *Information Packet on Surrogate Parents.* Washington, D.C.: Bureau of Education for the Handicapped, HEW, 1978.

University of Richmond Law Review. *Symposium: Children and the Law.* Richmond, Virginia: University of Richmond Law Review Association, Vol. 13, No. 4, Summer 1979.

Appendix 3

Recommended Films

9 Educational Films
Produced by Sally L. Smith, Director of the Lab School of Washington in collaboration with Joel Jacobson, independent filmmaker. Available through The Lab School of Washington, 4759 Reservoir Road, N.W., Washington, D.C. 20007.

Films One through Five: **Learning for a Lifetime:**
The Academic Club Method

The Academic Club method was developed by Sally L. Smith. It has been used to teach many students, with and without learning disabilities, in public and private schools, and in large and small groups. Any teacher can lead a club. The two elements needed are systematic objectives and creativity. Any subject can be taught through the club approach. The first five films give a teacher the necessary tools.

Part One: *Introduction*

In academic clubs students who have failed in regular classrooms are able to learn using the love of pretend and ingenuity that are a natural part of their play. Learning in a club involves the child's body, his mind, and all of his senses. Every aspect of a club is highly structured, including entry into a club, seating arrangements, formalized rituals, and approach to material. Under the cover of Secret Agents or Pirates, they acquire reading readiness skills. Students study history, geography, and civics as Cavemen, Greek Gods, Knights and Ladies, and Renaissance Councillors. (27½ minutes)

Part Two: *The Setting Up of a Club*

With a $10 investment in cloth, construction paper, posters, and tape, a classroom is turned into Mount Olympus where 12 learning-disabled children study history, geography and literature as members of a Greek Gods club.
 In the Greek Gods club, students act out the meaning of democ-

racy as practiced in Athens (the citizens vote) and tyranny as practiced in Sparta (the king orders). In the process they gain insights into a period of history and an understanding of an abstract concept.

An entirely different type of club is also shown in session—a Carnival Club in which novel games like "Guess the Grams" are used to teach mathematics. (27½ minutes)

Part Three: *Developing Reading Readiness Skills*

What skills does a child need to read? First academic club teachers answer this question. Then they gather in "brainstorming" sessions to invent and prepare club activities that will teach specific reading readiness skills within a particular dramatic framework.

Pirates point north, north-east, north-west from their ship; Keystone Cops march left, right, left, right, left. Both activities help students to orient themselves in space. Secret Agents, wearing individual identity cards, strengthen their powers of auditory and visual perception by decoding "secret" sound and light messages. Storekeepers, dressed in aprons, sort and classify their wares to develop a sense of organization and order. (27½ minutes)

Part Four: *Teaching History, Geography and Civics*

Lab School Students advance through six periods of history from 6-year-old Cavemen to 12-year-old American Revolutionaries and Industrialists. Knights of the Middle Ages become alchemists. Renaissance Councillors look for examples of perspective in art of the masters and then look at each other in perspective on a city street. Ritual, decor, and atmosphere are created to encourage students to think and to feel as cavemen, knights, guildsmen, or revolutionaries.

Students absorb great ideas and complex theories that are rarely taught to elementary school children while, at the same time, they acquire the skills needed to overcome their learning disabilities. (27 minutes)

Part Five: *The Teacher as Club Leader*

A public school teacher turns her large third grade class into a Smokey the Bear Club. Her students dissect a chicken as part of their study of nature, science, and animals. A Lab School teacher goes step by step through the setting up of an African Club to teach reading, math, geography, and history. Among the numerous other clubs shown in action are the Keystone Cops who acquire decision making skills by acting out the arrival of the cops to break up a family quarrel. (25 minutes)

Film Six: Tools for Learning: An Artist Teaches Academic Skills Through Woodwork

In the Lab School's woodwork shop, sculptor and artist Bert Schmutzhart and his students measure, saw, drill, hammer, and paint. The students concentrate on the product—a chair, a table, a boat, a musical instrument. The sculptor concentrates on the learning process.

A young boy and girl are introduced to anatomy as they build chairs to fit their own bodies. Another child learns about vibrations of sounds as she makes her own instrument. Two boys build a rowboat and learn about water displacement and buoyancy—an introduction to the principles of physics.

The important role of the arts and artists in elementary education is demonstrated. (27½ minutes)

Film Seven: **Linking Sound and Symbol:**
A Musician Teaches Reading Readiness

Anne Guiles, music teacher at the Lab School, uses innovative, easy-to-reproduce, home-made games to teach auditory and visual reading readiness skills to children, ages 6 to 12.

In daily music classes students learn to link a sequence of sounds to a sequence of moves on a game board. They link sound and color; they link sound and shape; and finally they link sound and symbol.

The techniques shown in this film have helped learning disabled children, but nursery school, kindergarten, and first grade students in regular classrooms can also profit from the similar reading readiness activities. (26½ minutes)

Film Eight: **Movement in Learning:**
A Dancer Teaches Academic Readiness

Louis Tupler, Lab School dance teacher and owner of a professional dance company, illustrates the ways in which learning disabled children are taught through dance to organize the movement of their bodies, to remember sequences, to follow directions, and to integrate several activities.

The film also shows the work of Lab School perceptual motor therapist Sheila Weiss who teaches individual children to isolate the parts of their body, to differentiate left from right, to cross the body midline and to integrate several motor activities.

Lab School teachers talk about learning disabilities and the important role of the body in learning. They note the relationship of organizing the body to organization of the mind affecting reading, writing, spelling, and arithmetic. (38 minutes)

Film Nine: **Passport to Literature—The Media Center:**
Listening, Understanding, and Acquiring Language
Skills

At the Lab School a love of literature is nurtured and sustained through regular and systematic use of the Library of Congress Talking Books and homemade tapes. As the student hears a story on tape, he also looks at the book and often touches concrete materials associated with the story. Later the student reports what he has heard—the who, what, where, why and how of the story.

Antoinette Mayer, Director of the Lab School Media Center, guides her students through these oral book reports. All Lab School children learn to locate their books on a map and on a time line. Eventually the students are also able to categorize and compare books and finally to discuss them with their peers. Methods of teaching vocabulary and of developing a child's memory are demonstrated by Mrs. Mayer. The film is narrated by a Lab School teenager who is now a reader and who recalls his feelings about the Media Center. (25 minutes)

Adolescence and Learning Disabilities

Describes the tasks of adolescence and relates them to the learning disabled adolescent.

Color/Sound, 40 minutes. Lawren Productions, P.O. Box 1542, Burlingame, California 94010.

Anyone Can

Teacher training guide for a program of motor development.

Sound/Color, 30 minutes. Bradley Wright Films, 309 N. Duane Avenue, San Gabriel, California 91775.

Bright Boy: Bad Scholar

Illustrates the diagnosis and treatment of children with learning disabilities.

Sound/Black and white, 28 minutes. Contemporary Films, McGraw-Hill, 330 W. 42d Street, New York, New York 10036.

If a Boy Can't Learn

Deals with a seventeen-year-old high school student with a learning disability and how he was helped to make progress.

Sound/Color, 28 minutes. Lawren Productions, P.O. Box 1542, Burlingame, California 94010.

I'm Not Too Famous At It

Shows the importance of knowing what children can and cannot do and exhibits the many and varied behavioral problems associated with learning disabilities.

Sound/Black and white, 28 minutes. Contemporary Films, McGraw-Hill, 330 W. 42d Street, New York, New York 10036.

I'm Really Trying

A segment of the "Marcus Welby, M.D.," television show about a learning disabled boy.

Sound/Color, 52 minutes. ACLD, 220 Brownsville Road, Pittsburgh, Pennsylvania 15210.

The Learning Series

Four films showing graphic episodes of children attempting to cope with life tasks for which they are not ready.

Sound/Black and white, 28 minutes. Contemporary Films, McGraw-Hill, 330 W. 42d Street, New York, New York 10036.

Thursday's Children

Presents three major areas: characteristics (especially sensory-motor problems), diagnostic evaluation, and educational programming.

Sound/Color, 32 minutes. Swank Motion Pictures, 201 South Jefferson Avenue, St. Louis, Missouri 63166.

A Walk in Another Pair of Shoes

Narrator Tennessee Ernie Ford explains to children some of the problems encountered by learning disabled children.

Sound/Color filmstrip, 18½ minutes. CANHC Film Distribution, P.O. Box 1526 Will Rogers Street, Los Angeles, California 96405.

Why Billy Couldn't Learn

Demonstrates problems, diagnosis, and education of children with neurological handicaps.

Sound/Color, 40 minutes. California Association for Neurological Handicapped Children, 6742 Will Rogers Street, Los Angeles, California 96405.

The Arts Central to Learning

Produced by Sally L. Smith, Director of the Lab School of the Kingsbury Center, a slide/tape documentary of the Lab School program emphasizing the arts.

Sound/Color, 30 minutes. National Committee, Arts for the Handicapped, 1701 K Street, Washington, D.C. 20006.

Albert Einstein: The Education of a Genius

Portrays Einstein's uniquely strong mode of thought; illustrates the importance of matching educational programming to individual differences. 44 minutes. Films for the Humanities, P.O. Box 2053, Princeton, N.J. 08540.

Early Recognition of Learning Disabilities

Shows young learning disabled pupils; interviews parents and teachers. 30 minutes. National Audiovisual Center, National Archives and Records Service, Washington, D.C. 20409.

Appendix 4

Recommended Professional Journals

Academic Therapy
20 Commercial Boulevard
Novato, California 94947

Interdisciplinary journal directed to an international audience of teachers, special teachers, parents, and specialists working in the field of reading, learning, and communication disabilities. All ages. Methods of identification, diagnosis, and remediation emphasized. Issued six times per year (September, October, December, February, March, and June).

Bulletin of the Orton Society
8415 Bellona Lane
Towson, Maryland 21204

Official bulletin of the Orton Society, a nonprofit scientific and educational organization for the study and treatment of children with specific language disability (dyslexia). All ages, international in scope. Many useful reprints available. Issued once per year.

Exceptional Children

Covers all of the areas of exceptionalities in children. It presents a variety of articles, including many on reading and language, for different types of children. Alternates every other month with *Teaching Exceptional Children*.

The Exceptional Parent
P.O. Box 101
Boston, Massachusetts 02117

A reassuring journal for parents; information and detailed articles. Issued six times per year.

The Journal of Learning Disabilities
101 East Ontario Street
Chicago, Illinois 60611

Multidisciplinary; primarily concerned with learning disabilities (diagnosis and treatment). All ages, international in scope. Theoretical and practical contributions. Issued ten times per year (June-July and August-September combined).

Journal of Reading
International Reading Association
800 Barksdale Road
Newark, Delaware 19711

Primarily directed to secondary teachers, the journal also concerns itself with older poor readers and motivational techniques. Its purpose is to exchange information and opinions regarding reading skills. Issued eight times per year (October through May).

The Journal of Special Education
Buttonwood Farms
3515 Woodhaven Road
Philadelphia, Pennsylvania 19154

Primarily devoted to all types of handicapped children in a special setting, the journal contains relevant material for remedial reading approaches. Issued four times per year.

Learning Disability Quarterly
Council for Exceptional Children
1920 Association Drive
Reston, Virginia 22091

Primarily research studies in learning disabilities directed to professionals. Issued four times per year.

Perceptions: The Newsletter for Parents
of Children with Learning Disabilities
P.O. Box 142
Millburn, New Jersey 07041

Published monthly, with practical suggestions and reports on the field directed to parents.

Teaching Exceptional Children
Publication of the Council for Exceptional Children
1920 Association Drive
Reston, Virginia 22091

Directed to the special class practitioner in both elementary and high school. Issued four times per year.

Appendix 5

Some National Legal, Advocacy and Service Organizations

American Coalition of Citizens with Disabilities
1346 Connecticut Avenue, N.W.
Washington, D.C. 20036

Association for Children with Learning Disabilities (ACLD)
4156 Library Road
Pittsburgh, Pennsylvania 15234

For parents, teachers, and other professionals. Provides needed information and support, follows the latest educational and medical research, and supports legislation for special classes and trained teachers in the field.

Closer Look
Parents' Campaign for Handicapped Children and Youth
Post Office Box 1492
Washington, D.C. 20013

A national information center for parents and professionals. Provides practical advice on how to find educational programs and other kinds of special services for handicapped children and youth.

Center for Law and Education
Gutman Library
6 Appian Way
Cambridge, Massachusetts 02138
(617) 495-4666

Primarily a research and information service for attorneys.

Children's Defense Fund
1520 New Hampshire Avenue, N.W.
Washington, D.C. 20036
(202) 483-1470

Not a service organization or a source of low cost legal service in most cases but will accept significant cases and conduct litigation. Carries out research, advocacy, and political lobbying. Will answer parent or lawyer questions. List of publications available on request.

Council for Exceptional Children
1920 Association Drive
Reston, Virginia 22091
(703) 620-3660

Developmental Disabilities Law Center
University of Maryland Law School
500 West Baltimore Street
Baltimore, Maryland 21201
(301) 528-6307

Mental Disability Legal Resource Center
American Bar Association
1800 M Street, N.W.
Washington, D.C. 20036
(202) 331-2240

Mental Health Law Project
1220 Nineteenth Street, N.W.
Washington, D.C. 20036
(202) 467-5730

Mexican-American Legal Defense Fund
28 Geary Street
San Francisco, California 94108

While P.L. 94–142 is not a specialization, they will offer consultation on the law as it affects Mexican Americans.

National Center for Law and the Handicapped
1235 North Eddy Street
South Bend, Indiana 46617
(219) 288-4751

Legal action and social science research. Primarily a service directly to lawyers seeking information at the local level but will answer questions for the general public. Publishes *Amicus,* a bi-monthly magazine on law and the handicapped.

National Committee for Citizens in Education
Wild Lake Village Green, Suite 410
Columbia, Maryland 21044
(301) 997-9300
(800) NETWORK = 638-9675 (National Hotline)

Takes parent point of view. Nationwide program to mobilize citizens to improve quality in education. Referral. Handbooks. Training sessions. Advocacy (will go to court in cases with precedent-setting potential). More than 300 affiliates in fourteen states.

National Education Association
1201—16th Street, N.W.
Washington, D.C. 20036

Teachers' organization. Publishes *A Teacher's Reference Guide to P.L. 94-142.*

National Juvenile Law Center
St. Louis University School of Law
3701 Lindell Boulevard
St. Louis, Missouri 63108
(314) 533-8868

National Network of Learning Disabled Adults
P.O. Box 3130
Richardson, Texas 75080

Native American Rights Fund
1506 Broadway
Boulder, Colorado 80302
(303) 447-8760

Has education specialist. Information on P.L. 94–142 and Section 504 as they affect native Americans.

Public Interest Law Center of Philadelphia
1315 Walnut Street
Philadelphia, Pennsylvania 19107
(215) 735-7200

Youth Advocacy Clinic
University of Richmond Law School
Richmond, Virginia 23173
(804) 285-6370

Youth Law Center
693 Mission Street—Second Floor
San Francisco, California 94105
(415) 543-3307

Appendix 6

Description and List of Tests Ordinarily Used to Diagnose Learning Disabled Students

At this time, the various specialists concerned with learning disabilities do not agree on the test battery to be used for diagnosis. Even when only one specific aspect of learning disabilities (such as language or visual perception) is under consideration, there is no consensus among professionals as to which tests are appropriate. Some advisory commissions have been set up to develop diagnostic models that can be tried in the near future.

A typical diagnostic battery includes tests of general intelligence or academic aptitude and tests of academic performance in reading, writing, spelling, composition, and arithmetic. Depending on the age of the child and the nature of the problem, tests of auditory and visual perception, sensory-motor integration, motor development, and language may be given. Young children may have tests designed to measure their general developmental level and academic readiness. Tests or rating scales to measure social and emotional adjustment may also be used.

The purpose of testing is to seek out the youngster's academic potential, identify his academic strengths and weaknesses, and determine how he learns best.

Some of the most frequently used tests are listed here. Never would all of these tests be used for one child and other instruments not mentioned here may be included in an evaluation. Tests which may be used for more than one purpose are listed in several categories. From the tests with which he or she is familiar, the examiner will select those which are most suited to each child's situation. Group aptitude and achievement tests primarily designed to monitor the school progress of nonhandicapped children are not included.

Tests of Cognitive or Intellectual Ability

These tests are used to indicate a youngster's intellectual potential. They measure general intelligence or academic aptitude.

Arthur Adaptation of the Leiter International Performance Scale. (Grace Arthur, C. H. Stoelting, 1950) This is a nonverbal measure designed to assess the intelligence of children 2 to 12 years of age. Appropriate for children who are deaf, hard of hearing, bilingual, nonfluent in English, or language impaired.

Boehm Test of Basic Concepts. (A. E. Boehm, Psychological Corporation, 1971) Measures mastery of space, quantity, time, and other concepts needed for school achievement. Provides norms for kindergarten through grade 2 at different socio-economic levels.

Columbia Mental Maturity Scale. (Burgemeister, Blum, Lorge; Harcourt Brace Jovanovich, 1972) Age range 3½ to 9 years. Measures general reasoning. May be used to assess children who have difficulty reasoning verbally.

Denver Developmental Screening Test. (W. K. Frankenburg and J. B. Dodds, LADOCA Project and Publishing Foundation, 1970) Detects delayed development in children aged two weeks to six years-four months. The test consists of four sections: personal-social, fine motor-adaptive, language, and gross motor. Can be used to screen for children with learning and behavior problems.

Illinois Test of Psycholinguistic Ability. (Kirk, McCarthy and Kirk, U. of Illinois Press, 1969) Assesses ability to process information through auditory and visual channels, ages 2 years to 10 years.

McCarthy Scales of Children's Abilities. (McCarthy, Psychological Corp., 1972) Assesses the general intelligence of children ages 2½ to 8½. Includes verbal, perceptual, motor, memory and quantitative scales.

Raven's Progressive Matrices and Colored Matrices. (J. C. Raven, Psychological Corp., 1960) A nonverbal test (colored matrices) suitable for children aged 6 to 11 years. Older children can take the standard matrices and adults can take the advanced matrices. The subject is asked to select a pattern to complete a design. It is a test of perception and spatial relations, useful for children with language difficulties.

Slosson Intelligence Test. (R. Slosson, Slosson Educational Publications, 1971) Measures primarily verbal ability, pre-school through high school level. Useful for screening since it is short and easy to administer.

Stanford-Binet Intelligence Scale. (L. Terman and M. Merrill, Houghton Mifflin, 1973) Used most often for younger or gifted children, although normed from age 2 to adult. It emphasizes verbal responses but assesses a variety of thinking skills.

Wechsler Adult Intelligence Scale (WAIS). (D. Wechsler, Psychological Corp., 1955) Tests verbal and nonverbal intelligence of adults aged 16 and up.

Wechsler Intelligence Scale for Children—Revised (WISC–R). (D. Wechsler, Psychological Corp., 1974) Designed to test general intelligence, ages 6 to 16. This test has established itself as one of the most useful tools for diagnosing learning disabilities. Verbal, Performance (nonverbal), and Full Scale scores are available. The profiles of subtest scores (as many as 12 subtests may be given) is extremely helpful for diagnostic-prescriptive teaching.

Wechsler Pre-School and Primary Scale of Intelligence (WPPSI). (D. Wechsler, Psychological Corp., 1967) For ages 4 to 6½. This test measures verbal and nonverbal reasoning and perceptual-motor abilities.

System of Multicultural Pluralistic Assessment (SOMPA). (J. Mercer, Psychological Corp., 1978) Not a test but a series of assessment devices using existing tests (WISC–R, Bender) to arrive at a culture fair evaluation of learning potential.

Woodcock-Johnson Psychoeducational Battery, Tests of Cognitive Ability. (R. Woodcock and M. Johnson, N.Y. Times Teaching Resources, 1977) A battery of cognitive tests from pre-school to adult level, measuring broad cognitive ability, verbal ability, reasoning, perceptual speed, and memory. Aptitude scores for reading, math, written language, and general knowledge are also available.

Tests of Information Processing

These tests are designed to give diagnostic information about the kinds of perceptual and communication deficits often found in learning disabled students.

Detroit Tests of Learning Aptitude. (H. Baker and B. Leland, Bobbs-Merrill, 1935) Measures various reasoning, memory and perceptual abilities from age 3 to 14+.

Illinois Test of Psycholinguistic Abilities (ITPA). (S. Kirk, J. McCarthy and W. Kirk, University of Illinois Press, 1969) Delineates abilities and disabilities in processing information through auditory and visual channels, involving receptive, organizing, and expressive processes.

Meeting Street School Screening Test. (P. Hainsworth and M. Siqueland, Easter Seal Society of Rhode Island, Inc., 1969) Screens kindergarten and first-graders for possible learning disabilities in language and sensory-motor areas. A pre-school version is available for pre-kindergarteners.

Slingerland Screening Tests for Identifying Children with Specific Language Disability. (Beth Slingerland, Educators Publishing Service, 1970) Screens for learning disabilities that relate to reading, writing, spelling, speaking, and listening. Emphasis is given to written, as opposed to oral, processes. Includes visual and auditory memory sequencing and discrimination. Available from pre-school through junior high level (Malcomesius test is for grades 6–8).

Visual-Aural Digit-Span Test (VADS). (E. Koppitz, Grune & Stratton, 1978) Assesses sensory-integration skills, using both auditory and visual reception and oral and written expression. Permits assessment of the best channels or modalities for learning.

Developmental or Readiness Tests

These tests are used to determine maturational lag in young children, evaluate academic readiness, and screen for children who may need special help upon entering school.

Boehm Test of Basic Concepts. (A. E. Boehm, Psychological Corp., 1971) Measures mastery of concepts needed for academic work: space, quantity, time, opposites, etc. Provides norms for kindergarten through 2nd grade at three socio-economic levels.

Columbia Mental Maturity Scale. (Burgemeister, Blum and Lorge; Harcourt Brace Jovanovich, 1972) Age range 3½ to 9 years. Measures general reasoning. May be used to assess children who have difficulty reasoning verbally.

Denver Developmental Screening Test. (Frankenburg and Dodds, LADOCA Project and Publishing Foundation, 1970) Detects delayed development in children aged two weeks to six years-four months. The test consists of four sections: personal-social, fine motor-adaptive, language, and gross motor. Can be used to screen for children with learning and behavior problems.

Evanston Early Identification Scale. (M. Landsman and H. Dillard, Follett Educational Corp., 1967) Identifies children aged 5 years to 6 years-3 months who are at low, middle, or high risk for learning problems in school. The child is asked to draw a human figure, which is scored on a scale of point values for missing body parts.

Goodenough-Harris Drawing Test. (Goodenough and Harris, Harcourt Brace Jovanovich, 1963) A child's human figure drawing is scored for number and proportion of body parts. For ages 3 to 15.

McCarthy Scales of Children's Abilities. (McCarthy, Psychological Corp., 1972) Assesses the general intelligence of children ages 2½ to 8½ and includes cognitive, verbal, memory, and gross and fine motor development.

Meeting Street School Screening Test. (P. Hainsworth and M. Siqueland, Easter Seal Society of Rhode Island, Inc., 1969) Screens kindergarten and first grade children for risk of learning disabilities. A pre-kindergarten level is available.

Pre-School Attainment Record (PAR). (E. Doll, American Guidance Service, 1967) Assesses social, physical and intellectual functions of children aged 6 months to 7 years. The parent is interviewed concerning the child's developmental behavior.

Slingerland Pre-Reading Screening Procedures. (B. Slingerland, Educators Publishing Service, 1977) May be given individually or in a group to kindergarten and 1st grade students. Assesses visual perception, auditory perception and both auditory and visual memory as applied to reading readiness tasks.

Test of Basic Experiences (TOBE). (M. H. Moss, California Test Bureau, McGraw Hill, 1972) This test is designed to assess the preschool, kindergarten, and 1st grade child's conceptual understanding of language, social studies, science, and math. The test is group administered.

Valett Developmental Survey of Basic Learning Abilities. (R. Valett, Consulting Psychologists Press, 1966) An adaptation of the Gesell and other developmental scales for ages 2 to 7 years.

Vineland Social Maturity Scale. (E. Doll, American Guidance Service, 1953) Parent is interviewed regarding the child's social maturity and independence.

General Achievement Tests

These tests provide an overview of a student's academic skills and establish the degree of aptitude-achievement discrepancy.

Brigance Diagnostic Inventory of Basic Skills. (A. Brigance, Curriculum Associates, 1977) Assesses basic readiness and academic skills from kindergarten to 6th grade level in reading, math, and language arts. A criterion referenced test designed to assist the teacher in developing instructional objectives for the classroom.

Handbook in Diagnostic-Prescriptive Teaching. (P. Mann, P. Suiter, and R. McClung, Allyn & Bacon, 1979) Skill inventories given informally to plan classroom instruction in reading, spelling, arithmetic and perceptual-motor skills.

Metropolitan Instructional Achievement Tests. (Farr, Prescott, Balow and Hogan, Psychological Corp., 1978) A battery of tests in mathematics, reading, and language arts for grades 1-12. May be given in a group or individually. Assesses a variety of component skills in math, reading, and language arts and provides instructional objectives and suggestions for teaching.

Peabody Invidual Achievement Test (PIAT). (L. Dunn and F. Marwardt, American Guidance Service, 1969) Measures general academic achievement in reading mechanics and comprehension, spelling, math, and general knowledge. For ages 5 to adult, with a variety of scores available that can be used in diagnostic profile with data from aptitude tests such as WISC–R.

Stanford Diagnostic Achievement Tests. (Beatty, Gardner, Karlsen, and Madden, Harcourt Brace Jovanovich, 1976) A battery of tests in mathematics and reading for grades 1-12. May be given in a group or individually. Assesses a variety of component skills in math and reading and provides instructional objectives and suggestions for teaching. Similar to the Metropolitan tests but with somewhat more emphasis on listening skills and oral vocabulary.

Wide Range Achievement Test. (Jastak and Jastak, revised, Jastak Associates, 1978) A screening test for academic skills in reading, spelling, and arithmetic from pre-school through college level. The test is quickly administered and scored but covers only selected component skills (spelling dictation, reading isolated words, and arithmetic computation).

Woodcock-Johnson Psychoeducational Battery, Tests of Academic Achievement and Interest. (R. Woodcock and M. Johnson, N.Y. Times Teaching Resources, 1977) For pre-school through adult level, these tests measure achievement in reading, math, written language and general knowledge. They also assess the level of academic versus nonacademic interests. These tests are designed to be used with the cognitive part of the battery to establish aptitude-achievement discrepancies.

Reading Tests

These tests may provide a grade equivalent or percentile ranking as a measure of the student's reading achievement, but are also used diagnostically to assess strengths and weaknesses in order to plan instruction.

Botel Reading Inventory. (M. Botel, Follett, 1970) Informal tests of word opposites, word recognition and phonics that can be used with grades 1-12 to determine a reading instructional level.

Durrell Analysis of Reading Difficulty. (Durrell, Harcourt Brace Jovanovich, 1955) Used for nonreaders through the 6th grade levels. Includes oral and silent reading and listening comprehension as well as word recognition, word analysis, and supplementary tests of visual and auditory skills needed for reading. Provides considerable diagnostic information.

Gates-MacGinitie Reading Tests. (Gates and MacGinitie, Houghton Mifflin, 1978) Can be used individually or for a group, grades 1-12. Measures vocabulary and comprehension.

Gates-McKillop Reading Diagnostic Tests. (Gates and McKillop, Teachers College Press, 1962) A diagnostic test of reading skills, including sight vocabulary, phonetic relationships, oral paragraphs, and spelling. Yields an instructional level and diagnostic analysis for nonreaders and above.

Gilmore Oral Reading Test. (Gilmore and Gilmore, Harcourt Brace Jovanovich, 1968) For grades 1-8, measures accuracy of oral reading (not including speed factor), comprehension, and rate of reading.

Gray Oral Reading Test. (W. Gray, Bobbs-Merrill, 1967) A measure of oral reading fluency yielding a grade equivalent score based on speed and accuracy. Since comprehension is not included in the scoring, the grade equivalent may not reflect the child's best instructional level. However, analysis of the child's errors provides much diagnostic information.

Roswell-Chall Diagnostic Reading Test. (F. Roswell and J. Chall, Essay Press, 1978) Informal assessment of word analysis skills including sight word recognition, single and combination consonant and vowel sounds and syllabication. For nonreaders and above.

Spache Diagnostic Reading Scales. (Spache, California Test Bureau, 1972) Can be used with students in grades 1-8 or higher, to determine instructional reading level and provide diagnostic information about word recognition, oral reading fluency, rate, and comprehension.

Sucher-Allred Reading Placement Inventory. (F. Sucker and R. Allred, The Economy Company, 1973) Gives instructional reading levels from kindergarten through 9th grade. Assesses oral reading fluency and comprehension.

Woodcock Reading Mastery Test. (R. Woodcock, American Guidance Service, 1973) Assesses reading abilities from grades 1-12 in letter identification, word identification, word attack, word comprehension (analogies), and passage comprehension (through a modified cloze technique).

Spelling and Written Language Tests

These tests assess strengths and weaknesses in a child's ability to communicate in written language. A child's skills should be assessed in actual composition as well as on a dictated spelling test.

Larsen-Hammill Test of Written Spelling. (S. Larsen and D. Hammill, Pro-Ed, 1976) Dictated word list for grades 1-8. Analysis of the types of spelling errors made to determine the child's use of phonics principles and visual memory. Also provides an instructional level.

Morrison McCall Spelling Scales. (J.C. Morrison and W. McCall, Harcourt Brace & World, 1923) Graded words from grade levels 1-12. Grade and age equivalents are provided. Eight alternate lists are provided.

Picture Story Language Test. (H. Myklebust, Grune & Stratton, 1965) Analyzes a child's ability to communicate in written language. Measures productivity, use of syntax and degree of abstract thinking. Norms for ages 7 to 17.

Test of Written Language. (D. Hammill and S. Larsen, Pro-Ed, 1978) A measure of a child's ability to communicate in written language, with norms for ages 8½ to 14½. Includes measures of vocabulary, thematic maturity, word usage, style (punctuation and capitalization), thought units (productivity), handwriting, and spelling. Composition is included along with separate tests of spelling, usage and punctuation and capitalization.

Webster Diagnostic Spelling Test. Assesses spelling abilities, grades 2-8. Measures phonic and structural analysis skills.

Diagnostic Arithmetic Tests

There are few standardized diagnostic arithmetic tests, so a math education specialist must use informal inventories and evaluations to assess a child. One-to-one interviewing and observing is necessary to diagnose the child's thinking process with numbers.

Key Math Diagnostic Arithmetic Test. (A. Connolly, American Guidance Service, 1976) An individual test, designed for children from kindergarten up, the Key Math is best used with youngsters functioning below 5th–6th grade level. The test assesses skills in numeration, fractions, geometry, symbols, addition, subtraction, multiplication, division, mental computation, numerical reasoning, word problems, missing elements, money, measurement, and time.

Inventory of Error Patterns in Basic Mathemathics. (B. Enright, Curriculum Associates Inc., 1979) A test designed to be administered individually to children experiencing difficulties in addition, subtraction, multiplication, division, fractions and decimals.

The Math Teaching Handbook, Informal Diagnostic Testing. (P. Herold, Selective Educational Equipment, 1978) A criterion referenced, informal diagnostic test is included in this handbook with many suggestions for diagnostic teaching.

Stanford Diagnostic Mathematics Test. (Beatty, Madden, Gardner, and Karlsen, Harcourt Brace Jovanovich, 1976) This test may be given individually or in a group and is suitable for students from the end of grade 1 through grade 8. It may also be used with high school students who are below the level of algebra. Skills in numeration, computation and applications (problem solving, tables and graphs, geometry, and measurement) are assessed.

Tests of Oral Language

These tests are used to assess a child's strengths and weaknesses in understanding oral language and in expressing himself through speech. The tests measure a child's organization of language, his understanding of and use of grammar, and knowledge of vocabulary. Obviously much can be learned from listening to a child talk.

Bankson Language Screening Test. (N. W. Bankson, University Park Press, Baltimore, 1977) For ages 4-8, measures psycholinguistic skills in areas of vocabulary, discrimination, syntax, auditory memory, and auditory sequencing.

Carrow Elicited Language Inventory. (E. Carrow, Learning Concepts, 1974) Evaluates a child's use of grammar. The child repeats sentences read to him by the teacher. The sentences are in both active and passive voice, and also include affirmative, negative, declarative, interrogative and imperative forms. For children aged 3-7. Standardized in English and Spanish.

Environmental Language Inventory. (Charles Merrill, 1978) Test is part of Environmental Language Intervention Program. Ages 2-5 and analyzes language in three different settings: imitation, conversation, free play.

Illinois Test of Psycholinguistic Ability. (S. Kirk, J. McCarthy and W. Kirk, U. of Illinois Press, 1969) Measures a child's communication skills: receptive, organizational, and expressive. For ages 2-10 years.

Northwestern Syntax Screening Test. (L. Lee, Northwestern U., 1969) Screens a child's receptive and expressive knowledge of syntax. Children select the correct sentence in response to a stimulus picture. For ages 3 years-11 months to 7 years-11 months.

Peabody Picture Vocabulary Test. (L. Dunn, American Guidance Service, 1965) Measure receptive vocabulary, or knowledge of word meanings by having child associate a spoken word with a picture. For ages 2½ to 18.

Pre-School Language Scale. (Zimmerman, Steiner and Pond, Merrill, 1979) Can be used with children of all ages who are presumed to be functioning at a pre-school or primary language level. Measures both auditory comprehension and expressive verbal ability. A Spanish translation is available.

Templin-Darley Test of Articulation. (M. C. Templin and F. L. Darley, U. of Iowa, 1960) Tests the child's ability to produce vowels, dipthongs, single consonants, and consonant blends in varying combinations.

Test for Auditory Comprehension of Language. (Carrow, Learning Concepts, 1973) Measures auditory comprehension in the areas of vocabulary, morphology and syntax. For ages 3-6, in both English and Spanish.

Test of Language Development. (Newcomer and Hammill, Pro-Ed, 1977) Used with children from 4 to 8 years-11 months, the test is a comprehensive measure of language ability. Subtests measure aspects of syntax and semantics and includes picture vocabulary, oral vocabulary, grammatic understanding, sentence imitation, grammatical completion, word discrimination, and word articulation.

Token Test. (DiSimoni, N.Y. Times Teaching Resources, 1978) Measures subtle receptive language skills by having the child listen to and carry out instructions of increasing length and complexity. For pre-school through grade 6.

Utah Test of Language Development. (M. Mecham, J. Jex and J. Jones, Communication Research Associates, 1967) Tests expressive and receptive verbal language skills in children from ages 1-15 years.

Vocabulary Comprehension Scale. (Tina Banks, Learning Concepts, 1975) For ages 2-5 (norms are the words-age at which 80 percent of subjects understood meaning). Comprehension of words of position, size, quality, quantity, and pronouns.

Wiig-Semel Test of Linguistic Concepts. (E. H. Wiig and E.M. Semel, Charles Merrill, 1974) For grades 1-8. Evaluates comprehension of linguistic relationships. Five subtests with four requiring yes/no answers (comparative, passive, temporal and spatial) and fifth (familial) requires child to produce response, i.e. "What do you call your mother's mother?"

Tests of Auditory Perception

These tests measure children's ability to perceive and discriminate speech sounds, to sequence auditory material, and to remember what they hear.

Goldman-Fristoe-Woodcock Test of Auditory Discrimination. (Goldman, Fristoe and Woodcock, American Guidance Service, 1970) This test assesses speech sound discrimination under quiet and noisy conditions.

Goldman-Fristoe-Woodcock Auditory Skills Battery. (Goldman, Fristoe and Woodcock, American Guidance Service, 1976) This test battery provides a comprehensive diagnosis of auditory perception for individuals from 3 years of age to adulthood. It measures auditory selective attention, auditory discrimination, memory and sound-symbol association.

Lindamood Auditory Conceptualization Test. (Charles H. Lindamood and Patricia C. Lindamood, Teaching Resources Corp., 1971) Measures discrimination between speech sounds and the perception of the number and order of sounds within spoken words. For grades K-12.

Roswell-Chall Auditory Blending Test. (F. Roswell and J. Chall, Essay Press, 1963) A quick test of children's ability to blend a sequence of spoken sounds into a meaningful word. Suitable for non-readers or beginning readers of any age.

Wepman Auditory Discrimination Test. (J. Wepman, Language Research Associates, 1973) Measures child's ability to recognize differences between phonemes of English speech. The child is asked to listen as the examiner reads pairs of words and then to indicate whether the words read were a single word given twice or two different words. Ages 5-9 years.

Tests of Motor Development

These tests are used to assess a child's gross and fine motor coordination. Obviously much can be learned from watching how a child moves as well.

Bruininks-Oseretzky Test of Motor Proficiency. (R. H. Bruininks, American Guidance Service, 1977) A recent modification of the Lincoln-Oseretzky tests. For children from 4-18 years. Subtests include running speed and agility, balance, bilateral coordination, strength, response speed, visual motor control and upper-limb coordination, speed, and dexterity.

Harris Tests of Lateral Dominance. (A. Harris, Psychological Corp., 1974) Used with any age student to determine preferred hand, eye and side of body. Can be used for screening for developmental immaturity.

Meeting Street School Screening Test. (P. Hainsworth and M. Siqueland, Easter Seal Society of Rhode Island Inc., 1969) The first part of this test for kindergarten and first grade children surveys bilateral sequential movement patterns and awareness of the body in space.

Purdue Perceptual-Motor Survey. (E. Roach and N. Kephart, Merrill, 1969) An informal survey which evaluates motor performance and its relation to perceptual awareness. Skills include balance and posture, body image, perceptual-motor matching, ocular control and form perception. Norms for children from 6-10 years of age.

Southern California Sensory Integration Tests. (A. J. Ayres, Western Psychological Services, 1966) Assesses a variety of sensory-motor and perceptual skills. For ages 4-10 years and suitable for use with retarded and cerebral palsied children, as well as the learning disabled.

Tests of Visual Perception and Visual-Motor Integration

These tests are used to assess the kinds of perceptual-motor problems that are typical of learning disabled children.

Beery Buktenica Developmental Test of Visual-Motor Integration. (K. Beery and N. Buktenica, Follett Educational Corp., 1967) Assesses visual-motor functioning by having the child copy designs, using pencil and paper. For children from 2-15 years, it may be given individually or in a group.

Bender Visual-Motor Gestalt Test for Children. (L. Bender, American Orthopsychiatric Association, 1968) The Bender test requires a subject to copy nine geometric designs, using pencil and paper. Elizabeth Koppitz has developed a scoring system for use with children ages 5-11 years. The test is used with children primarily to measure visual-motor integration, but also gives indications of general organizational problems and emotional adjustment.

Benton Visual Retention Test. (A. Benton, Psychological Corp., 1955) This test of visual memory can be used with ages 8 years and up. The subject must reproduce the design after the forms have been exposed and removed.

Frostig Developmental Test of Visual Perception. (M. Frostig, Consulting Psychologists Press, 1961) Measures eye-hand coordination, figure-ground perception, form constancy, position in space and spatial relationships. For ages 3-8 years.

Motor-Free Test of Visual Perception. (R. Colarusso and D. Hammill, Pro-Ed, 1972) Tests visual perception without involving motor integration. Assesses spatial relationships, visual discrimination, figure-ground, visual closure, and visual memory. For ages 4-8 years.

Slingerland Screening Tests for Identifying Children with Specific Language Problems. (B. Slingerland, Educators Publishing Service, 1970) Assesses visual perception, visual memory, and visual-motor integration by having children match, copy, recall, and write letters and numbers. Evaluates the degree to which perceptual deficits actually affect children's writing and spelling. For kindergarten through grade 5 (Malcomesius test for grades 6–8)

Visual-Aural Digit-Span Test (VADS). (E. Koppitz, Grune & Stratton, 1978) Assesses children's ability to perceive sequential information auditorily and visually and to respond orally or in writing. For ages 5-11.

Tests of Social and Emotional Adjustment

These tests measure a child's emotional development and his ability to relate to others in social situations. In addition to tests, informal observations by teachers and parents are important.

1. *Projective Tests:* These tests provide an in-depth assessment of personality and emotional functioning. They should be administered only by a trained clinical psychologist.

Children's Apperception Test (CAT). (L. Bellak, Western Psychological Services, 1955) Children are asked to look at animal pictures and respond with a story. For younger children, but similar to the TAT test.

Rorschach Inkblot Test. (H. Rorschach, Western Psychological Services, 1966) Subjects, from pre-school to adult, are asked to look at ink blots and respond by telling what they see.

Tasks of Emotional Development (TED). (H. Cohen and G. R. Weil, TED Assoc., 1975) Projective story-telling technique similar to CAT but uses pictures designed for both latency and adolescent boys and girls. Assesses social, developmental, and family issues.

Thematic Apperception Test (TAT). (H. Murray, Western Psychological Service, 1943) Older children and adults are asked to look at pictures and respond with stories. Themes and topics chosen by the subject can reveal inner drives and fantasies.

House-Tree-Person Technique. (J. Buck, I. Jolles, Western Psychological Services, 1964) The child is asked to draw a house, tree, and person. These drawings may reveal the child's view of himself and his world.

2. *Rating Scales:* Teachers, parents, or other persons acquainted with the child answer questions regarding his behavior and development. Established norms enable the examiner to interpret the results.

AAMD Adaptive Behavior Scales. (American Association of Mental Deficiency, Washington, D.C., 1969) A behavior rating scale for ages 3 to adult and suitable for emotionally maladjusted, mentally handicapped, and developmentally disabled persons.

Burk's Behavior Rating Scales. (H. Burk, Arden Press, Calif. Association for Neurologically Handicapped Children, 1969) Identifies children, grades 1-8 with pathological behavior.

Deveraux Behavior Rating Scale. (G. Spivak and M. Swift, Devereaux Foundation, 1967) Provides a profile to measure 15 behavior dimensions for children and adolescents.

Vineland Social Maturity Scale. (E. Doll, American Guidance Service, 1953) Assesses personal and social competence.

Walker Problem Behavior Checklist. (H. H. Walker, Western Psychological Services, 1970) Provides a profile for elementary school children of behaviors that interfere with successful achievement. Measures acting out, withdrawal, distractibility, peer relations, and immaturity.

Appendix 7

Sample IEP

prepared for the child named Gilbert (Chapter 11)
placed in a public school self-contained classroom
written by Karen Duncan.

Individualized Education Program

I. Identifying Information for School Year 19<u>80</u> to 19<u>81</u>.

Student: ___Gilbert___ Birthdate: ___May 27, 1972___

Age: _8½_ School District: _____

Hours/days per week in regular education: ___none___

Hours/days per week in special education program: ___fulltime 5 days/week___

Hours/days per week in physical education: ___7½ hours/week___

Initiation and duration dates of IEP: ___9/80 to 6/81___

Interim review date: ___2/81___

II. Health Status, Vision, and Hearing

Gilbert's general health is good. Examination done in May 1980 indicates good visual and auditory acuity.

III. Performance Levels

Reading: Gilbert is unable to score on all subtests of the Woodcock Reading Mastery Test except on Letter Identification where his knowledge of a few alphabet letters gave him the score 2.4. He is currently functioning on the pre-primer level. See goal area for specific strengths and weaknesses.

Math: Key Math Diagnostic Arithmetic Test (5/80). Overall score at 2.5 grade level. Subtests in written computation on low first grade level. Subtests in concept areas reached mid-third grade level. See goal area for additional information.

Spelling: Unable to score on formal spelling test. See goal area for additional information.

Status on Communication Skills (Speech/Language and Writing): The WISC–R demonstrates his excellent fund of general information; excellent descriptive vocabulary; excellent reasoning ability and processing of information. Classroom work demonstrates age appropriate grammar, but he is unable to express himself in writing.

Motor and Perceptual Skills: Severe visual motor problems and poor visual perception skills especially in areas of visual memory and visual discrimination. Koppitz Developmental Bender Score 3 years below Chronological Age (C.A.). On visual memory subtest of ITPA (5/80) scored 2½ years below C.A.

Social/Emotional Status: Records indicate Gilbert relates well to classmates and teachers in small groups. History of isolating behavior in large groups. When confronted with difficult task, he can become resistant to instruction and verbally aggressive. History of distractibility, poor focus and attention, difficulty with transitions, extremely disorganized, poor approach to tasks.

Other (self-help, vocational, relevant family information, etc.): Disorganized in care of belongings and work space; forgets where he is supposed to be.

IV. **Special Conditions and Support Services Needed to Implement IEP**
Gilbert needs to be in a small, highly individualized fulltime special education class; one-to-one tutorial instruction; supportive counseling; low pupil/teacher ratio; limited transitions in schedule; occupational therapy.

V. **Special Procedures and Schedule for Assessing Progress**
Weekly consultation between classroom teacher and special education curriculum advisor to assess Gilbert's progress. Daily consultation between classroom teacher and classroom teaching assistants. Formal testing in May 1981. See separate goal areas for individual methods of evaluation.

VI. Child Study Team   Date of Meeting: _____
     Members Present   Name/Position

_____   Representative from Special
     Education Dept. _____

_____   Special Education Teacher

_____   Classroom Teacher

_____   Diagnostician _____

_____   _____

Signature of Parent/Guardian (signature verifies involvement in development of this Individualized Education Program)

_____   _____
                                                Date

VII. Prioritized Annual Goals and Short-term Objectives

Area # 1

Visual Motor

Visual Perception

Responsible Person/s:

Special Education Classroom Teacher

Occupational Therapist

Pertinent information to implement program (include strengths, weaknesses, needs, etc.):

Gilbert does not grasp a pencil correctly. He writes very slowly with poor size and spacing. His poor visual memory makes it difficult for him to write manuscript letters from memory. He can trace and copy manuscript letters from a model but finds writing in general to be a very laborious task. He reverses and rotates letters (p,q,b,d) and numbers (2,3,5,7,9). He demonstrates poor spatial planning in paper/pencil activities. Pediatrician recommends occupational therapy to improve visual-spatial problems and motor planning on fine motor tasks. Gilbert's gross motor skills are fair.

Method of Evaluation:

Teacher observation; Southern California Sensory Integration Tests given by Occupational Therapist.

Annual Goal:

Gilbert will demonstrate improved visual-motor and visual-perception skills through daily remedial activities in the classroom and twice weekly sessions with licensed occupational therapist trained in sensory motor integration.

Area # 1 :   Visual Motor & Visual Perception

Short-term Objectives	Projected Start	Dates End	Materials/Methods/Techniques/Special Resources
1. Gilbert will complete visual-motor readiness activities on a daily basis with 90% accuracy.	9/80	6/81	Daily classroom activities with visual-motor readiness materials:
2. Gilbert will complete daily practice sheets in the following areas with 80% accuracy: part/whole figure-ground spatial relations visual closure	9/80	6/81	mazes pegboard geoboard Daily practice sheets to improve: part/ whole figure-ground spartial relations visual closure
3. Gilbert will track from left to right pictures, symbols and letters without moving his head with 90% accuracy.	9/80	12/80	
4. Gilbert will be able to complete simple mazes with 90% accuracy.	9/80	12/80	Teacher-made manuscript handwriting sheets.
5. Gilbert will be able to copy lower case manuscript letters from a model with accurate letter formation and proper size and spacing.*	9/80	12/80	Eye-tracking exercises
6. Gilbert will be able to write lower case manuscript letters from dictation with accurate letter formation and proper size and spacing.*	12/80	2/81	

*Accuracy/mastery based on teacher judgment.

Area # 1 :   Visual Motor & Visual Perception

Short-term Objectives	Projected Start	Dates End	Materials/Methods/Techniques/Special Resources
7. Gilbert will be able to copy upper case manuscript letters from a model with accurate formation, proper size and spacing.*	2/81	4/81	
8. Gilbert will be able to write upper case manuscript letters from dictation with accurate formation, proper size and spacing.*	4/81	6/81	
9. Dictated consonant-vowel-consonant (CVC) words, from reading, Gilbert will be able to write them in manuscript with correct letter formation, proper size and spacing.*	2/81	6/81	
10. Gilbert will be able to hold writing instrument with proper grasp: between thumb, index, and middle finger.	9/80	12/80	
11. Gilbert will demonstrate improvement in pace and fluency in handwriting.*	9/80	6/81	
12. When writing without a model, Gilbert will write without reversals and rotations 80% of the time.	9/80	6/81	

*Accuracy/mastery based on teacher judgment

Area # 1 :   Visual Motor & Visual Perception

Short-term Objectives	Projected Start	Dates End	Materials/Methods/ Techniques/Special Resources
13. Gilbert will complete activities designed to promote sensory motor integration (to include tactile discrimination, motor planning and eye-hand coordination activities):			Twice weekly sessions with licensed occupational therapist trained in sensory-motor integration.
a. Gilbert, with vision occluded, will be able to pick object out of a group of 3 common objects and name it.	9/80	1/81	
b. Gilbert will navigate through an obstacle course of 4 obstacles placed 3 feet apart while lying prone on a scooterboard.	9/80	1/81	
c. Gilbert will hit a 3 inch ball suspended at eye level, alternating hands, 20 times in succession.	9/80	6/81	
d. Gilbert will bounce a 7 inch ball within a 2 foot square with his right hand, 25 times in succession.	9/80	6/81	

Area # 1 :   Visual Motor & Visual Perception

Short-term Objectives	Projected Start	Dates End	Materials/Methods/Techniques/Special Resources
e. With therapist creating a left to right pattern with flashlight on wall in darkened room, Gilbert will follow it with his flashlight.	11/80	6/81	
f. With therapist creating an unpredictable sequence with flashlight on wall in darkened room, Gilbert will follow it with his flashlight.	2/81	6/81	

| | | Responsible | Special Education |
| Area # 2 | Reading/Spelling | Person/s: | Classroom Teacher |

Pertinent information to implement program (include strengths, weaknesses, needs, etc.):

Currently reading at pre-primer level. Unable to score on formal test. Can sing alphabet but cannot consistently name letters in isolation from model. Knows short vowel sounds *a* and *i* and consonant sounds *c,m,n,b,t,f*. Difficulty tracking letters from left to right on a page. Relatively strong auditory channel indicates ability to learn phonics rules. Could benefit from being taught phonics in conjunction with linguistics to lessen visual memory load and improve visual discrimination.

Method of Evaluation:

Selected subtests from the Gates-McKillop test. Informal teacher-made tests.

Annual Goal:

Gilbert will progress from pre-primer to primer level in the SRA Basic Reading Series, demonstrating improved ability to link sound with symbol, to visually discriminate letters within words and to increase long-term visual memory for limited sight words. He will demonstrate commensurate progress in spelling consonant-vowel-consonant (CVC) words from his reading series.

Area # 2 :   Reading/Spelling

Short-term Objectives	Projected Start	Dates End	Materials/Methods/Techniques/Special Resources
1. Gilbert will identify letters of the alphabet in sequence from written model with 80% accuracy.	9/80	10/80	Combination phonics/linguistic reading program using SRA Basic reading Series.
2. Gilbert will identify letters of the alphabet in isolation from written model with 80% accuracy.	9/80	11/80	Keep student sourcebook of words learned.
3. Given 10 pairs of letters, Gilbert will be able to discriminate which are the same and different with 80% accuracy.	10/80	12/80	Teacher-made games to improve visual memory and discrimination.
4. Gilbert will be able to put alphabet letter in correct sequence A–Z. (magnetic letters)	9/80	12/80	Daily drill with Language Master.
5. Gilbert will be able to write letters in correct sequence A–Z.	10/80	1/81	Multi-sensory reinforcement of reading words in spelling and hand-
6. Shown a consonant, Gilbert will be able to give correct sound.	10/80	12/80	writing.
7. Shown letters a,e,i,o,u Gilbert will be able to give short vowel sound.	11/80	1/81	Daily individual tutoring in both reading and spelling.

Area # 2 :   Reading/Spelling

Short-term Objectives	Projected Start	Dates End	Materials/Methods/Techniques/Special Resources
8. Given short vowel sounds, Gilbert will be able to name letter, give a key word and write the letter.	11/80	1/81	
9. Given 10 consonant-vowel-consonant (CVC) words in each of following areas, Gilbert will be able to automatically decode without sound blending with 80% accuracy:			
Short *a* CVC words	12/80	1/81	
Short *i* CVC words	1/81	2/81	
Short *o* CVC words	1/81	2/81	
Short *u* CVC words	2/81	3/81	
Short *e* CVC words	2/81	3/81	
10. Gilbert will be able to read the following small sight words: *the, a, is, was, and*	3/81	5/81	
11. Gilbert will be able to orally spell and then write with 80% accuracy ten reading words in each of the following groups:			
Short *a* CVC words	12/80	1/81	
Short *i* CVC words	1/81	2/81	
Short *o* CVC words	1/81	2/81	
Short *u* CVC words	2/81	3/81	
Short *e* CVC words	2/81	3/81	

Area #2 : _____ Reading/Spelling

Short-term Objectives	Projected Start	Dates End	Materials/Methods/ Techniques/Special Resources
12. Dictated the words *the, is, a, was, and,* Gilbert will be able to spell them orally and then write them with 80% accuracy.	3/81	5/81	
13. Given 10 pairs of look-alike CVC words from reading, Gilbert will be able to read pairs with 80% accuracy.	3/81	5/81	
14. Given Michigan Tracking worksheets, Gilbert will be able to track for a given letter with 80% accuracy.	9/80	6/81	
15. After reading a passage from his reading, Gilbert will be able to answer factual questions with 90% accuracy.	3/81	6/81	

Responsible Special Education

Area # 3   Math   Person/s: Classroom Teacher

Pertinent information to implement program (include strengths, weaknesses, needs, etc.):

Gilbert demonstrates a relative strength in the concept areas (time, money, measurement); however, in written computation the visual complexity of problems interferes with his performance. Because of his weak visual memory, he still does not automatically recall math facts. He learns best through experiential activities, games and using manipulative materials. He needs drill for math facts, but he understands the process of regrouping in addition.

Method of Evaluation:

Key Math Diagnostic Arithmetic Test

Annual Goal:

Gilbert will progress in computation skills and application of mathematical concepts from the mid-second grade level to beginning-third grade level.

Area # 3 : _____ Math _____

Short-term Objectives	Projected Start	Dates End	Materials/Methods/Techniques/Special Resources
1. Presented with addition flashcards (1-20), Gilbert will be able to give correct answer within 5 seconds with 90% accuracy.	9/80	12/80	Multi-sensory approach using concrete manipulatives. (Dienes blocks, number line, chip trading).
2. Presented with subtraction flashcards (1-20), Gilbert will be able to give correct answer within 5 seconds with 90% accuracy.	9/80	12/80	Language master to drill facts. Aids such as graph paper to organize math problems.
3. Presented with multiplication flashcards (tables 1-6), Gilbert will be able to give correct answer within 5 seconds with 90% accuracy.	11/80	2/81	Daily one-to-one individual tutoring. Teacher made worksheets and games.
4. Given 10 addition problems (3 digit + 3 digit with regrouping), Gilbert will be able to compute the sums with 90% accuracy.	9/80	1/81	Minimize paper and pencil tasks; stress experiential math activities and games such as classroom bank program or mini-business course.
5. Given 10 subtraction problems (up to 3 digit without regrouping), Gilbert will be able to compute answers with 90% accuracy.	9/80	1/81	

Area # 3 : ___ Math _____

Short-term Objectives	Projected Start	Dates End	Materials/Methods/Techniques/Special Resources
6. Given 10 subtraction problems (up to 3 digit with regrouping), Gilbert will be able to compute answer with 90% accuracy.	12/80	3/81	
7. Given worksheet of 20 multiplication facts (tables 1-6), Gilbert will write correct product with 85% accuracy.	12/80	3/81	
8. Gilbert will be able to chip trade to 100's place with 90% accuracy.	10/80	1/81	
9. Shown Dienes blocks representing 15 numbers (Ex: 4 hundreds, 3 tens, 0 ones), Gilbert will be able to write the numerals they represent (430)	12/80	3/81	
10. Dictated 10 numbers (up to 5 digits long), Gilbert will be able to write numbers in proper sequence with 90% accuracy.	12/80	3/81	
11. Dictated 5 2-digit math problems (+ or −), Gilbert will be able to space them on a page reflecting improved spatial planning.	3/81	6/81	

Area #3 : ___Math___

Short-term Objectives	Projected Start	Dates End	Materials/Methods/Techniques/Special Resources
12. Read a word problem (with addition or subtraction solution), Gilbert will be able to determine process necessary for solution and compute answer with 90% accuracy.	1/81	6/81	
13. Given oral problems involving the concepts of: time (5 each) money (5 each) measurement (5 each) at the mid-second to beginning-third grade level, Gilbert will be able to solve problems with 80% accuracy.	1/81	6/81	

		Responsible	Special Education
Area # 4	Social/Emotional	Person/s:	Teacher

Pertinent information to implement program (include strengths, weaknesses, needs, etc.):

Gilbert is extremely disorganized as seen in his poor care of belongings, work space, poor approach to tasks and difficulty with transitions in schedule. He must be in a small group, as he tends to isolate himself from peers and teachers in large groups. He exhibits a pervasive fear of failure and when especially anxious he talks incessantly. He must be given short, success-oriented tasks since he becomes resistant, highly distractible and impulsive when confronted with difficult ones. He needs a highly structured, closely monitored classroom environment where every aspect of the day is systematically organized for him.

Method of Evaluation: Teacher observation.
Mastery of objectives based on teacher judgment.

Annual Goal:

Gilbert will demonstrate a more positive self-image, increased tolerance for frustration, improved organizational skills; and he will exhibit less distractibility in his behavior.

Area # 4 :   Social/Emotional

Short-term Objectives	Projected Start	Dates End	Materials/Methods/ Techniques/Special Resources
1. Gilbert will display a greater degree of self confidence as evidenced by an openness to new and challenging work and to unexpected changes in routine.	9/80	6/81	Supportive counseling by special educa- tion teacher. Low pupil/ teacher ratio: 3:1.
2. Gilbert will demonstrate increased control of vol- ume and tone of voice when confronted with difficult tasks.	9/80	1/81	Short success- oriented activi- ties.
3. Gilbert will increase his appropriate verbaliza- tions concerning his feelings, personal skills, strengths and learning problems.	9/80	3/81	Integrate his in- terests into his total curricu- lum. Organize work for him at first.
4. Gilbert will ask for assis- tance from teacher when necessary.	9/80	1/81	Self-charting system to encourage bet-
5. Gilbert will respond positively to teacher re- quests more often than in a negative manner.	9/80	1/81	ter organization and improved independent functioning.
6. Gilbert will put his pen- cil, markers, papers, lunch and other belong- ings in his desk at the appropriate times.	9/80	3/81	

Area # 4 : Social/Emotional

Short-term Objectives	Projected Start	Dates End	Materials/Methods/Techniques/Special Resources
7. Gilbert will work one-to-one with teacher on challenging material in a positive manner.	9/80	11/80	
8. Gilbert will increase independent working time without becoming distracted up to:			
10 minutes	11/80	2/81	
15 minutes	2/81	3/81	
20 minutes	3/81	4/81	
30 minutes	4/81	6/81	

An IEP in the Arts

IEP's are written in the areas where a student needs support services. Traditionally, these are written for the language arts, reading, mathematics, spelling, composition, handwriting areas of the program and, sometimes, for science and social studies. Since the arts are central to a student's education at the Lab School of the Kingsbury Center, we have written IEP's in these areas as well. Systematic teaching and remediation can take place in the arts! A child named Douglas is used as an example here. ONLY THE ARTS PORTION OF THE IEP HAS BEEN INCLUDED.

Student Profile

Student: Douglas

Age: 11

Intelligence: Verbal and performance scores on WISC indicate average intelligence. Above average scores on subtests—similarities (13), vocabulary (13), and picture completion (13). Score of 6 on digit span, arithmetic, and coding subtests.

Behavior: Very immature

Highly distractible—hyperactive

Extremely impulsive

Perseverative

Disorganized with belongings, work space, and in his work.

Organized with use of free time.

Very defensive, often angry with adults, bosses, peers.

Learning Disabilities:

Poor visual memory and discrimination and visual sequential memory.

Poor spatial relationships as shown in large, poorly spaced handwriting.

Poor auditory memory and auditory sequential memory.

Focuses on detail, misses main point.

Very literal, confused by inferences and subtleties.

Disorganized in thoughts and therefore in speech.

Rigid and concrete in reception and expression of language.

Word retrieval problems.

Strengths: Good gross motor coordination, good skier.
Good auditory discrimination.
Very determined, hard worker; good artist.

		Media Center Teacher Language
Expressive/		Therapist
	Responsible	Special Education
Area #__ Receptive Language	Person/s:	Teacher

Pertinent information to implement program (include strengths, weaknesses, needs, etc.):

Douglas' expressive language is inhibited by poor memory. He has difficulty organizing his thoughts; and he possesses a limited descriptive vocabulary. Douglas' listening skills and ability to follow oral directions are weak. He is concrete and rigid at times in his comprehension and use of vocabulary. He could benefit from language development activities which are integrated into multiple curriculum areas (i.e. language therapy, classroom and media center).

Method of Evaluation:

Test of Language Development; Subtests from the ITPA; teacher observation and record keeping.

Annual Goal:

Douglas will demonstrate improved receptive and expressive language skills as evidenced by expanded descriptive vocabulary, improved ability to follow oral directions, understand abstract ideas, identify the main idea and make inferences and generalizations.

Area #___ :   Expressive/Receptive Language

Short-term Objectives	Projected Start	Dates End	Materials/Methods/Techniques/Special Resources
1. Douglas will be able to listen to a recorded story with headphones for a period of 15 min. without teacher supervision.			Media Center 3 times weekly (30 min. each)— Library of Congress Talking Books.
2. Douglas will be able to respond in complete sentences to questions concerning the main idea of recorded story with 90% accuracy.			Peabody Language Kit

Language therapy |
| 3. Douglas will be able to answer in complete sentences questions concerning the sequence of events within the story with 90% accuracy. | | | Student keeping list of new descriptive words in personal notebook.

Class discussion. |
| 4. Douglas will be able to answer in complete sentences (when appropriate) questions concerning the characters in the story with 90% accuracy. | | | |
| 5. Douglas will be able to follow 3-step oral directions with no more than 2 inputs 80% of time. | | | |

Area #___ :   Expressive/Receptive Language

Short-term Objectives	Projected Start	Dates End	Materials/Methods/ Techniques/Special Resources
6. Douglas will be able to relate two personal experiences orally with appropriate grammar and descriptive vocabulary during Monday class discussions of weekend activities.			
7. Given new vocabulary words relating to a special topic, Douglas will be able to use them in the proper context 80% of the time.			
8. After listening to a 6 sentence story, Douglas will be able to answer questions of who/what/ when/where with 80% accuracy.			
9. Douglas will demonstrate comprehension of multiple-meaning words by (a) identifying the meaning which applies to the word in a given sentence and (b) by generating sentences illustrating given meanings of words with 90% accuracy.			

Area # ___ : __Expressive/Receptive Language__

Short-term Objectives	Projected Start	Dates End	Materials/Methods/ Techniques/Special Resources
10. Douglas will demonstrate comprehension and use of simile by (a) choosing and/or explaining the real meaning of the figurative language and (b) by substituting similes for simple descriptive adjectives in given sentences with 90% accuracy.			
11. Douglas will use inference to choose and/or explain the mood of a character when the mood is implied, by using descriptive action words and modifiers in sentences and short paragraphs with 90% accuracy.			

VII. Prioritized Annual Goals and Short-term Objectives - continued

Responsible

Area # ___   Drama   Person/s: Drama Teacher

Pertinent information to implement program (include strengths, weaknesses, needs, etc.):

Douglas is most successful following oral directions when they are supplemented with visual cues. He has difficulty focusing at times due to his distractibility. He is very imaginative in pantomime. He tends to focus on details rather than the main idea. He has difficulty interpreting facial gestures.

Method of Evaluation:

Teacher observation.

Annual Goal:

Douglas will demonstrate improved ability to integrate organization of thought with language and movement through drama.

Area #____ : ____Drama____

Short-term Objectives	Projected Start	Dates End	Materials/Methods/ Techniques/Special Resources
1. After being told a simple story supplemented by visual props (flannel-board, hats, costumes, hand props) Douglas will be able to imitate the characters and their actions in the proper story sequence.			Teacher-made props, cos-tumes, flannel-board displays. Teacher dem-onstration and step-by-step di-rections.
2. After watching the teacher role play both appropriate and inap-propriate actions in a restaurant, Douglas will be able to act out the same situations and be able to discriminate what is "appropriate."			Drama teacher trained in learn-ing disabilities.
3. Given a large face card of a specific feeling (happy, sad, angry, etc.), Douglas will be able to act out this feeling in face and body.			
4. Given the same face card of specific feeling, Douglas will be able to add words to body movement expressing feeling. (Initially, teacher may provide ap-propriate words.)			

Area #___ : ___Drama___

Short-term Objectives	Projected Start	Dates End	Materials/Methods/ Techniques/Special Resources
5. As teacher pretends to handle a substance in an empty bowl and says, "What am I handling?" Douglas will focus on bowl and guess imaginary substance.			
6. Douglas will pretend to handle an imaginary substance (sand, water, honey, etc.) and say, "What am I handling?" while other students guess.			
7. Assuming the role of a weather broadcaster, Douglas will be able to "report" on weather while taking cues from pantomimer experiencing a certain type of weather.			
8. In a space improvisation in which he assumes the role of an astronaut, Douglas will be able to follow 3 oral directions one at a time as given by "Mission Control" (the teacher): 　　"Take seat" 　　"Count down" 　　"Freeze during take-off"			

Area #___ : ___Drama___

Short-term Objectives	Projected Start	Dates End	Materials/Methods/ Techniques/Special Resources
9. After he executes each single action in this space improvisation, Douglas will respond "Roger, Mission Control."			
10. Given teacher modeling three actions in sequence with a chair, Douglas will pantomime actions in correct sequence. (ex: stand behind, pullout, sit down)			
11. After viewing teacher performing 3 actions with chair, Douglas will be able to perform same actions in reverse.			
12. With teacher playing role of a shopkeeper and Douglas as a customer, he will employ gibberish and body/hand movement to ask for specific items. (ex: "Blah, blah, blah," etc.)			
13. As the customer in the same improvisation, Douglas will be able to verbalize and employ appropriate body and hand movements to obtain specific items.			

Responsible

Area # ___   Music   Person/s: Music Teacher

Pertinent information to implement program (include strengths, weaknesses, needs, etc.):

Douglas' auditory memory is weak; however, he is able to encode and decode a sequence of two red (loud) and yellow (soft) sound symbols. He can decode and encode two different instrument sounds with symbol cards. He can play a rhythm of four beats per measure using single hands. Douglas' rhythm and timing skills are inconsistent.

Method of Evaluation:

Teacher observation.

Annual Goal:

Through participation in the music program, Douglas will demonstrate improved auditory perception skills, especially in his ability to link sound to symbols, and improved visual-motor skills.

Area # ___ : Music

Short-term Objectives	Projected Start	Dates End	Materials/Methods/ Techniques/Special Resources
1. Given a drum and 2 drumsticks, Douglas will be able to play a rhythm of 4 beats to a measure with alternating hands 4/5 times.			A variety of concrete manipulatives and highly motivating, colorful materials.
2. Given 6 different instrument sounds and accompanying symbol cards and pocket board, Douglas will be able to discriminate those 6 sounds and place proper symbol cards for each sound in pocket from left to right.			Instruments which vary greatly in sound and playing technique Teacher-made games with symbol cards for a variety of interesting themes.
3. Given a complete sequence of 3 instrument sounds, Douglas will be able to place correct 3 symbol cards in pocket board from left to right in proper order.			Step-by-step instructions and highly structured lessons.
4. Given a series of 2, 3, and 4 handclaps, Douglas will be able to reproduce them.			Music teacher trained in learning disabilities
5. Given a simple rhythm (3/4 or 4/4) of handclaps Douglas will be able to reproduce this rhythm pattern correctly 4/5 times.			

VII. Prioritized Annual Goals and Short-term Objectives - continued

Area # ___ : ___ Music ___

Short-term Objectives	Projected Start	Dates End	Materials/Methods/ Techniques/Special Resources
6. Given rhythm sticks and other simple instruments (drums, castinets, etc.), Douglas will listen to a series of rhythm patterns (3/4 or 4/4) and reproduce them correctly.			
7. Douglas will listen to a non-meaningful word (such as "taboo") and reproduce it correctly.			
8. Douglas will listen to a 2-syllable word with a drum-beat played per syllable, and he will say the word and beat the drum on the right syllable simultaneously.			
9. Given a series of 6 loud and soft sounds, Douglas will place the appropriate red (loud) or yellow (soft) symbol cards in the pocket board from left to right as he hears the sound.			
10. Given a series of 4 red and yellow symbol cards, Douglas will play a drum-beat loudly or softly to correspond to the cards as they are presented.			

Area # ___ Wood Workshop

Responsible
Person/s: Wood Workshop Teacher

Pertinent information to implement program (include strengths, weaknesses, needs, etc.):

Douglas is able to communicate his ideas graphically; but he has problems organizing and integrating his ideas for shop. He loses focus easily. He has good gross motor skills enabling him to use the larger workshop power tools with accuracy. He exhibits some clumsiness with smaller manual tools such as a screwdriver and hammer.

Method of Evaluation:

Finished product; teacher judgment.

Annual Goal:

Through involvement in woodwork projects, Douglas will demonstrate improved ability to plan, organize and correctly sequence his ideas and movements; he will demonstrate improved visual-motor skills.

Area #____ : ___Wood Workshop___

Short-term Objectives	Projected Start	Dates End	Materials/Methods/ Techniques/Special Resources
1. Given pencil and paper, Douglas will be able to draw a simple plan of a project which he has pictured in his mind.			Specially trained workshop artists.
2. With teacher assistance, Douglas will discuss and determine the proper dimensions of his project and notate them accurately on the drawing.			Close teacher supervision, instruction, and assistance.

Power tools. |
3. With teacher assistance, Douglas will discuss the proper sequence of steps necessary to make his project.			Models provided as examples of projects.
4. With teacher assistance, Douglas will choose the appropriate materials (size and quantity) to construct his project.			
5. With teacher assistance, Douglas will measure and mark correct dimensions on wood.			
6. After instruction, Douglas will use power tools to cut, drill or sand wood for purposes of assembling his project.			

Area #____ : ___Wood Workshop_____

Short-term Objectives	Projected Start	Dates End	Materials/Methods/ Techniques/Special Resources
7. Given hammer, screw-driver, nails, screws, etc., Douglas will assemble his project in the correct sequence.			
8. Given finishing implements and materials (sandpaper, shellac, paint, etc.) Douglas will complete his project.			
9. Verbally with visual cues (completed project and drawings), Douglas will be able to relate to another child in the correct sequence, the steps necessary to build his project.			

Responsible _____

Area # ___ _____Dance_____   Person/s: ___Dance Instructor___

Pertinent information to implement program (include strengths, weaknesses, needs, etc.):

    Douglas has difficulty following oral directions in dance, especially those of a spatial nature. At times he is insecure in his movements. Although he enjoys dance, he has difficulty maintaining focus.

Method of Evaluation:

    Teacher observation.

Annual Goal:

    Through involvement in the dance program, Douglas will demonstrate improved gross motor planning, ability to follow spatial directions and self-confidence in dance movement.

VII. Prioritized Annual Goals and Short-term Objectives - continued

Area #____ : __Dance__

Short-term Objectives	Projected Start	Dates End	Materials/Methods/Techniques/Special Resources
1. With teacher as a model, Douglas will be able to flex and extend the head, arms and feet; and elevate and depress shoulders as warm-up exercises.			Dance instructor trained in working with learning disabled children
2. Given a verbal cue, Douglas will be able to flex head forward, to right side, extend to back and flex to left in coordination with rhythmic beat.			
3. Seated on the floor, Douglas will be able to flex and extend arms and feet simultaneously to a rhythmic beat.			
4. During a dance activity where Douglas pretends to be made of metal, and the teacher aproaches a specific part of his body with a large magnet, he will pretend that part of his body is drawn to the magnet.			

Area #___ : Dance

Short-term Objectives	Projected Start	Dates End	Materials/Methods/ Techniques/Special Resources
5. Given a specific starting point and area in which to move, Douglas will be able to perform the following activities, one at a time, to music: Leep forward in a straight line 3 times. Gallop forward 5 steps. Slide to the left and to the right.			
6. Assuming the role of one of a pair of "fighters" in a dance (such as "West Side Story"), Douglas will be able to perform fighting type movements without touching his partner.			
7. Douglas will be able to imitate a series of 4 basic steps from an African dance.			
8. While singing the appropriate African song, Douglas will be able to perform an African dance which involves a series of simple movements.			

Area #____ : ___Dance___

Short-term Objectives	Projected Start	Dates End	Materials/Methods/Techniques/Special Resources
9. After observing visual picture cues and the teacher as a model, Douglas will be able to form his body into a given shape such as a circle or triangle.			
10. Given a 5 ft. piece of elastic with loops to hold onto, Douglas will be able to use hands and feet with the elastic to copy the teacher in making a triangle, rectangle, and 5-pointed star.			
11. After observing the teacher using the elastic in a dance, Douglas will be able to take part in a group dance using the elastic.			
12. Using a flashlight in a darkened room, Douglas will be able to follow various parts of his body in movement with the flashlight (arms, legs, etc.).			
13. As a member of a group holding a parachute, Douglas will be able to raise and lower parachute on cue.			

Area #___ : ___Dance_____

Short-term Objectives	Projected Start	Dates End	Materials/Methods/ Techniques/Special Resources
14. As parachute is raised by the group, Douglas will be one of two who will run across under the parachute and assume proper position in the group on the opposite side.			

	Academic Club-	Responsible	Academic Club
Area #	Museum Club	Person/s:	Teacher

Pertinent information to implement program (include strengths, weaknesses, needs, etc.):

Douglas possesses a good fund of general information. He is usually able to understand and remember vocabulary words related to history. His behavior is inconsistent from day to day. When he is focused, he can make outstanding display projects for the museum. He is extremely resistant to any activity involving handwriting. When attentive, he is quick to learn within the dramatic framework of the club.

Method of Evaluation:

Teacher judgment.

Annual Goal:

Through involvement in the Museum Club, Douglas will demonstrate improved understanding of historical, geographical, and civic concepts; and improved perceptual, language, socialization and organization skills.

Area #___ : Academic Club-Museum Club

Short-term Objectives	Projected Start	Dates End	Materials/Methods/Techniques/Special Resources
1. Assuming the role of a museum curator, Douglas will be able to describe to a visitor his function as a curator of a museum, the purpose of a museum and how material is gathered and displayed.			Club teacher trained in working with learning disabled children. Teacher-made materials, activities.
2. Given a daily password (from vocabulary relating to museum and periods of history being studied), Douglas will be able to remember password each day and be able to explain its meaning.			
3. Presented with a specific period of history (Old Stone Age; Ancient Egypt, Ancient Greece, Ancient Rome; the Middle Ages or Renaissance), Douglas will be able to: a) Locate the center of civilization of that period on a map. b) Name an important historical event of that period. c) Name important discoveries or scientific inventions of the period. d) Name important figures of the time.			

Area #___ : Academic Club-Museum Club

Short-term Objectives	Projected Start	Dates End	Materials/Methods/Techniques/Special Resources
4. Presented with a specific period of history, Douglas will be able to discuss with the teacher in a guided interview important civic concepts relating to the period. (ex: emergence of governing patterns, importance of religion, survival of the fittest, the feudal system, democracy)			
5. Presented with a map of the world, Douglas will be able to locate and label Europe, Italy, the Mediterranean Sea, Africa, the Atlantic Ocean, Greece, Egypt and other areas related to the periods of history studied.			
6. Given a map of an area of civilization which he has studied, Douglas will be able to locate and label major topographical features (rivers, mountains, isthmus, peninsula, etc.), surrounding countries and important cities.			

Area #___ :   Academic Club-Museum Club

Short-term Objectives	Projected Start	Dates End	Materials/Methods/Techniques/Special Resources
7. Douglas will be able to assume the role of an important person of a particular historical period and portray him in a significant event of the time. (ex: Columbus sighting land; caveman discovering fire; feudal lord assessing guilt and punishment for a crime; renaissance councilman)			
8. In a guided interview with the club teacher, Douglas will be able to compare and contrast daily life in feudal towns during the Middle Ages with daily life in cities during the Renaissance. (should include information concerning food, shelter, clothing, occupations, entertainment, education, etc.)			
9. In a guided interview with the club teacher, Douglas will be able to compare and contrast the cultural aspects of two different historical periods (paintings, music, drama, literature)			

Area #___ :   Academic Club-Museum Club

Short-term Objectives	Projected Start	Dates End	Materials/Methods/Techniques/Special Resources
10. Given 20 different pictures or word cards representing historical, geographical, cultural or civic concepts of a period, Douglas will be able to sort cards into the correct historical periods. (ex: fire-Stone Age; Democracy-Greece; guild emblem-Renaissance; Nile River-Egypt, etc.)			
11. Douglas will demonstrate improved auditory, visual and tactile skills by successfully completing two and three dimensional drawings, models, diaramas, maps to serve as museum displays, following auditory and visual cues. (ex: Pyramids, Greek Temple, Medieval Castle, Renaissance guild emblems, etc.)			
12. Assuming the role of a museum curator, Douglas will take part in the writing of a behavioral code for museum curators.			

Area #___ : __Academic Club-Museum Club__

Short-term Objectives	Projected Start	Dates End	Materials/Methods/ Techniques/Special Resources
13. As a museum curator, Douglas will adhere to the standards of behavior designated in this code.			

Index

ABOUT THE AUTHOR

SALLY L. SMITH is Full Professor in charge of the Learning Disabilities Program at American University in Washington, D.C. She is also the Director of The Lab School of Washington, which she founded in 1967 for intelligent children with severe learning disabilities. Mrs. Smith has pioneered a curriculum where the arts are central to the educational program of each child. Her previous books include *Nobody Said It's Easy*, a book of advice for teenagers, and *A Child's Guide to a Parent's Mind*. An earlier edition of *No Easy Answers* was published under the auspices of the National Institute of Mental Health. She is the author of many articles in professional magazines, and speaks frequently on panels, as a guest lecturer, and on radio and television concerning the problems of learning disabilities. She has also been a consultant to the U.S. Government and to the U.N. Secretariat, International Year of the Child. Sally L. Smith attended Bennington College and the New York University School of Education. She is the mother of three sons.

Bantam
On Psychology

☐ 28037 **MEN WHO HATE WOMEN & THE WOMEN WHO LOVE THEM** Dr. Susan Forward $4.95
☐ 26401 **MORE HOPE AND HELP FOR YOUR NERVES** Claire Weekes $4.50
☐ 27376 **HOPE AND HELP FOR YOUR NERVES** Claire Weekes $4.50
☐ 26754 **PEACE FROM NERVOUS SUFFERING** Claire Weekes $4.50
☐ 27043 **THE POWER OF THE SUBCONSCIOUS MIND** Dr. J. Murphy $4.50
☐ 34367 **TEACH ONLY LOVE** Gerald Jampolsky, M.D. (A Large Format Book) $8.95
☐ 27087 **CUTTING LOOSE: An Adult Guide for Coming to Terms With Your Parents** Howard Halpern $4.50
☐ 28496 **SUPER JOY: IN LOVE WITH LIVING** Paul Pearsall $5.50

ALSO AVAILABLE ON AUDIO CASSETTE

☐ 45047 **BREAK YOUR ADDICTION TO A PERSON** Howard Halpern, Ph.D $7.95
☐ 45080 **MEN WHO HATE WOMEN AND THE THE WOMEN WHO LOVE THEM** Susan Forward, Ph.D $7.95
☐ 45142 **WHEN AM I GOING TO BE HAPPY? BREAK THE EMOTIONAL BAD HABITS THAT KEEP YOU FROM REACHING YOUR POTENTIAL** Penelope Russianoff, Ph.D $8.95
☐ 45167 **TEACH ONLY LOVE** Gerald Jampolsky $8.95
☐ 45218 **LIFE IS UNCERTAIN, EAT DESSERT FIRST: Finding the Joy You Deserve** Sol Gordon and Harold Brecher $8.95

Buy them at your local bookstore or use this page for ordering.

We Deliver!
And So Do These Bestsellers.

LWA